D1745230

100 Years of the Los Angeles County Fair, 25 Years of Stories

•

David Allen

Inland Valley Daily Bulletin columnist

Pelekinesis

100 Years of the Los Angeles County Fair, 25 Years of Stories by David Allen
ISBN: 978-1-949790-64-1
Library of Congress Control Number: 2022935026

The columns in this book first appeared in the *Inland Valley Daily Bulletin*
1998 to 2021 and are used with permission of the *Inland Valley Daily Bulletin*.
All rights are retained by the *Inland Valley Daily Bulletin*.

Book design by Mark Givens

Cover photograph of David Allen and then-Fairplex CEO Miguel Santana
    on the Sky Ride, 2019, by Renee Hernandez

First Pelekinesis Printing 2022

For information:
Pelekinesis
112 Harvard Ave #65,
Claremont, CA 91711 USA

Pelekinesis
www.pelekinesis.com

100 Years of the Los Angeles County Fair, 25 Years of Stories

David Allen

FAIR COVERAGE BY YEAR

This book is dedicated, with affection and
respect, to the grape sno cone.

ONE-FOURTH OF THE FAIR:
AN INTRODUCTION

As a relative latecomer to Southern California, my attendance at the Los Angeles County Fair started at the ripe age of 33. That's how old I was when I was hired by the *Inland Valley Daily Bulletin*, the newspaper for Pomona, and for which the fair is local news.

By then, the fair, which debuted in 1922, had been an annual fixture for about 75 years, minus a few years off during World War II. A few locals had attended all of them, starting with when they were children, and many more had been going for decades. But I had no misty childhood memories of the fair. When I went as an adult, I was there as a working professional and part-time wiseacre, looking for stories for the newspaper.

I'm no longer sure if I attended in 1997, my first year here – more on that in a moment. My first writing from the fair came in 1998: a few paragraphs of color written to accompany a layout of night photography in our Features section and a review of a Smokey Robinson concert.

The next few years, though, I really cut loose. Let me explain how that came about.

First off, I hail from a rural part of Illinois, where our county fair was a big deal and a spark of interest in a very small town. Even if Pomona's fair is a vastly more complex enterprise that takes place almost entirely on asphalt and under smoggy skies, something in my DNA makes me susceptible to its charms.

In the late 1990s, our fair coverage was in a rut, at least as far as I was concerned. Our editors would meet with the fair's public relations staff to get an overview, then come up with a list of stories. Half were about new elements or attractions and the other half were perennials, like "is the fair safe?" and "what work goes on at the fair after hours?"

These stories, scheduled one per day, were put on a sign-up sheet. Reporters could write their name by one they were willing to cover. In other words, our fair coverage was predetermined before the fair even opened, and by editors who never actually left the office to attend.

The coverage was predictable in both senses of the word: Stories would appear like clockwork, but they weren't always that interesting. While the reporters were happy to get out of the office and some reveled in the change of pace, not all of them had a feel for the fair, and the ideas they were given felt canned.

Where was the spontaneity? It's the Los Angeles County Fair, and somehow we made it seem boring. You wouldn't think that was possible, but we managed it.

To digress to 1997, I remember the sign-up sheet had only one idea that interested me, an exhibit about aliens and Area 51. The reporter who got to the clipboard moments ahead of me had the good sense to pick that story. She handed me the clipboard, chortling at having taken the sole fun idea. I looked at what was left and, disheartened, took a pass on them all.

There was evidence that fair coverage could be done better. Other than a perfunctory preview story, the Los Angeles Times never covered the fair – except in 1997.

That year, a young reporter named Mayrav Saar wrote a daily feature, often about people around the fairgrounds such as performers or longtime vendors. Her lively stories were clearly the product of someone with a sense of humor who relished the human element.

Many of these stories I clipped for future reference as I sought to grasp the possibilities. My favorite was her interview with a mime, who did not speak but rather pantomimed his answers. One reply was a mimed tear trickling down his cheek in response to some hurt that had led him to this career. Almost 25 years later, this detail and this story are lodged in my memory.

I may have been the only journalist who was paying attention, but to me, Saar laid out a template for how the fair could be covered with intelligence and imagination. (I just looked up her LinkedIn page, and here's how she describes her *Times* period: "Specialized in the kind of witty stories people stuck to their refrigerators.")

Two years later, I got my chance. I was a general assignment reporter at the *Bulletin* (as well as a twice-a-week humor columnist), and I made a pitch: Let me cover the fair daily. I'll go there with a photographer and find stories.

City editor Christia Gibbons, who was already in my corner, was sold immediately by my enthusiasm. She had to fend off the editors at one of our sister papers who would have felt a lot more comfortable if we'd planned every story before the fair opened. To placate them, we had to, with a wink, invent some placeholder ideas each week that we could scrap if I came up with better ones – which I did.

Finding fun feature stories at a county fair, it must be said, was not exactly hard labor. I mean, stories were everywhere, from absurd daily contests to performers roaming the grounds, from a sheep shearer to the kiddie rides.

Sometimes identifying story subjects simply required seeing the fair with fresh eyes – which I had. The fair was all new to me.

From 1999 to 2002 I wrote a lot of stories and a few columns about the fair. Then my column was elevated to three times per week and became my full-time job – no more general assignment reporting.

Still, I attended the fair every year anyway to look for column material. The columns tended to be a little snarkier or have more attitude than my stories had. But I hope my genuine affection for the fair still came through. And over time, the attitude lessened and the affection became more pronounced. My column on the simple pleasure of a grape sno cone was an example of the latter

Over time, I did become a little jaundiced. The fair changes from year to year, but not that much. And all the permanent food stands and many of the permanent features, even the beloved Clock Tower, were gradually razed to make the grounds more flexible year-round.

Eventually a lot of the homey, hokey flavor seemed to be slipping away.

In May 2022, a few weeks away as I write these words, the fair will celebrate the centennial of its humble 1922 start. And I will have attended for 25 years. I was a little surprised myself when I did the math, but 25 years out of 100, one-quarter of all the fairs, that's beginning to sound respectable.

And that brings us to this book.

In recent years Pelekinesis publisher Mark Givens and I have put together three books of my columns, with *Pomona A to Z* collecting a 26-part alphabetical look at the city, and *Getting Started* and *On Track* presenting my best from 1997 to 2000 and from 2001 to 2005, respectively.

This book is a little different. Rather than a "best of," it contains virtually everything I've penned about the fair from 1998 to 2021. Columns, feature stories, concert reviews, previews of the fair (complete with prices for entry and parking), short items, a blog post, even a news story about a lawsuit. It's all here.

You see, figuring out what pieces were "the best" began to seem foolish. How would I measure those? Because virtually all of these pieces, which after all chronicle an annual event, are out of date. Very little of what I've written can serve as a guide to whatever the 2022 fair will consist of.

Yet isn't the fair worth remembering? With that in mind, we decided to go all in. This book takes the approach that the Los Angeles County Fair – via these stories of people, attractions, concert lineups, pricing, sights, sounds and smells – is worth documenting. Because even if nearly all of the particulars have come and gone, the last quarter-century of the fair is worth setting down in detail.

Only a very few redundant pieces were left out, as well as a column on the now-defunct Dr. Bob's ice cream operation, which appears in *Pomona A to Z*.

The contents are heavily weighted to the 1999 to 2002 period in which I covered the fair in some depth. In some years of the 2010s,

I wrote only one column from the fair. But there hasn't been a year in which I didn't write at least one – even in 2020 and 2021, when the fair didn't take place due to the coronavirus. Because even the lack of a fair was worth writing about. Every year, therefore, is represented.

Not every important development is covered in these pages. We had news and feature reporters writing about the fair. The loss of 4-H involvement, the departure under fire of the fair's longtime CEO and the end of horse racing got plenty of ink in our news or sports sections and, to avoid overlap, I wrote about other things. So you'll find those topics mentioned only glancingly.

But you'll find a lot of fun stories, some silliness, a few changes noted as they were happening, moments that may bring back memories, elegies for elements now lost. Also, a lot of jokes about foods on a stick.

Incidentally, in the mid-2000s at a journalism conference in Orange County, a woman walked past me whose name tag read, in big letters, "Mayrav Saar." I stopped her, introduced myself, gushed about how great her fair coverage had been a few years earlier and told her it had inspired me. Then with the *Orange County Register*, she was appropriately startled but accepted the compliment.

Readers, I hope you'll find plenty in these pages to delight you, just like at the actual Los Angeles County Fair. As Neil Young once sang about his favorite cars, I'll say to the fair: "Long may you run."

David Allen
March 2022

GOT SPORTS? MILKING NEWS FROM THE FAIR

SEEKING relief from the murky news out of Washington, a weary nation has turned to the world of sports, specifically, to a high-profile contest with a refreshingly clear-cut outcome.

I'm speaking, naturally, of the Senior Citizens Milk Drinking Contest, which captivated a couple dozen spectators Tuesday in a livestock barn at the Los Angeles County Fair.

The showdown began at high noon in the sawdust-covered ring, which was surrounded by a chain-link fence, presumably to keep the crowds at bay.

Over the public address system, the announcer put out the call as the moment of truth approached:

"Milk drinking contest for senior citizens! ... Age 50 and over! ... It's not how MUCH you can drink, it's how FAST you can drink a half-pint of milk!"

This put Al Gysegem of Arcadia in a tough spot. Moments before, he had polished off a half-pint of milk – for fun. Now someone was asking him to drink ANOTHER half-pint. Should he try it?

"Heck, why not?" the 73-year-old told me recklessly before entering the ring, which by the way was square.

Excitement built as the announcer recited the list of prizes:

"We have a cow cutting board! A glass that changes color when milk is in it! And a cow towel!"

Eight men and three women eagerly lined up. Each chose a container of milk, either white or chocolate.

Meanwhile, in the bleachers, excitement had reached a fever pitch.

"Go, Grandma!" one fan yelled.

The judge explained the rules: Place the straw so that it touches the bottom of the container. Hold the container at arm's length until told to begin.

He counted down: "One ... two ... three!"

In a blur, the seniors began slurping. Within 10 seconds, it was all over.

Third place was captured by Regent Burulle, 63, of San Dimas, who told this reporter that no, he had not practiced, although once, a few years back, he had drunk from a bottle of milk with a nipple as a gag.

Thanks for sharing, Regent.

Al Gysegem took second, his earlier half-pint apparently not throwing him off his game.

"I got a large capacity," he bragged.

But what of the champ? Why, it's polo-shirt-and-shorts-clad Richard Land, 57, of Upland. What do you do for a living, Richard?

"I almost don't want to tell you," he said sheepishly.

Aw, cmon.

"OK," he said. "I'm the fire chief."

Right. And I'm the governor.

No, really, Richard Land is the fire chief. Of Pomona. He had the day off and was enjoying the fair with his wife, Shirley, when she nudged him into the ring.

In an exclusive post-contest interview, Richard said he trains continually, drinking everything through a straw – "sodas, you name it."

The dizzying number of rules had complicated matters, he told me gravely, especially having to start from an arm's-length position.

"I had had a plan on how I was going to win it," he confided, "but I had to alter my strategy."

One final question if I may, champ. Could you sum up your feat for the folks at home?

"With concentration, skill and determination," Richard told me firmly, "I sucked my way to victory."

Maybe I can sell this to *Sports Illustrated*.

Richard, by the way, retires effective today after 33 years in the Los Angeles County Fire Department, where he's served as chief in Claremont, Glendora and San Dimas before Pomona.

Maybe he'll kick back today with a tall, cold one. And a straw, natch.

CARNIVAL RIDES LIGHT UP THE NIGHT AT THE LA COUNTY FAIR

IT'S not Paris, or even Las Vegas, but the Los Angeles County Fair lights up beautifully at night.

As the sun sets and natural light fades, the task of illuminating the fairgrounds falls to the fair's attractions. At night, after biding their time during the day, the neon tubes and fluorescent bulbs adorning the carnival rides and refreshment stands burst into luminous life.

Strings of colored lights blaze, flash and ripple in waves. Rides like the Zipper, the Tornado, the Spinout and the Yo-Yo gain glamour, mystery and, seemingly, speed as they whirl against the night sky. Funnel cakes and cotton candy seem exotic, yet oddly comforting, when bought from glowing stands and consumed in the dreamlike half-darkness.

You haven't seen the fair until nighttime – when, if it weren't for the magic of the manmade lights, you couldn't see it at all.

TRACKS OF HIS CHEERS

GOING to see a 1960s-era singer at a (gulp) county fair, you expect a mechanical performance, even when the singer is as beloved as William "Smokey" Robinson.

But Robinson's concert Tuesday at the Los Angeles County Fair was inventive and soulful, joyful and sincere. He had the audience singing along en masse, on its feet, roaring its approval, totally captivated.

It's hard not to love Robinson's songs, of course: the hits from his time with the Miracles, "You Really Got a Hold on Me," "Tears of a Clown" and "Tracks of My Tears"; the solo hits "Being With You" and "Cruisin'"; and the early Temptations hits he wrote, "The Way You Do the Things You Do" and "My Girl."

Those songs are memorable not only for the melodies but for their nuggets of truth, expressed through clever rhymes and playful turns of phrase. Whole songs are based on extended metaphors and comparisons: "I'm sticking to you like a stamp to a letter, like birds of a feather we'll stick together," he once wrote for Mary Wells.

Robinson fed on our love for the songs to express his love for performing. His own love for his songs was evident. He never condescended to words he wrote 18, 26 or 38 years ago.

He sang his heart out. And he sounded humble and happy that he had such great songs to sing, to people who appreciated them.

After a pleasant but rather stiff warm-up medley of four early hits, Robinson launched into "Ooo Baby Baby": "I - did - you - wrong, my heart went out to play/But in the end I lost you, what a price to pay..."

With the tempo slowed in half, Robinson put maximum emphasis on the emotion, virtually reinventing the song. The song sounded so fresh you'd have thought he wrote it that morning instead of in 1965.

"Whew!" Robinson said when he was done, acknowledging our enthusiasm and sounding a bit startled by how he'd been swept away. "We should have played that one first!"

A similar sprightliness transformed "One Heartbeat," a 1986 ballad that sounds anonymous in its recorded version but comes across like a Smokey Classic in live performance.

Robinson, clad in a cream-colored suit and olive shirt, was a warm and engaging presence.

Between songs, he spun anecdotes about the Motown days and his songwriting for the Tempts. He kidded his band members, most of whom have been with him for years, and said they were like his family. He complimented US on OUR singing.

Maybe, when he sang "More Love," the opener, he was singing about his relationship with us: "Each day I'm livin' to, make sure I'm givin' you, more love, and more joy, than any age or time could ever destroy."

When he sang a medley of some of his favorite songs he'd written for the Tempts, he took care to include two little-known gems, "It's Growing" and "Don't Look Back."

For "My Girl," he sang the first third slowly and soulfully, backed only by guitarist Marv Tarplin, the man who wrote the delicate, instantly recognizable intro and contributed to so many other classic Robinson songs.

The show's climax was the 1975 hit "Cruisin'," with an extended audience-participation bit, a "feel-good contest," in which Robinson pitted half the crowd against the other half to see who could sing the phrase "I love it when we're cruising together" louder.

Silly? Sure. But boy, does he know how to work an audience.

Robinson huddled with his band and then announced a tie.

"We have got to settle this," Robinson said, with mock firmness. "We cannot leave this unsettled. Next time we play here, I want everybody in these same seats!"

Deal.

LEAPIN' LIZARDS!

WITH a roar, three dinosaurs swept through the streets of La Verne on Wednesday, heading for the population center of Pomona.

Well, OK, on a flatbed truck.

Sadly, the dinosaurs weren't here from the misty dawn of time, they were here from Irvine. The remote-controlled reptiles were bound for Fairplex, where they'll be the main event at next month's Los Angeles County Fair.

Fifty dinosaurs will set up home in a 43,080-square-foot "jungle" for an attraction called DinoQuest, which fair officials say will be both edifying and terrifying.

"They all move. We have one that actually pumps blood. One spits. They all breathe," said exhibits manager Kathy Wadham.

None of them are reported to eat little boys and girls, but the fair might want to review its liability coverage, just in case.

The first trio of dinosaurs – for the record, a Stegosaurus, an Amargasaurus and a Parasaurolophus – arrived Wednesday, and more will show up in the coming days, fair spokesman Sid Robinson said. The fair runs from September 9 to 26.

Dinamation, an Irvine company that specializes in animatronic dinosaurs, is supplying the dinosaurs for the $500,000 attraction.

A 28-foot truck carried the docile dinos up Highway 57 to La Verne, where, for publicity's sake, they were propped upright for the final leg along Foothill Boulevard, D Street and Arrow Highway to Fairplex.

Topped by a blue fin, the head of the Amargasaurus hung over the truck's side gate, leering at motorists – perhaps to show his displeasure over their use of fossil fuels.

The long neck of the Parasaurolophus leaned over the truck cab.

Protecting their back, the Stegosaurus glared at drivers to the rear.

Reaction varied:

A boy skating along Foothill stared, open-mouthed.

Two pedestrians crossed D Street at their own pace, unheeding of the risk of delaying a truck loaded with dinosaurs.

A landscaper downtown stopped work to watch the truck rumble by.

Two young girls on D Street pointed in amazement.

Motorists on Foothill craned their necks for a better view.

Other motorists, though, impatiently swerved around the truck to make better time. One shook his fist.

Hmph. A puny example of road rage, to a dinosaur.

LOS ANGELES COUNTY FAIR TO CELEBRATE DIVERSITY

IT'S a theme park, art show, food court, horse race, museum, amphitheater and infomercial rolled into one.

And even that description doesn't fully describe the event that draws 1.3 million visitors a year to Pomona: the Los Angeles County Fair.

The $26 million extravaganza – the best-attended county fair in America – opens Thursday and continues through September 26.

"Diversity" is the theme, exemplified by an Asian Festival, art displays, the Fiesta Village, gospel music and performances by Chinese acrobats.

Diversity is the 77th annual fair's mantra, too.

How many places on Earth, after all, feature both an extreme sports park and a diaper derby? Or live hip-hop music and a mime?

" 'Something for everybody' is such a cliche, but this is a place where we can say it and be honest about it," said fair spokesman Sid Robinson. "We've got something for everybody – regardless of gender, age or ethnicity."

It wouldn't be a fair without farm animals to see, pet and smell. Showcasing agriculture was once the mission of county fairs like Pomona's, launched in 1922 on land that had been a beet and barley field.

As agriculture has been crowded out by suburbia, the fair has become far more than cows and pigs.

DinoQuest, the fair's big gun this year, puts the focus on the scariest animals of all: dinosaurs.

To paraphrase the pitchman, these aren't real dinosaurs but an amazing simulation. Fifty life-sized robotic dinosaurs that spit, chew, roar and swing their tails will fill a supermarket-sized exhibit hall, made up to look like a prehistoric jungle.

It's almost certainly the fair's most ambitious attraction ever – and one that seems destined to send little kids running for their lives, then begging to go back. Note to mom: Entry is free with fair admission.

Young children who have seen the exhibit-in-progress are fascinated, but they aren't always up to the experience, reported Don DeLano, the fair's horticulturist, who helped design the interior.

"Some pretend to be dinosaurs: 'Aarr, I'm a T. rex!' Others edge away," DeLano said. "The girls actually seem more comfortable in here than the boys."

DinoQuest is supposed to be edifying as well as terrifying. An accompanying comic book will describe each dinosaur. Hands-on displays will teach more. World-renowned paleontologist Robert Bakker, an adviser for the *Jurassic Park* movies, is scheduled to speak September 11.

This year's other big gun is the extreme sports park.

Traveling skateboarders, in-line skaters and BMX bikers will show off their skills and compete in nationally televised contests. Fair visitors can rent skates and skateboards to challenge the half-pipe and other obstacles.

Pro skateboarder Tony Hawk and pro biker Dave Mira – the Mark McGwire and Sammy Sosa of extreme sports – will offer demonstrations on September 21 and 25, respectively.

Uh, all this at a county fair? That IS extreme.

"It's totally different from anything we've ever done," Robinson admitted. "We want people to think it's cool to come to the fair."

The coolness factor will heat up September 24 when soul icon Isaac Hayes performs on the Los Angeles Newspaper Group stage.

Hayes is best known for his "Theme From 'Shaft,'" but a whole new generation of fans doesn't even know the song. (Hush your mouth!) They know him as the voice of Chef, the worldly wise school cook on *South Park.*

Swing revivalists Big Bad Voodoo Daddy are due onstage September 21. The group's high-octane updating of classic 1940s big band music landed them in the movie *Swingers.*

Other standouts among the musical acts include country singer Randy Travis, the fair's headliner on opening day, as well as pop sensation Monica and the need-no-introduction Beach Boys.

Thankfully, perhaps, little else about the fair has pretensions of hipness.

There's a quilt whose patches showcase all 58 California counties. A petting zoo. An outdoor model railroad. Thoroughbred racing. A mother-daughter lookalike contest.

A cross-cut redwood tree tracing history to the time before Christ. Student artwork. A competition in, of all things, table setting. Consumer products of varying degrees of usefulness and tackiness.

Such attractions are "part of the charm of the county fair," Robinson said. The garden railroad, perhaps the most elaborate in America, isn't glitzy like DinoQuest, but people have loved it for decades, he said.

No fair is complete without carnival rides. Among the 76 rides is the return of a 1997 favorite, the Ejection Seat – a gigantic human slingshot that flings riders 150 feet in the air in two seconds.

People pay to do this?

In the midway and elsewhere, more than 258 food vendors will sell all sorts of cuisine, from Thai to Greek to Mexican to American, including everything on a cardiologist's no-no list.

Rounding out the guilty pleasures, monster trucks and the "Pileup in Pomona" demolition derby are also on the fair's entertainment menu.

The fair can be gloriously unsophisticated, but there are oases of culture, too.

The Flower and Garden Pavilion's imaginative exhibits are curated by the Rose Parade's floral director.

And the Millard Sheets Gallery displays museum-quality art and artifacts. This year's highlights include Pre-Columbian clay figures as old as 200 B.C. and Indian baskets with intricately woven patterns. "Any of these would take a person a year to do," said curator Christy Johnson.

The fair is what it is: a populist pleasure that comes around but once a year, one of the pre-eminent spots in Southern California to rub elbows with a broad cross-section of humanity.

Not only that, but there's funnel cakes.

Fair admission ranges from free (for children 5 and younger) to $1 for adults on weekends. General parking is $5.

Roaring back to life

GOING to a county fair can be a trip back in time – but more than 65 million years?

That's exactly the effect sought by the designers of DinoQuest, the main attraction of this year's Los Angeles County Fair in Pomona. They've turned an exhibit hall into a prehistoric jungle filled with robotic dinosaurs that spit, roar, gnaw and claw.

In all, 50 life-sized dinosaurs – including three mighty T. rexes – will shake up visitors, who will walk through foliage-lined pathways in dim lighting, surrounded by the sounds of shrieks, growls and thunder.

"Everything is animated. Everything has sound," said exhibits manager Kathy Wadham. "It's way cool."

DinoQuest opens Thursday as a highlight of the 77th annual fair, which runs through September 26.

Fair officials say the $580,000 attraction may be the most ambitious in the fair's history. Entry to DinoQuest is free with fair admission, which ranges from free to $18.

Children and adults alike love dinosaurs, which have become a staple at natural history museums, said Mike Converse, who is creative director for Dinamation International, the Irvine-based company that made DinoQuest's animatronic critters.

"Let's face it," Converse said, "anything that will eat you gets your attention, whether it's a great white shark or a dinosaur."

Based closely on fossil evidence, with some guesswork thrown in, DinoQuest's dinosaurs are robotic skeletons covered by urethane rubber skin, driven by air cylinders and controlled by computers.

The robots can do a lot, including simulated breathing – but, crucially, they stand in place.

"We've yet to come up with one that runs around," Converse said.

"Frankly, it's probably just as well."

DinoQuest is set up as a journey through time. Visitors pass through a "time portal" – the building's entrance – which supposedly sends them to the era of the dinosaurs, 258 million to 65 million years ago. Visitors must negotiate the pathway through menacing monsters to reach the time portal at the far end of the building, where they'll encounter something more soothing: hands-on learning stations and a snack shop.

As they enter the main hall, one of the first dinosaurs they'll see is a Dilophosaurus.

"He rears up, his head goes about 18 feet off the ground, he swings his head from side to side, and without warning spits a stream of water 26 feet," Converse said.

Nearby, a Baryonyx standing in a stream will chomp on a fish. On a plain, two Pachycephalosauruses (whew!) will square off in battle, butting heads.

Gore-loving boys are sure to love the Utahraptor – a cousin to the Velociraptors of *Jurassic Park* – which chews on a Sauropod's bloody, severed head.

In the last and largest tableau, a herd of Triceratops battles back against three attacking T. rexes. The largest T. rex rears 20 feet in the air and bellows.

"When he opens his mouth, roars and makes direct eye contact with you, it can be pretty chilling," Converse said.

Past that scene, visitors walk, or perhaps run, through a curtain of fog to return to "present day."

As if to reassure everyone that they are indeed back in 1999, Dino-Quest ends with a souvenir store.

FLOWERY BLOOMS AT THE FAIRPLEX

THE Mayans built some nifty pyramids, sure, but they never thought of turning the steps down the side into a waterfall powered by a Jacuzzi pump.

Leave it to the enterprising folks at the Los Angeles County Fair, who built an indoor, 48-foot-high replica Pyramid as the Flower and Garden Pavilion's centerpiece.

At first, though, the pump-driven flow down the 13 steps to the waterfall produced a torrent of water. That's when designer John Chartier added molding and pebbles to the tops of the steps.

"That was probably the hardest part, to get the water to ripple and stay under control," said Chartier, the exhibit's horticulturist and construction manager. "Otherwise, it just rushed down."

Rushing down, by the way, is a common reaction to the Flower and Garden Pavilion.

According to exit polls, the pavilion – not the carnival rides, not the pigs, not Fiesta Village – is the most popular attraction at the fair, which opens Thursday and ends September 26.

"People like the flowers. It's a nice place to regroup from everything else out on the fairgrounds," said Jim Blythe, assistant coordinator for the exhibit, during a tour on Tuesday. "We'll get at least 78 percent of the fairgoers through here."

Not everyone there is a garden lover.

"Feel this breeze?" Blythe said, spreading his arms. "It's a nice cool place to get in out of the heat."

Speaking of wilting, the pavilion replaces its flowers every two to three days. By the end of the fair, 18,088 blooms may be used, said Susan Overton, the floral exhibit's assistant coordinator.

Inside the graceful A-framed building, the real eye-catcher may not be flowers at all, but the Mayan pyramid built by Chartier.

Rather than stone blocks, Chartier used two-by-fours. "Carvings" and figures of cavorting monkeys are made of foam.

Also dominating the room are two reflecting pools – one modern, one Greco-Roman – surrounded by lilies, chrysanthemums and kalencoa.

A display of wedding dresses from each decade of the century line one wall, each with an accompanying bouquet.

Outside are a lagoon and a variety of small gardens, designed to give tips to homeowners, and even apartment dwellers, on sprucing up a tiny bit of earth. On the hillside behind are more gardens, some planted by students.

Impressive. But with the high-profile DinoQuest attraction, will the bloom be off the rose this year for the Flower and Garden Pavilion?

Pavilion workers are realistic.

"I'm afraid we may lose out this year to the dinosaurs, but we'll do our darndest to keep it No. 1," Overton vowed. She added: "Not that we're in competition."

YOUNG CHINESE ACROBATS BRING BALANCE TO FAIRPLEX

CONTORTIONIST Zhang Chun Yan does a back bend so severe, she can gaze at the back of her ankles.

When Zhang shuffles a few steps – walking on her hands and feet, head bobbing just off the floor – she looks like a spider.

Suddenly you feel ashamed that you can barely touch your toes.

Zhang is one of a troupe of seven Chinese acrobats from Beijing who are amazing and delighting audiences on the Community Stage of the Los Angeles County Fair.

The 28-year-old Zhang started training at age 12. She tried several disciplines and found she likes contortion best.

All that bending looks painful. Is it?

"Before, I hurt. Now, it's OK," Zhang said through an interpreter. "I start every morning for a couple of hours, stretching."

Fellow acrobat Wan Yabo, who's only 11, is nearly as limber. She balances five stacked bowls on her head, then climbs onto the shoulders of Zhang, who's 28. Then she climbs onto his head.

After several minutes of maneuvers up there, Wan does a one-armed handstand on Zhang's scalp. The bowls remain perched on her head, only slipping once.

It's just as well they slipped. Otherwise, we might have suspected tape.

Another acrobat, Wang He, specializes in low-wire balancing. It's like a high-wire act, only without the high part.

The wire is supported on the stage between two braces, perhaps 8 feet high. When Wang stands on the wire, it sags like a V, the low point a foot off the stage.

Obviously there's no net. The main danger in falling is death by embarrassment.

Wang, who's 16, doesn't fall, although he gets laughs by pretending he's about to tumble, flashing a broad smile to show his relief that he didn't.

With no balance stick, just his own sense of balance and a pair of feet that can curl around the wire, he walks a few steps in each direction. Lies down on the wire like it's a hammock. Stands, faces the crowd, grabs the wire in each hand like the rope on a swing set, then begins swinging.

The show culminates with group somersaults and a display of strength, as Zhang holds three acrobats aloft.

Fairgoers may have seen the troupe before, but not these acrobats.

"They rotate members depending on what acts they want. Visas also have a role in it," said Jean Hollingshead, the fair's entertainment supervisor.

"Every group we've had ... we're just blown away," she added.

These young acrobats are on their first tour outside of China. They started in Australia, then hit Alaska for a fair. "Very cold," Wang said.

They'll go to New York, Texas, Miami, "some big cities," said troupe director Ken Hai. With three shows a day, there won't be much time for sightseeing before their 18-day run at the Pomona fair is over.

Based on their initial impression, though, Los Angeles comes up short compared to Alaska.

"Much better there," Hai said with a smile. "Air clean."

CHILLY CON CORNY: PENGUINS FIT THE BILL

FOR birds that are supposed to be flightless, these penguins spend an awful lot of time in the air.

On the midway of the Los Angeles County Fair, penguins jump on a trampoline. Some dive into a pool, from heights of up to 50 feet.

Others don skis – skis?! – to fly down a ramp into the pool.

All of them do twists and somersaults before hitting the water.

If their athleticism seems unusual for penguins, get this: The lead penguin, Chilly, wears a mustache.

Um, don't all penguins look alike, Chilly? Or is that just an unthinking stereotype?

"Each penguin," Chilly explained during a post-show interview, "is unique in its own way, with its own characteristics."

Very P.C. (Penguinally Correct). This wasn't quite a flippers-across-the-water moment, though. By this point, Chilly had unzipped his penguin suit to stand revealed, in swim trunks, as Bill Brown, Olympic-style diver.

Brown and his four fellow fake fowl are performing in Arctic Splash and Crash, a free midway show that combines diving, gymnastics and ski jumping.

Costumes, too.

Brown said his globetrotting troupe likes to perform in costume, dressed as penguins, clowns or pirates. Pomona's fair, however, is the first time they've done a whole show, nearly, in costume. It's also the first time the high divers and skiers have performed together.

Fair officials "wanted a cuter show, one that's more appealing to the kids, of all ages," Brown said. "And this one fit the bill."

The other penguins are Willy (Bill Howe) and Piccadilly (Selena

Laniel), who dive, and Snow (Ryan Snow) and Slasher (Dustin Wilson), who ski. Silly (Lucie Arcand) is sidelined by a twisted ankle. (Unasked question: Do penguins have ankles?)

For part of the show, the penguins perform dives and jumps in exchange for treats of licorice tossed by trainer Craig Peterson. When Peterson leaves to get more licorice, the penguins take over the show.

As a capper, one diver climbs a ladder to a tiny platform 75 feet off the asphalt, followed by a looooong dive into the pool.

For that stunt, the diver doffs his or her penguin suit to make the leap in swimwear. The costumes are made for "funny dives," not serious dives, Brown said.

"The height is not a problem," Laniel said. "The depth of the pool is a problem." It's 9 feet deep.

To help, the other divers, also out of costume, sit on the lip of the pool and stir the water with their feet, disturbing the glassy surface. Otherwise, the diver can see clear to the bottom and might misjudge the distance.

Scary? Not really, Brown said. To the Florida native, it's the thought of ski jumping – which the divers refuse to do – that gives him the willies.

By the way, Brown knows penguins are from the Antarctic, not the Arctic.

"We hope no one notices that," he said. "It's creative license." He must have left that license in his other suit.

WILD WEST WANNABES HIT THE ASPHALT TRAIL FOR ANNUAL CATTLE DRIVE

PAST a Bakers Square they rode, within spittin' distance of the Bagelry, as suburban cowboys led 299 head of cattle Friday morning down the streets of La Verne.

It was the annual cattle drive from the foothills to the Los Angeles County Fair, a popular publicity stunt that mixes the old and new wests.

Steers were herded from La Verne's Palmer Equestrian Facility to Pomona's fairgrounds, a 7-mile route. They passed gated subdivisions, tract homes, retail stores and freeway construction, asphalt streets standing in for the dusty trail.

The event was no thundering stampede. The two-hour "drive" was more of a walk.

Some 138 riders, most of them local horse owners, herded the steers, which had been trucked in from a ranch in Santa Margarita for the occasion. Riders paid $150 for the adventure and said it was worth every penny.

"It's a blast," said Pam Heisinger, a 43-year-old supermarket checker from Walnut who has ridden in each drive since the 1996 debut. "It's just so much fun that you keep coming back every year."

Families lined the streets, traffic stopped and construction workers gawked as riders herded the mooing steers down Wheeler Avenue past Base Line Road and Foothill Boulevard, then along Bonita Avenue.

"People love a parade," said Doug Lofstrum, the Fairplex official who led the drive. "That's what this is, a parade."

For riders, the trick was negotiating paved streets. Manhole covers and other slick spots can trip up horses, who wear metal shoes, said three-time rider Paula Miller of La Verne.

Bushy mustached Dan Needham, who owns a direct-mail advertising business, was one of many riders dressed in cowboy finery: a white hat, leather chaps, boots and a gold star identifying him as "Sheriff Dan."

Needham, a 56-year-old San Dimas resident, is a horse lover who rides his quarter horse, Shi Shi, each afternoon and goes on *City Slickers*-type cattle drives each year.

Does he ever wish he'd lived in the Old West?

"Getting up at dawn and using an outhouse, that's not too appealing," Needham admitted. "Dressing in western clothes and being around pals, that I like."

The celebrity rider was a politician, Assemblyman Bob Margett, R-Arcadia. Margett, who dressed down in jeans, said after the ride that he'd had a great time – to a point.

"The people at the turn of the century were on cattle drives three or four months," Margett, 70, reflected. "I was on it for three hours and that was probably enough for me."

The biggest cheers came as the riders and steers passed the elementary school students lined up outside Oak Mesa School. Many of the young buckaroos wore cowboy hats and vests made from brown butcher-block paper. They kept up a continuous shriek of delight for several minutes straight, as if they'd sighted 'N Sync.

"Little kids' faces, that's worth all the time and trouble right there," two-time rider Garry Nichols of Alta Loma said.

In fact, it was the reaction of a little girl last year that led to a new element of this year's drive.

Nolena Prouty, 3, was pictured in the *Daily Bulletin* wearing a huge hat, riding a stick horse and waving to riders from the sidelines. That inspired Lofstrum, Fairplex's vice president of operations, to invite students to ride stick horses behind the riders this year as they entered the fairgrounds horse track.

More than 1,100 students ages 4 to 8 signed up to participate, waiting outside the track gates to follow the riders in.

Kindergarten students from Pomona's Kingsley Elementary School had perhaps the most elaborate stick horses, fashioned from cereal boxes, brown paper and plastic pipe. Students enjoyed riding their horses and seeing real horses close up.

"I loved it," said Jennifer Sanchez, 5, who dubbed her horse Little Mermaid.

"I want to be a cowboy," declared 5-year-old Alberto Berumen. "I like the bulls and the horses. I dress like a cowboy and go to rodeos."

Offering what might be a mixed message, would-be cowboy Alberto was also dressed in a Cleveland Indians cap.

SQUEAL OF THE CENTURY: POMONA MAYOR WINS LAST HOG-CALLING CONTEST AT FAIR BEFORE THE YEAR 2000

To squeals of delight, the mayor of Pomona won the Los Angeles County Fair's hog-calling contest Tuesday, beating all comers, including Claremont's mayor, an Elvis impersonator and three children.

"Let's hear it for Pomona!" Mayor Eddie Cortez proclaimed after two hogs made a beeline for him inside the ring, drawn by his high-pitched series of "sooey" calls.

A livestock barn at the Pomona fairgrounds was the setting for the tongue-in-cheek contest, which had gained national publicity on *The Tonight Show.*

Contestants took turns stepping into a ring and attempting to coax a hog to join them. The eight entrants, however, were far more energetic than the five hogs, which studiously ignored everyone but Cortez.

Contestants begged, sang, tossed straw and even tried commanding hogs to step into the ring, to no avail.

"Here pig pig pig pig," Claremont Mayor Karen Rosenthal called, extending a lemon. "Do you want this lovely lemon from a Claremont lemon tree?"

The unimpressed porkers continued rooting around in the straw.

A jumpsuit-clad Elvis belted out versions of classic songs rewritten for the occasion, closing with "Love me tender, love me sweet, you pigs make such good meat."

Not surprisingly, the hogs weren't at all shook up.

Before leaving the building, Elvis identified himself as Shawn Kottkamp of Claremont. His three children also competed.

Bill Kottkamp, 6, rocked back and forth, repeating, "Mosey on down, pardners! Mosey on down, pardners!" The hogs refused.

With all five hogs inches from the ring as she entered, Betsy Kottkamp, 9, seemed assured of victory, but they fled as soon as she began calling.

The assertive Rachel Kottkamp, 10, used the vinegar over honey approach, loudly demanding, "Come here! Come here!"

Maybe that works better on her siblings.

Veteran callers Rick Jansson and Joseph Mangrich found that well-honed technique was no match for a bored animal.

Afterward, Mangrich, a 38-year hog caller, said he's practicing a dying art.

"Hog calling doesn't mean what it used to because hogs today are fed by machine," said a genial Mangrich, 75, of Pomona. "Calling means nothing to these hogs."

To what did Cortez attribute his victory? His boyhood as a migrant farm worker's son, which gave him plenty of opportunity to slop the hogs and call them to dinner.

Perhaps, as a politician, he also knows a thing or two about pork.

NO TEARS, JUST LAUGHS FROM THIS CLOWN

SHE'S a little girl on a big tricycle who goes out of her way to talk to strangers.

"Helloooooo!" Shylo the clown says, pedaling by a couple of older women at the Los Angeles County Fair. "Do you want a ride?"

She tells a knobby-kneed gent in shorts that he's cute, then calls out to a middle-aged couple, holding hands: "Oh, look at these two lovebirds comin' up! Are you in loooove?"

The stonefaced man breaks into a grin.

Shylo, who cashes her paycheck as Linda Siples Hulet, makes her living by making people smile. As one of the ground entertainers, she roams the fair, greeting visitors and, with luck, leaving them laughing.

"Want some duck tape?" Shylo likes to ask, displaying a long strip of tape on which plastic ducks are stuck.

Not everyone is in the mood for a clown. Teenagers in school uniforms shift their eyes away as Shylo rides up.

Children are more easily charmed.

"Gimme five!" Shylo tells 5-year-old Harmony Karimi of Chino Hills, who happily slaps palms.

Shylo pedals up the row of vendors. To a pool salesman perched on the edge of a water-filled pool on this muggy Wednesday, she asks: "Wouldn't you like to fall backward?" He utters a grunt.

Some children are immune, too. Asked if he'd like to be her boyfriend, a little boy shakes his head "no" and runs to daddy.

Flirting goes better with two delivery men. Shylo asks them to kiss her, puckering up in vain, eyes closed, as the men stand there embarrassed, laughing.

Elementary school students relaxing in the shade get the clown's full-court press. At first the Long Beach students are shy, but she loosens them up, calling their young teacher "grandma" and telling corny jokes.

"Why did the turkey cross the road?" she asks. "Because the chicken was on vacation!"

Soon she's made Brandon Raphiel, 8, the center of attention, getting him to help with a magic trick and razzing him about various classmates being his girlfriend. The students are won over by the time her five-minute routine is done.

To an older couple, Shylo calls out: "Hi, Mom! Hi, Dad!" They wave back.

She adds: "I'll be home at 10 o'clock!"

FAIR'S DIAPER DERBY IS SLIGHTLY SOILED BY BATTLE OF THE SEXES

BABY Tori Spaulding turned the Los Angeles County Fair's wholesome diaper derby into a WWF-style brawl Thursday, pushing her opponent in the face and making him cry.

A look of shock and hurt creased Miles DeBruin's face in the moments before he burst into tears.

The drama between the two toddling titans, both 11 months old and both hailing from Upland, had only begun.

But first, the background: Tori and Miles had won their respective heats there on the Community Stage, crawling past the finish line to their parents faster than the other babies.

As preliminary champs, Tori and Miles had to face each other in a crawl-off to see which was the fastest baby.

Tori, clad in a pink dress, and Miles, wearing a blue jumper, got off to good starts before stopping on the mat to play.

That's when Tori got a bit too friendly and pushed Miles in the face, pressing him to the mat.

Tori crawled another two feet, until she heard Miles' sobs. Turning, she crawled back – and kissed his cheek.

Miles stopped crying. Pressing her advantage, Tori grabbed his face and kissed his forehead, hard enough to knock him over.

As he righted himself, she pushed him in the chest.

Before the confused Miles knew whether to cry or propose marriage, his mother pulled him away.

Tori crawled back to the starting line and sat down, looking innocent.

"I think we'll call it a draw," said a practical Jean Hollingshead, the fair's entertainment supervisor.

Tori's parents, Don and Julie, said having older siblings has made her friendly and physical.

"She's very playful," Don said.

Miles, whose only words are "mom," "dad" and "ball," had no comment.

A related fair event took place a half-hour earlier, one that didn't involve infants, just infantile behavior: the belching contest.

In a welcome sign for humanity, only seven contestants showed up.

Through the bullhorn provided by contest officials, Damien Ulloa, 15, of Lynwood emitted a low, glottal belch.

Explaining his technique in an exclusive interview, Damien said: "I put air into my stomach and then I wait for a while until my system pushes it out."

"I could have done it longer," he added, but the air was only in his stomach 30 seconds before his turn came.

In the adult competition, Juan Melendez, 22, of Pomona uttered a little "urp," which he later re-enacted upon request.

How was he able to belch at will? "I drank some beer," he said. "I had a few."

BLIND MAN CONQUERS HIS OWN MT. EVEREST

DOUG Davidson is blind, but each year at the Los Angeles County Fair, he has one goal clearly in sight.

For 30 years, Davidson has visited the fair solely to climb to the top of the Giant Slide, glide down the wavy slide on a burlap mat, then climb the stairs to do it again. And again.

Davidson, 42, has made the slide his personal Everest. In 1998, he set a personal record of 60 trips. On opening day this year he hit 61.

"The only reason he stopped then was he wanted to see the Randy Travis show," said his dad, Ken Davidson, who's 77.

That many trips takes three to four hours.

On Friday, Davidson returned to his favorite ride to shoot for 65 trips, or more.

He has trouble explaining his obsession with the Giant Slide, which may have begun as early as 1965, the year the attraction opened. Familiarity is one reason. Exercise from the repetitive climbing is another. Another reason: "It's just plain fun," he said.

"It's like a breath of fresh air," he said. "It may be fall, but it's like a breath of spring."

Ken Davidson said his son gets a taste of freedom on the slide, the way a sighted person does behind the wheel of a car.

By himself, Doug Davidson climbs the 95 steps to the top of the 50-foot slide. A slide employee lays out his mat. Davidson steps on, sits, pushes himself off and rides silently down the four humps to the bottom.

An employee, or his father, leads him to the steps so he can go again.

"That was 29," he'll say, to keep the numbers straight. "Thirty is next."

Blind since birth, Davidson lives with his parents, Ken and Margaret, in Los Angeles. His life has been as normal as possible, his father said.

He went to the movies with his two brothers. He was a kicker on his high school football team, which got him a letterman's jacket. A college graduate with a degree in communications, he plays the piano, reads Braille, takes computer classes, swims and competes in an annual marathon.

"He doesn't look at blindness as a handicap," Ken Davidson said. "He looks at his diabetes as a handicap ... because he likes to eat."

His parents planned to cut him off at 66 trips to eat because of low blood sugar.

Giant Slide manager Nancy Maxwell, who's worked the ride for 23 years, lets Davidson on the $1.80-a-trip attraction for free.

"He's a tradition of the slide," Maxwell said proudly. Her daughters grew up helping him.

Other disabled people ride the slide, including people with Down syndrome and multiple sclerosis, "but nobody who's gung-ho like Doug," Maxwell said.

Slide employee Michael Murakami was among those who helped Davidson lay out his mat Friday and opening day.

"It's unbelievable," Murakami said. "Sixty-one times up the stairs." Other people ride "at most, four or five times," he said. "They're huffing and puffing. This guy does it like it's nothing."

Jennifer Reid of Riverside, whose children were contemplating a second slide, was delighted to hear about Davidson's feat.

"Oh my gosh, how fun," Reid said, watching Davidson on another trip down. She had a guess as to what a blind person would get out of the effort.

"It's the thrill," Reid said. "Most people close their eyes when they go down it anyway."

Los Angeles County Fair to open with a twist

THE Los Angeles County Fair opens today, boasting the usual assortment of thrill rides, cotton candy and cows and one unusual attraction: a presidential candidate.

George W. Bush is expected to make a brief stop at the fair at 2:15 p.m. as part of a campaign swing through the region.

"He will give a short speech (and) he's going to kind of officially open the fair for us," fair spokeswoman Wendy Talarico said.

Bush plans to appear in the Heritage Farm area, which seeks to recreate the activities of a farm of a century ago.

No president or presidential candidate appears to have dropped by the fair since its founding in 1922, according to Talarico's research, but a future president, Ronald Reagan, visited in 1966. Bush will be the second offspring of former President Bush to take part in the fair. Son Neil Bush lent his voice to the hog-calling contest in 1988.

But enough of that. The 18-day county fair runs through October 1 and, presidential politics aside, the newest and biggest attraction is Expedition Earth.

Housed in a 50,000-square-foot building, the attraction will mimic seven ecosystems, from tropical rainforest to desert to the frozen arctic. Animatronic whales and woolly mammoths will be joined by 300 live animals, including sharks, armadillos and lizards. Educational exhibits at the end will put it all in perspective.

Gravity Zone, the traveling skate park for in-line skaters, skateboarders and BMX bikers, is returning with a difference.

"It's three times as large as it was last year," Talarico said.

Bigger wheels will be on display in Thunder Alley, a tribute to motorsports presented by the National Hot Rod Association. Dragsters, sprint cars and a simulated racing pit should rev up enthusiasm among race fans.

The fair isn't all new and different, needless to say.

Carnival rides, high-calorie food, novelty products, street performers and concerts are among the regular attractions of the event, which is billed as the largest county fair in North America. Last year nearly 1.2 million people attended.

Amid the bustle are places of sanctuary that offer a chance for quiet contemplation.

The Millard Sheets Gallery this year will focus on young artists with the theme "Revolutionary Art." The Flower and Garden Pavilion, one of the fair's perennial favorites, is devoted to geometric shapes found in flowers. The lavish, imaginative displays, not to mention the cool shelter from the heat, make for a popular escape.

The fair opens today at 11 a.m. and closes at 10 p.m. In a bonus for first-day visitors, admission is only $2, courtesy of the *Inland Valley Daily Bulletin* and its sister publications in the Los Angeles Newspaper Group.

Fair opens with a flair

I T'S not as glitzy as the Olympics, it's not on television, but the Los Angeles County Fair kicked off Thursday with an array of pleasures designed to entice people out of their recliners.

Staples like thrill rides, sinful food and barnyard animals were joined by more surprising fare: a skate park and a lavish indoor zoo featuring live and robotic animals. There was even a presidential candidate.

Fair officials hope they can reverse an attendance slide. This year, there's the added hurdle of the summer games.

"They've got to out-compete the Olympics," Pomona Councilman Elliott Rothman said. "But we've got something the Olympics don't have. We've got pig racing."

Thursday's wilting heat didn't dissuade people from packing into Pomona's Fairplex for the 73rd edition of the fair. By the time the 18-day event ends October 1, the fair expects to draw 1.2 million people.

"Expedition Earth," the glitziest of the new exhibits, was an immediate hit Thursday. The 43,000-square-foot building displays six environments and habitats, from prehistoric rain forest to desert to ocean. Three hundred live animals and 22 robotic ones tantalize and terrorize.

A robotic great white shark is one of the stars. Hanging from wires, the shark sways menacingly and opens its famous jaws to bare its double row of teeth.

"Why is it moving?" one girl asked nervously as she hurried past.

Frank Sandoval of Pomona teased his 5-year-old grandson as they passed by. "Look at those big teeth! The better to bite you with," he said.

"It's a great exhibit," Sandoval said outside. "The kids are having a ball in here."

Thursday's heat – perhaps the least welcome of all fair traditions – was especially noticeable in "Expedition Earth," where the simulation of a steamy rain forest was all too realistic. But the binturong, a furry mongoose-like critter from Southeast Asia, was in his element.

"He's used to the heat," trainer Amy Langdale said. "I think the animals are more used to it than we are."

Among the other big attractions this year is the Gravity Zone skate park, where in-line skaters, skateboarders and BMX bike riders can show their chops.

Another draw was a one-day only event, a speech by Republican presidential nominee George W. Bush. Hundreds of people crowded into the Heritage Farm area to see him.

Bill Deschene of Upland, who was sporting a Bush-Cheney sticker on his shirt, said he didn't come to the fair specifically for Bush but wasn't going to pass up the opportunity to see him.

"I think his father did a good job. I think he'll follow," Deschene said.

Nearby was the Davidson family from Los Angeles, who have their own tradition. Doug Davidson, 43, is a blind man who comes to the fair each year to ride the Giant Slide as many times as he can in one day.

"Doug is trying to beat his record from last year, when he did 68," said his father, Ken Davidson.

One of the most popular traditions is the Flower and Garden Pavilion. It has the same elaborate floral arrangements as always, but the flowers will be changed five times over the course of the fair, curator Jim Hynd said.

"The visitor can come back several times and see something new each time," Hynd said.

Among the first-day fair visitors was Karen Griffin of Claremont. She likes the first day because the crowds are thinner and the vendors seem friendlier.

"There's something here for everybody," said her friend, Jeff Gardner of Pico Rivera.

That's music to the ears of fair officials, who are fighting to keep their event relevant. Attendance has been slipping for several years. 1999's attendance of 1,190,814 was the lowest in 20 years.

Competition for attention, the fair's limited run and a population unused to county fairs are among the challenges to overcome, said Jim Kostoff, chairman of the fair association.

The fair has added the skate park for young people, created Asian and African "village" areas to appeal to Southern California's diverse population and, in answer to complaints, improved its directional signs, Kostoff said.

"We're just trying harder and harder to bring our presentation up to the level people want," Kostoff said. "I think we're getting there."

FAIR OFFERS BITE-SIZE FUN FOR PINT-SIZE PEOPLE

THE red-and-silver prop planes "flew" no more than 8 feet off the ground – low enough that those things on the ground that looked like ants really were ants.

But to 4-year-old Ben Sweeney, who was aloft in the Red Baron kiddie ride Friday at the Los Angeles County Fair, he was soaring through the wild blue yonder.

"It's like I'm going to go flying off somewhere!" the Upland youngster said excitedly once back on terra firma.

It wasn't all smooth flying, though. After all, the ride not only goes around but up and down. And the planes travel at a pulse-quickening 2 mph.

"It was a little bit scary," Ben admitted.

Welcome to Kiddieland, where the pace and scale of the rides are suited to the fair's pint-sized patrons.

Three kiddie areas offer rides in miniature rockets and cars, inside spinning strawberries and atop flying elephants, among other delights.

Sure, they're a far cry from the Grand Wheel, Ejection Seat, Hi-Miler and other scary rides on the carnival midway – but, hey, everybody's got to start somewhere.

Enjoying his first fair, Michael Shoemaker of La Verne took on the Dragon, a lizard-shaped roller coaster that makes a gentle loop no more than 6 feet off the ground.

"Hold on! Hold on!" his mother, Sue, called out as the dragon started rolling. Michael, 3, quickly complied, gripping the safety bar.

After a couple of times around, though, Michael raised his arms high, the better to experience the hair-raising dips of – gasp! – 5 feet.

"He's brave. He's a thrill-seeker," his mom said with a chuckle.

On the final loops, though, Michael's face grew clouded. He looked a little unsure of the wisdom of his decision to tackle such a perilous ride.

Afterward, though, he appeared unruffled.

"It was fine and fun," he declared.

Not all the rides end so happily.

As the jets in the F-80 ride gently circled, the only thing in full throttle were co-pilot Hudson Logie's tear ducts. Luckily, his sister Isabelle, 4, was there as co-pilot to comfort the wailing 2- year-old.

Back in his mother's arms, the tears drying on his cheeks, the young pilot from Whittier consented to a debriefing on his rough flight.

"I didn't like the choo-choo train," said Hudson, obviously still rattled.

Most children make it through the kiddie rides with a smile, but some cry, either because they don't want the ride to end or because it can't end soon enough for them, ride operator Curtis Stewart said.

He'll stop a ride if a parent requests. Otherwise, he keeps it going. Unless "a kid tries to jump out ... because they're scared," he said. "I've had that happen."

Over at the Peter Paul Elephant Ride, which sends smiling pink pachyderms spinning through the air in tight rotation, Sean Yost, a 17-month-old Rancho Cucamonga toddler, shared a ride with his mom, Cara.

Sean had a nice time. Cara? Not so much.

"It goes in too many circles," she admitted. "I got a little sick. I never used to."

SHEARER HELPS SHEEP COOL OFF

LIKE a boy getting his first haircut, the lamb getting his first shearing did not look happy.

He sat tensely on his butt against the legs of the shearer, who stood over him with the clippers.

But the 4-month-old lamb was in good hands. Don Paulson, the shearer, expertly guided the motorized clippers, moving the lamb's head to the side to better get at his neck, scooting around the ears, over the eyes and up and down his belly.

Within 10 minutes, it was all over. The lamb stood on the platform at the Los Angeles County Fair, looking white and nude, shorn of his blanket of oatmeal-brown wool.

"That's gotta feel good in this heat," one sweating man in the crowd remarked.

Probably so, Paulson said later.

"I think it feels good when it's off," Paulson said. "They do eat better when they're shorn. But on the other hand, the wool does give them some insulation."

Each day at the fair, Paulson demonstrates the art of sheep shearing. Four times a day, five times on weekends, he leads a lamb onto the platform and starts clipping. Crowds instantly gather.

Children gape and wince, perhaps recalling bad haircuts of their own. Some finger the wool and take a piece away. This lamb lost 3 pounds of wool to the power clippers, about a half-inch all over. He was left with a one-eighth-inch dusting.

"To regrow that much, give it four to five months," Paulson said. "Wool's growing all the time. Just like hair."

This lamb is a Rambouillet, a breed that produces a high-quality fine-wool fleece, which might be used in a man's suit. Unfortunately, the wool market isn't so hot right now, so the wool sheared at Paulson's station is given away or thrown out.

Sheep typically are shorn once or twice a year. They have other ways to keep cool besides a shearing, Paulson said. Like dogs, they pant. Unlike dogs, they perspire.

"Some of their cooling is through perspiration, but they also breathe fast to cool off on the inside," Paulson explained.

It's his second fair, but he's been shearing sheep off and on for 60 years, in between stints in the U.S. Navy and at General Dynamics.

But he's no expert, he's quick to say. He once spent a few months in New Zealand and found himself outclassed by men who could shear 300 to 400 sheep in an eight-hour shift. He could manage only 128 – or one every four minutes.

At age 83 – his birthday was Tuesday – the Pomona man still shears on occasion.

"Tired," he joked, "not quite retired."

DENNIS FOREL'S BIG WHEEL

YOU might say Dennis Forel is the Los Angeles County Fair's good-wheel ambassador.

It's hard not to smile at the sight of Forel weaving through the fairgrounds a head above everyone else, riding an old-fashioned bicycle with a 52-inch front wheel.

But creating smiles is the reason he's there.

"My job is to help brighten people's day," Forel said. "And they're already here to have their day brightened."

Forel tools around the fairgrounds daily, meeting and greeting visitors. He's one of the grounds entertainers, whose ranks include clowns, a Dixieland band and costumed characters. They roam the property offering quick pick-me-ups.

As he makes his rounds, Forel goes out of his way to offer tips on fair sights – they're giving away free cheese in the next building! – as well as directions and even balloon animals, which he's expert in crafting.

"He just loves what he does," fair spokeswoman Wendy Talarico said. "You can see it in his face and the way he likes to get people involved in the fair and make sure everyone's enjoying themselves. That's what he cares about, that everyone has a good time."

Forel sits about 7 feet high on his racing bicycle, a replica of a turn-of-the-century model – high enough to look Shaquille O'Neal in the eye.

The high perch gives him a great view, an advantage in navigating through the crowds. On the other hand, he's vulnerable. His bike's center of gravity is high, the turning radius is large and his hand brake, for emergencies, locks the wheel immediately.

He's taken a few spills over his five years at the fair. No one's ever knocked him over. Yes, he carries liability insurance.

"People are pretty gracious about getting out of the way," Forel said.

Fairgoers pepper the 47-year-old Torrance man with questions. The main ones: How does he get on the bike? How does he get off?

He stands behind the bicycle, puts his left foot on a step by the small rear wheel and pushes the bike forward, hopping on his right foot once, twice, three times until he's got the momentum to swing himself onto the leather sling seat.

"It's like a scooter," he said. "Hop on, put your feet forward and ride away."

To get off, he slows down and dismounts on the left side with another hop.

Matching his quaint bicycle, his fair garb is pure Americana: a red, white and blue sequined vest, a straw boater, a bow tie and round wire-rimmed glasses.

Although he looks as though he stepped out of a time warp, Forel generally prefers modern times and technology. What hasn't been improved upon over the last century, he said, are human beings.

"People are people. They're not really going to change," he said, a kindly smile creasing his face. "They have a need. Sometimes all they need is a hello."

THESE PIGS AREN'T POKEY

THESE little piggies go "whee-whee-whee" all the way to the finish line.

At the Los Angeles County Fair, horses aren't the only four-legged animals racing around an oval track. Pigs also run on a small oval in mock races staged by a Kansas-based exotic animal farm.

Wearing racing silks with numbers on the side, four pigs at a time squeal out of the starting gate. They tear around the fenced-in track on Pepper Street and descend on the prize at the finish line: an Oreo cookie on a silver platter.

"Sometimes we use a 'Pig' Newton," explained trainer Tim Hart. "It's just a little treat for them. They like those cookies."

A fair staple, Hedrick's Pig Races take place five times each weekday and six times on weekends. The action is a little less intense than in the Budweiser Grandstand, where horse-racing fans pore over the odds before placing bets for favorites and longshots.

For the low-key pig races, which are free, the crowd – dominated by children – gathers in bleachers around the oval. No betting was observed Monday. Some fans were seen studying a printed program beforehand, but it turned out to be the fair schedule, not the Daily Racing Form.

Hart gets the crowd in the mood for racing excitement by playing recorded versions of "Old MacDonald," "Jimmy Crack Corn" and "The William Tell Overture."

His partner, Chris Ellsworth – introduced as "the pig whisperer" – herds the porkers from the trailer into the starting gate.

A recorded bugle call is played, the lever is pulled and they're off!

No, the pigs don't have jockeys.

Before the noon post time on Monday, Hart promised good racing that day. Friday's rain had wetted down the sawdust-covered concrete track, sending the pigs "slipping and sliding around" over the weekend, he said. "Now the track's pretty dry and they should be speeding up."

In an exclusive to this newspaper, Hart handicapped the three races, picking the pigs named Sylvester Stalloin, NStink and Kevin Bacon.

"Kevin Bacon's been coming in pretty good the last couple of days," Hart revealed.

Luckily, no wagers were made, because Hart was wrong two out of three times.

Stalloin won his race against such fellow musclemen as Jean-Claude Van Hamme, but in the "battle of the bands" contest, 98 Piggees beat out New Pigs on the Block. The celebrity-studded third race saw Forrest Grunt get the Oreo ahead of Leolardo DiPigrio.

Don't shed any tears for the also-rans.

"We give them all something after every race so the losers don't feel bad they didn't get the cookie," Hart said.

That's enough on the pig races. We don't want to boar you.

FAIRPLEX TERMINATES ANNUAL CATTLE DRIVE

BID "happy trails" to the cattle drive through the streets of La Verne, because the event, perhaps the Los Angeles County Fair's most popular publicity stunt, has bitten the dust.

The annual cattle drive sent 300 head of cattle trotting through city streets to Fairplex, herded by 130 amateur cowpokes on horseback. Several thousand people lined Wheeler and Bonita avenues to watch the parade-like procession go by.

But Fairplex officials quietly dropped the cattle drive this year from their roster of events. They said Thursday that the drive, begun in 1996 and held each year through 1999, had run its course.

The 18-day fair in Pomona, billed as the largest county fair in North America, ends Sunday and attracts about 1.2 million people a year.

La Verne City Manager Martin Lomeli is among those disappointed to see the sun set on the cattle drive.

"I'm sorry the event's not here," Lomeli said. "It's something our residents looked forward to. It was a unique event, obviously." But he defended Fairplex's right to change its entertainment.

Businesses got into the spirit of the cattle drives by decorating their facades in an Old West theme. Inspired by the horses passing by, young children galloped around the sidewalk on stick horses.

Many of Grace Miller Elementary School's 500 students dressed in cowboy hats and paper vests to watch the parade.

"It was such a sight for children, who sometimes don't even have cats and dogs at home, to see cattle and horses going down the street," Principal Lori Morris said.

Cattle drive riders, many of whom had little to no experience on horses, also got a kick out of the *City Slickers*-type event.

Two-time rider Garry Nichols, a 53-year-old accountant and financial planner from Upland, said the event was "great fun" and that he was sorry to see it go.

Nichols admitted that the $150 participation fee didn't cover the fair's expenses. But he questioned whether Fairplex officials realized how much positive publicity they gained from the camera-friendly cattle drive.

"How much would they have to pay to get that TV coverage and press coverage?" Nichols wondered. "We even had Channel 5 news. You can't quantify that stuff. But apparently somebody did and decided it wasn't worth the effort."

Nichols said he assumes the event was canceled because the Fairplex vice president who had introduced and organized the cattle drives, Doug Lofstrum, left the fair in February.

Fairplex spokeswoman Wendy Talarico acknowledged that Lofstrum had been "heavily involved" in the drives but said the decision to drop the event was made before his exit. Lofstrum, now a consultant for the Orange County Fair, deferred questions to Fairplex.

Regardless of the timing, Talarico said Fairplex officials want to keep the fair different and interesting, and that means adjusting the entertainment mix.

"We wanted to offer something fresh and new for everyone," Talarico said.

Special attractions include an indoor zoo called Expedition Earth, a larger skate park and the Thunder Alley motorsports section, Talarico said.

"We have eight nights of grandstand entertainment and that has been very successful," she said.

However, the 1999 fair had 18 nights of grandstand entertainment. Two of those events, the demolition derby and the monster truck rally, were dropped this year.

Talarico said the fair is concentrating on weekend concerts, all of which have nearly sold out the 10,000-seat grandstand. Last year's weeknight concerts were lightly attended, she said.

"Every year is just different. We look at it every year with a clean slate and try to come up with the best lineup we can. So far they (visitors) seem to be enjoying what we're offering them," she said.

COUPLE JUGGLE MARRIAGE, CAREER

JUGGLING fire, as she does onstage, takes guts.

But Takako Hayes showed fearlessness from the start, when she decided to join her husband's act as an equal partner – despite having no experience.

"After we were married, my husband was always practicing. I was bored, so he taught me the tricks," she said.

It was important to her that she not be window dressing. "I don't want to be the assistant, handing over the props: 'Ta-da!' " she joked.

As Terrell and Takako, they perform in California and Japan at corporate parties, theme parks and county fairs – including the Los Angeles County Fair, where they play the Good Music Stage each day for free at noon, 2 and 4 p.m. The fair ends Sunday.

The husband-and-wife duo juggle balls, blocks and lighted torches, the latter while riding unicycles. He mimes with his hat, which seemingly has a mind of its own. She does tricks on the Chinese yo-yo, a barbell-sized spool manipulated on a string suspended between two hand-held sticks.

Terrell, 47, is a former lawyer from Tennessee who found he'd made the wrong career choice. He hooked up with a street performer in San Francisco for two weeks and decided he liked that life better.

"It was tough, though, for a lawyer," he said. One minute he was informing clients of his rate: "$100 an hour, please." Next he was saying, hand outstretched: "A dollar, please? ... Change?"

He met Takako, who's now 36, while playing in Japan in 1989. She was a tour guide at the venue. Both were immediately smitten. They married a few months later, after learning each other's language.

In 1990, Terrell was back in Japan, performing solo, as he always had. Takako had a brainstorm.

"She saw a man and woman juggling act and felt the woman wasn't all that good," Terrell said, "and felt she could do better."

He taught her enough to get her onstage with him. Crowds liked her. He taught her the basics in the next six months. They got a five-year booking at a Japanese resort as a duo.

"From there, it was 'Takako and her husband Terrell,' " he said with a grin. "I don't try to compete with her. Whatever I do, all eyes are on her anyway."

Takako, who before marriage worked in a department store, loves the life of a performer.

Her family in Japan is behind her – now.

"At first they said, 'Oh, get a normal job,'" she admitted. "Once they saw the show, they can tell how happy I am. They totally support me."

Jury says stands belong to fair

Food stands at the Los Angeles County Fair are owned by the fair, not the vendors, a jury said Wednesday, deciding that the razing of stands last year without payment to the vendors wasn't at all unfair.

After their seven permanent stands were demolished in August 1999, the Fuerst family sued the Los Angeles County Fair Association, which owns and operates the complex in Pomona where the fair is held each September.

The Fuersts, who sought $595,000 in damages, claimed they owned the stands and had the bills of sale from previous owners to prove it.

But after six hours of deliberation, a Superior Court jury in downtown Los Angeles ruled otherwise.

"We're pleased with the jury verdict. We think it was very just," fair spokeswoman Wendy Talarico said.

In 1999, fair officials asked food vendors to sign rights of ownership contracts as a condition of being allowed to operate. The contracts, which basically defined the stands as storage lockers, formalized the fair association's belief that it owned the buildings, officials said at the time.

The Fuersts, who had been concessionaires for 18 years, declined to sign the contract for their booths, including Marsha's Chicken, the Spaghetti Pot and the Lucky Cuss Saloon, which they said were among the fair's most popular.

The booths, all located near the Clock Tower, were bulldozed by the fair in August 1999, allegedly because they were outdated and in need of extensive renovations. The Fuersts contended that plans for a proposed year-round entertainment complex, Fairplex Village, prompted the contracts and demolition.

Marsha Fuerst of West Covina, who talked to jurors after the verdict, said some were sympathetic but explained to her that provisions in the lease between the fair association and the Los Angeles County government for the 487-acre Fairplex property tied their hands.

"We were asking for damages, but since they determined this lease provision made it that we didn't own the stands, they couldn't" award damages, Fuerst said. She didn't agree with the verdict. One son, Mitchell Fuerst of San Dimas, said an appeal of the verdict is possible, as is a request to return to the fair at some future date.

Their attorney, Mitchell Shapiro, did not return a call seeking comment late Wednesday and Talarico did not have details of the case.

Marsha Fuerst said the family – including her husband, four children and their spouses and children – gave "18 years of their life" to the fair and felt "sad, to say the least" about their absence from the 1999 and 2000 fairs. The family grossed nearly $1 million in sales through the 18-day run of the fair.

Still, they were proud to have stood up for what they believed were their rights, Fuerst said.

"You might be able to fight city hall, but you can't fight the fair," Fuerst said.

The Fuersts were the only concessionaires to sue over the agreement but not the only ones affected. Jim and Beverly Bowen also refused to sign the agreement in 1999 and their stands, Pie A La Mode and Bev's Cafe Siesta, were also bulldozed.

The fair has about 250 concession stands and all remaining concessionaires have signed the agreement, Talarico said.

MAKING MAGIC AT FAIRPLEX

WITH a little technical wizardry, a magic castle is taking shape at the Los Angeles County Fair, designed to delight young readers who love fairy tales – as well as a certain series of books about a boy magician-in-training.

The Castle of Magical Discoveries is the gee-whiz attraction at this year's fair, which opens Friday. Those who venture inside can gape at robotic dragons that roar and belch smoke, cross a moat into a castle and learn some of the tricks of the magician's trade.

Budding Harry Potters can watch objects levitate, whisper to each other from across a room and marvel at lightning in a bottle.

They'll do so in the Boggleway Academy of Science and Illusion, a name that may sound vaguely familiar.

Call Boggleway an unofficial offshoot of the Hogwarts School of Witchcraft and Wizardry from the Potter series of books.

While there's no tie-in with the Potter phenomenon, fair officials certainly hope some of the magic rubs off.

"Harry Potter became so popular, that definitely had an impact on the planning," fair spokeswoman Wendy Talarico said. "But that's not why we created the exhibit."

It was the availability of robotic dragons from Dinamae, the company that provided robotic dinosaurs and sharks in previous years, that got the exhibit going, Talarico said.

In the Dragons Courtyard that greets visitors, a 14-foot-tall dragon looms over a European-style castle. Claws dug into the parapets, the dragon moves his head, roars, spews smoke and even blinks.

Nearby, a mother dragon teaches her two babies how to breathe fire. Another dragon guards its hoard of jewels. Behind glass, Quetzalcoatl, the Aztec god of life, transforms from a human image into a magnificent plumed serpent. (It's done with mirrors, literally.)

Early reviews from pint-size patrons are promising.

"We've been bringing in the smaller kids and they're just fascinated," said John Chartier, coordinator of the exhibit, during a walk-through Wednesday.

Why? Probably because it's one thing to see dragons in a fairy tale, Chartier theorized, and another to come face to face with three-dimensional dragons that writhe and roar.

"It's storybooks coming alive," Chartier said.

Much of the exhibit was still being installed Wednesday, but the dragons were in place and one whimsical touch gave a hint of the flavor. In the laboratory area, a shelf on a "stone" wall held jars labeled with such magic compounds as snake's liver, dragon's teeth, lizard lips ... and Viagra.

Math, science, art and magic tricks will be incorporated in hands-on ways. Children and adults can make test tubes bubble, for instance, and test the properties of gravity, inertia and friction in a giant marble maze.

At the very end of the exhibit will stand the Coat of Arms Cafe and a gift shop – illustrating the modern sleight-of-hand of separating parents from their money.

L.A. COUNTY FAIR STARTS DAY LATER

THERE'S lots to do at this year's Los Angeles County Fair – but not today. Unlike past years, the fair is closed today and kicks off Friday.

The change from a Thursday opening is part logistics and part marketing, fair officials said.

They wanted to distance the fair from the crunch of Labor Day, children's return to school and the just-ended state fair in Sacramento, which featured some of the same concessionaires.

Fair officials "also felt Friday would be a stronger opening day," spokeswoman Wendy Talarico said. "Thursday is hard to get people out for. Friday is just a better day to start out."

With the later start, the fair, which ends September 23, will run 17 days instead of the typical 18.

A 17-day fair, however, is actually a longer tradition. Historically, the fair was 17 days for most of its life until 1980. From there the event grew as long as 24 days before being scaled back to 18 in 1997.

Opening day will carry a bonus this year. Admission, typically $10 on weekdays, will be lowered to $1, courtesy of this newspaper and its sister publications in the Los Angeles Newspaper Group.

FIRST DAY OF FAIR FEATURES FANTASY

NIFTY rides, animal contests, good-bad food and miracle mop demonstrations are probably the first things that come to mind when you think of the Los Angeles County Fair, which opens today.

You probably don't think of castles, dragons and wizards. But Building 7A, which in recent years has housed glitzy exhibits of robotic dinosaurs and world ecosystems, this year features the Castle of Magical Discoveries, a 43,000-square-foot, $1 million monument to science and sorcery, sure to appeal to Harry Potter fans.

Visitors can gawk at robotic fire-breathing dragons, learn magic tricks and, in preparation for a possible career as a knight errant, test their reaction time and endurance.

At the Pomona fair, which runs through September 23, other aspects also defy expectations.

Twenty human-sized angel sculptures will be displayed around the Millard Sheets Gallery, having relocated from their perches in downtown Los Angeles, where they caused a mild sensation this spring. Even Pershing Square, which had the most sculptures in one place, didn't have this many.

"I think they have more impact when they're concentrated," said Christy Johnson Micheli, curator of the gallery.

The gallery will also feature a collection of still life paintings and photos and, in a twist, visitors can sit for a free photo that will be posted on the website of the California Museum of Photography in Riverside. Its goal is to photograph 20,000 fair visitors.

A few touches this year are new, so don't doubt your memory if things don't seem quite the way you remember them from last year.

Heritage Farm is now California Heritage Square, for instance, and the livestock area now has a formal name: Fairview Farms.

Also, sections of the sprawling 487-acre grounds are now designated as "neighborhoods." Shades of Ontario Mills!

The biggest change is to Fiesta Village, a fair staple since 1952. One building is gone, transforming the formerly boxed-in village into an open plaza. The remaining buildings have been freshly painted, the stage has been enlarged and trees have been added. There's also a new name, Plaza de las Americas, intended to reflect Central and South American cultures, not just Mexican.

A castaway theme takes over the adjacent America's Kids building, which features an "Island Adventure" with an erupting volcano, thatched umbrellas, parrots and monkeys, and a mock shipwreck – everything but Wilson the volleyball.

"We do have Lyle Lyle Crocodile," event coordinator Tricia Bassett said, referring to an appearance by the popular children's book character.

Over at the Flower and Garden Pavilion, the theme is "The Fragrances of France," and the building remains a good place to escape the heat and bustle.

It wouldn't be a county fair without contests for hog calling, butter churning and tortilla tossing, among other competitions. More refined talents are on display in the Creative Expressions building, formerly Creative Living, where table settings, needlework and baked goodies are judged.

Thrills of a more visceral sort can be found on the carnival midway. New this year is the Mega Drop, which takes you 133 feet in the air before dropping you at 50 mph. More than 70 rides will test your ability to keep down the corn dog you just ate.

Speaking of corn dogs, more than 250 food stands will offer the usual array of diet-busting junk food.

One downside this year for cash-strapped families is the increased price for admission, parking, hamburgers and sodas. Enough deals exist, however, that fair officials say calendar-watching families can avoid paying full price for everything.

Today, for instance, the usual $10 weekday admission is just $1, courtesy of this newspaper and its sister publications in the Los Angeles Newspaper Group.

From behind the counter of her New York Deli, 20-year concessionaire Mary Lee Ricketts is cautiously optimistic that crowds will pack Fairplex despite the increases.

"We all hate to see prices go up, but it's not $2.95 anymore anywhere," Ricketts said.

END RESULT OF TOO MANY SWEETS

SPOTTED at the L.A. County Fair, a cinnamon roll booth with a large sign declaring: "Ten Pound Buns."

How refreshing. Food vendors usually aren't so upfront about the after-effects.

* * *

Time Flies Dept.: Can it really have been a year since I asked someone to meet me at the Clock Tower?

Smokey Robinson Gets Intimate With Crowd At Fairplex

"Let's get intimate," Smokey Robinson told nearly 10,000 listeners midway through his show, and based on the roar of approval, nobody seemed sad about his plans.

Indeed, soul crooner Robinson was able to convey warmth and, yes, intimacy during Sunday's concert at the Los Angeles County Fair, despite the size of the crowd and the grandstand seating.

Robinson encouraged the audience to sing along on several songs, not that anyone seemed to need encouragement. "Tears of a Clown," "You Really Got a Hold on Me" and "I Second That Emotion," among other hits with the Miracles, are indelible. "My Girl," "Get Ready" and "The Way You Do the Things You Do," some of the equally catchy classics he wrote for the Temptations, also were revived Sunday.

In his between-song comments, Robinson reminisced about the Temptations, complimented the audience on its singing and, in one touching segment, spotlighted guitarist Marv Tarplin, the co-writer of many Motown hits, who now plays in his band. They performed one of the classics they co-wrote, "The Tracks of My Tears," with Robinson singing and Tarplin picking out the familiar, delicate riff, before the rest of the band joined for the finale.

Robinson's hitmaking days are probably behind him, but the 61-year-old Motown singer still knows how to work a crowd and put a song across. He manages to be slick and heartfelt at the same time. Much of his 90-minute set mirrored his 1999 fair performance, even down to the patter, yet his joy in performing seems authentic.

On his version of his 1981 solo hit "Being With You," he sang the last chorus, "I don't care about anything else but being with you," then made a sweeping gesture to the crowd. In other words: This is where I want to be, onstage.

Or, as he put it in one song that on Sunday also seemed addressed to longtime fans in his audience: "If you feel like giving me/A lifetime of devotion/I second that emotion."

Looking trim and fit, Robinson wore a white banded collar shirt and a gray frock coat. He doffed the coat a few songs in and, later, unbuttoned the shirt, causing more than a few shrieks of delight. Three bouquets of roses were delivered to the stage during his 90-minute set.

His vocal showcase was a stunning version of "Ooh Baby Baby" (best known through Linda Ronstadt's hit version) in which the wounds of romantic loss seemed fresh, as if the "mistakes, I know I've made a few" had occurred yesterday, not 35 years ago, when he wrote the song. As he pulled the notes from somewhere deep inside, he really did seem "about at the end of (his) rope."

Besides the classics, Robinson sang two songs from his most recent album, 1999's *Intimate*. ("Thank you both," he joked about the album's sales.) "Sleeping In" and the partly Spanish-language "Tu Me Besas Muy Rico" had little of the verve of his classics, but the live performances had more spark than the recorded versions.

Robinson's hallmarks as a songwriter are clever comparisons, unusual rhymes and the contrast between sadness and gladness. "Tracks of My Tears" is about a man who always wears a smile to cover the hurt inside. "It's Growing" compares the singer's growing love for a woman to the way a fisherman exaggerates the size of his catch and a story grows the more it's passed around.

The same playfulness and warmth in his songwriting comes across in performance. The show ended with "Cruisin'," one of his best-loved solo hits. Robinson split the crowd in half and got each side to compete with the other on singing the line "I love it when we're cruisin' together," a surefire rouser.

The way he swept us off our feet, he could have been a broom.

ONE OF A KIND: PHOTOGRAPHERS TAKE PORTRAITS, POSE QUESTION 'WHAT MAKES YOU UNIQUE?'

THEY'LL snap your photo – and also get a flash of insight.

Photographers from a Riverside museum are asking people at the Los Angeles County Fair to sit for a free portrait. They've shot more than 10,000, in a booth inside the Millard Sheets Gallery, and plan to post them all online as an art project.

Naturally, since art's involved, there's a twist. After the portrait, fairgoers are asked a question: What makes them unique?

If the free photo doesn't floor them, the introspective question usually does.

"It takes people by surprise," said Ryan Swoverland, one of the photographers. "People say 'I don't know' or 'Ask someone else what makes me unique.'"

Swoverland and his colleagues at the UC Riverside Museum of Photography don't take "I don't know" for an answer. They'll keep asking until they get something, then dutifully type the answer into their laptop computer, along with the subject's first name, age and ZIP code. The information will be posted along with the person's photo on the museum's Web site.

(There should be no privacy concerns about the pictures on the Internet because last names are not asked and there is no way to contact any of the subjects, Swoverland said. Some subjects even give phony names, which is fine.)

The project is called 20,000 Portraits, and one goal is to get people to think about themselves. While the project documents a large group of people, each can stand out as an individual.

Understandably, most people's immediate response to the question about their uniqueness is generic: their personality, their smile or simply themselves.

Some, though, come up with an answer as original as they are. "One woman said she's raising a one-eyed, one-winged crow named One-Eyed Stanley," Swoverland said. "Another guy said what made him unique is his ghetto booty."

"Some of the answers," Swoverland added, "are awesome and diverse."

Over a few minutes Monday afternoon, answers given included "My eyes," "Myself," "Everybody loves me," "I like swimming," and "I like to do everything once."

The latter answer was from Campbell Cu, a 53-year-old ex-Canadian who lives in Los Angeles and is studying to become a dog groomer.

No one had ever asked him what makes him unique, Cu said afterward with delight. "Whether it's unique or not," Cu said, "it's us at the moment."

Photos are shot with a digital camera, meaning there's no film involved, just computer space.

Subjects sit on a stool in front of a metal frame showing the boundaries of the image. They're encouraged to do whatever they like. For her picture Monday, Pamela Semple waved at Swoverland, the photographer. Within seconds, he was able to show her the picture on his laptop. Semple, a 34-year-old from Redondo Beach, liked the way her hand blurred next to her still face. The experience was fun, she said, "because you didn't care what you looked like."

Perhaps it's the quasi-anonymity, but the photo doesn't carry the usual anxiety of having your picture taken. Still, most adults, reacting to the prompt that it's a portrait, merely sit and smile, said Karen Barber, one of the photographers.

"It's the kids who'll make funny faces and stick out their tongues,"

Barber said. "With the events of the last week, some people will wave a flag."

Printouts of the portraits are not possible at the fair, but they are supposed to be posted online soon.

Fairgoers will be able to search for their photo by ZIP code, age or first name. Or they can create their own custom search.

If, say, a man named John types in his name, he should find photos and responses of everyone else who gave the name John. He could do the same with his ZIP code or age.

Or someone could type in a random word and see if that pops up in any "what makes you unique" responses.

"You could even type in 'giraffe' and get something," Swoverland said. "One person said she collects giraffes."

POMONA'S JUST TOYING WITH US

THE co-founder of Wham-O Inc., Arthur Melin, died June 28, and the news reminded me of Pomona's role in launching one of the company's signature goofy products: the Frisbee. Let's take a spin through history, shall we?

Melin and his partner, Richard Knerr, were college pals who founded their San Gabriel-based company in 1947 to sell a slingshot. Soon they were peddling other sporting goods by mail order, but hadn't hit the big time – not until a fateful walk along the beach in 1955.

Melin and Knerr saw people playing with a small disc that resembled a flying saucer as it spun through the air. They asked its owner where he'd bought it. "He said, 'The Los Angeles County Fair,'" said fair spokeswoman Sharon Autry.

Intrigued, Knerr and Melin visited the Pomona-based fair to check out the product themselves, Autry said. They met Fred Morrison, the man selling the flying discs, and negotiated rights to the novelty. Introduced by Wham-O in 1957, the discs were called Pluto Platters until a name change the next year to the now-familiar Frisbee.

And to think: If it weren't for Pomona, people might still be tossing around pie tins.

PLUTO PLATTER TALE STILL SPINNING

THE inventor of the Frisbee got his start hawking his flying discs at the L.A. County Fair in Pomona, as mentioned in this space last week.

Well, I've since found more information on Walter Frederick Morrison and his Pluto Platter – which is what the discs were called before he sold the rights to Wham-O.

In the early 1950s, Morrison and his wife would travel to beaches, parks, department stores and, yes, the Pomona-based fair to demonstrate his flying saucers, which capitalized on the then-popular UFO craze.

Morrison reportedly employed the flair of a P.T. Barnum as he explained to baffled fairgoers, circa 1955, how the strange discs stayed aloft.

"At the Pomona fair in Los Angeles," according to a 1987 *Sports Illustrated* article, "he pretended that the disc was connected to an invisible wire."

As Morrison told the magazine: "Feeling kind of stupid, we started walking through the crowd and yelled, 'Watch out for the wire!' And people started looking out!'"

A path was cleared, the Pluto Platter was demonstrated, and Morrison made fairgoers a deal too good to pass up: He'd sell 100 feet of invisible wire for $1 – and throw in the Pluto Platter for free.

"Sales were pretty good," Morrison recalled. "Maybe because we were right across from the beer tent."

Meanwhile, reader Jay Williams of Pomona tells me he remembers Morrison in his later days as a hardware store owner in La Verne.

Morrison once explained one inspiration for his invention of the Frisbee, the 81-year-old Williams says: "(Morrison) worked for movie studios. At lunchtime they'd go in the alley and take the lids off film tins and would sail (the lids) back and forth."

The clatter didn't go over so well on the set.

"A director came out and told them he didn't mind them doing that but wished they'd use something that didn't make so much noise," Williams related.

Morrison later found something quieter.

One word: plastics.

ICONS OF THE FAIR TURN 50

GIVEN its function, a clock tower really can't be described as timeless.

But as the Los Angeles County Fair's Clock Tower is now 50 years old, it seems the visual landmark – which helps fairgoers tell time, find their way and meet up with friends – has become a true landmark as well.

Introduced in 1952, the Clock Tower isn't the only structure at the fair hitting the half-century mark this year.

The Flower and Garden Pavilion, whose fragrant, and cool, displays are among the fair's most popular, debuted in 1952 as well.

So did the former Mexican Village, now known under a more politically correct name, Plaza de las Americas.

While it's coincidence that they all debuted the same year, the clock tower, flower pavilion and Latino village all became icons of the fair, which began in 1922 and opened Friday for its latest run.

The three structures are "very recognizable and yet so unique from one another," said fair spokeswoman Wendy Talarico. "Just seeing them, people know where they are, immediately."

No ceremonies or special events are planned for the anniversaries, so you'll have to plan your own solemn observances.

Standing 50 feet tall, the Clock Tower was predicted from the start to become a landmark for fairgoers trying to get their bearings on the 487-acre grounds. The fair promoted the phrase "Meet me at the Clock Tower" that very first year and the wording caught on.

Generations of fairgoers have reconnoitered under the tower.

"It was erected as a central meeting place," Talarico said. "The phrase "Meet me at the Clock Tower' has really stuck through the years."

It's also been dubbed "the hub of the fair," and several features make that designation true today.

An information booth and lost-child area are just a few steps away. Benches and shade make the tower a perfect place to catch your breath – as does a Krispy Kreme doughnut stand added two years ago. And an automated teller is nearby.

Visually, the tower's top is a four-sided box with clocks on each face and flags on top. In its lower section, the tower's walls are angled, forming the shape of an X on the ground.

The tower's distinctive look is, believe it or not, French.

It was styled after the clock tower at 1925's Paris Design Exhibition, according to author and pop historian Charles Phoenix, who has researched the fair's history.

"Can you imagine that clock was inspired by 1925 Paris?" Phoenix said. "But it's true."

Whether the color was also Parisian isn't known, but Pomona's tower was originally orange. It's now a tasteful white.

The Flower and Garden Pavilion's design also was an artful borrowing from another source, this one from South America.

Architect Everett L. Tozier's domed rotunda was based on a futuristic church in Brasilia, the capital of Brazil, designed by famed modern architect Oscar Niemeyer, Phoenix said.

A sweeping arched roof and a facade almost entirely constructed of glass marks Tozier's creation. Over the entrance, a neon sign – made by Pomona's Williams Sign Co. – spells out "Flower and Garden" in script, with an "F" that looks like a rose.

The Flower and Garden Pavilion, Phoenix said, is "an outrageously spectacular piece of modern architecture. There's not another building like it in Southern California. ... It's nothing short of a miracle that it's still there."

Of course, the Flower and Garden inside are pretty, too.

Originally known as the Flower and Nursery Building, the inaugural display in 1952 made use of the talents of wholesale florists from downtown Los Angeles.

Whether the theme is "The Fragrances of France" or "Geometric Shapes," the pavilion's floral designers still strive to create a sensuous experience for fairgoers. This year's theme is "Reflections of the South." Gardens will mimic New Orleans' French Quarter, southern plantations, bayous and steaming swamps.

Year after year, the pavilion is one of the fair's most popular exhibits.

"It's sort of an escape," Talarico said. "All the flowers! It's a calming, cool escape from the rest of the fair."

Less calm and cool is the Latino village area, a bustling plaza with Mexican food, jewelry and entertainment.

Surrounded by walls simulating adobe, the village debuted in 1952 as the Mexican Village. It was sponsored by Los Angeles' Mexican Chamber of Commerce.

As time went on, the village began to seem anachronistic, or worse. The name was changed in 1996 to Fiesta Village, and again in 2001 to Plaza de las Americas, accompanying a remodeling job.

The plaza is now more open, physically, and more inclusive of other Latin cultures, hence the new name, Talarico said.

This year, the plaza will continue during the day as a "cultural marketplace" with food and other vendors, and with performers such as the Ballet Folklorico, Talarico said.

At night, chairs will be cleared away and the plaza will become akin to a dance club, with live performances of salsa and *Tejano* music.

And so the old becomes new – but, comfortingly, not too new.

FAIR OFFERS CALORIES ON A STICK

TODAY'S health advisory: The L.A. County Fair is selling Deep-Fried Snickers Bars on a Stick.

As gourmands know, Pomona's fair is a pioneer in the cuisine concept of food items on sticks.

"This year we'll have 31 food-on-a-stick items," fair spokeswoman Wendy Talarico bragged recently, and I was glad to hear it, because I'm a stickler for details.

Corn dogs, ice cream and popsicles, sure, but you can also experiment with cheese on a stick, linguica sausage on a stick, teriyaki on a stick and even pork chops on a stick.

As far as I know, no one is yet selling spaghetti on a stick – but in a year with Snickers on a stick, I may be proved wrong.

The Snickers are sold at a Texas Donuts stand near the Flower and Garden Pavilion. They're three bucks, and given the cost of a Snickers, this means the fried batter, powdered sugar and wooden stick must be worth $2.50.

My colleague Will Matthews was at the fair with me for lunch Friday, and while I couldn't bring myself to buy a deep-fried chocolate bar, Matthews, our investigative reporter, felt duty-bound to investigate.

The Snickers was handed over in a paper tray like a corn dog. It was battered and speared like a corn dog too. "Be careful, it's hot," the server told Matthews – a warning not typically associated with candy bars.

Soon Matthews was biting into his piping-hot Snickers bar, which was sliding off the stick dangerously. Meanwhile, the powdered sugar on top was blowing all over his red shirt.

In an exclusive interview, Matthews told me the candy bar was gooey and not good. After eating about one-third, or $1 worth, he threw the other $2 worth away. Finally, something our investigative reporter was unable to get to the bottom of.

His verdict: "Deep-fried Snickers suck."

Put that on a stick and eat it.

* * *

I also checked out the fair's "Lights! Camera! Science!" extravaganza, which features hands-on science experiments related to the movies, as well as movie posters, vintage movie and TV actors signing autographs and, near the front, a theater-style concessions stand.

A large popcorn, I noticed, is six bucks.

Yes, six bucks.

A 32nd item on a stick: fairgoers.

* * *

For a couple of years, I'd been looking forward to the 2002 fair, its 80th anniversary, so I could write about MacPherson's Ice Cream, which is also celebrating its 80th.

Known for its "custom-built ice cream bars" (on a stick, naturally), root beer floats and soft serve cones, MacPherson's had a stand way back at the inaugural 1922 fair.

Not a year has gone by without a MacPherson family member behind the counter. It's now run by Margaret MacPherson, the founder's granddaughter.

A family-run ice cream stand! Now there's a heartwarming human-interest story, eh?

I tracked down Margaret at her stand on Friday to inquire cheerfully about an interview.

"No," she snapped. "I don't want to be in the newspaper. I'm very busy. I've got customers lined up. I don't have time for this."

Um, well, we could do it later...

"I have no interest in a story. All right? I think I've made myself clear. Goodbye."

A 33rd item on a stick: me.

CAMEL MILKING? THAT'S UDDERLY RIDICULOUS

SPOTTED at the L.A. County Fair: A bluesman named Brother Yusef, sitting in a gazebo near the Pie A La Mode stand, picking songs on an acoustic guitar and moaning the blues.

No, none of his sad songs were about the price of parking.

* * *

This year the fair has a demonstration of camel milking – yes, camel milking – which puts me in mind of the scene from *Meet the Parents*, where Ben Stiller tells his girlfriend's parents he once milked a cat. "Anything with nipples, you can milk," he tells Robert De Niro, who responds, deadpan: "I've got nipples, Greg. Could you milk me?"

Well, just like cats and Robert De Niro, camels have nipples too. A bunch of us gathered around a pen in Hidden Meadows Park as a man wearing a headset microphone brought out a mama camel and her baby camel for a dromedary demonstration.

Camels only "drop" their milk after a certain amount of coaxing, and then only for 90 seconds, the man, Gil Riegler, said, explaining that the speedy feeding is a legacy of the animals' nomadic lifestyle.

At the fair, the milk doesn't always pour – pressure of a public performance and all – but this time, the juice started flowing. Riegler let the baby camel get a good gulp, then elbowed his way in and, pulling on mama's udder with one hand, holding a bucket with the other, began, yes, milking a camel.

That's it. I can die happy.

After witnessing a man in Pomona milk a camel, I can truly say I've seen it all.

Riegler showed off the white, frothy stuff in the bucket, and while tastes were ruled out because of health regulations, he reported that camel's milk is sweet, naturally low in fat and loaded with vitamins.

Don't tell Chino, but Oasis Camel Dairy, Riegler's farm in San Diego County, hopes to get camel's milk on the market in 2003.

Can a drive-through Alta Dena camel's milk stand be far behind?

In the meantime, the milking shows are not to be missed.

"This is the first time in the U.S. that anybody has publicly seen anyone milk a camel," Riegler told me.

See? And you thought you were too sophisticated for the fair!

So why is Riegler milking camels? A jeweler by trade, he became acquainted with camels while volunteering at a camp where disabled people mix with exotic animals as therapy.

When he heard that camel's milk is rich in insulin, which could help diabetics, he thought he'd try opening a dromedary dairy.

If you're wondering how Riegler learned to milk camels, he took lessons in Israel from a professor who specializes in camel milking.

Riegler, whose only relevant experience was milking goats as a child, became adept at camel milking – but only after learning to vary his approach from camel to camel.

"Camels are like women," the professor told him sagely. "Everybody has a different touch."

I'd better stop here before my editor busts my hump.

* * *

Truth in advertising: A tamale contest today at the fair has a sponsor: The Gas Company.

Don't say you weren't warned!

SNO CONES GOOD TO A FAIR-THEE-WELL

EVERYONE who enjoys the L.A. County Fair enjoys it for a different reason.

For me, it's the joy of wandering aimlessly on baking-hot asphalt under a broiling sun, sweat spritzing from my body like I'm a human lawn sprinkler.

Kidding.

What I like is the mix of humanity, the charming exhibits and the all-American (i.e., greasy) food.

What I like best, though, are sno cones.

Granted, sno cones seem like the biggest ripoff at the fair – which is saying something.

There's virtually no "there" there to a sno cone. There's ice, there's flavored syrup, there's a paper cone. Oh, and that funky straw, the one with the scoop at the end.

Its inventor, I'm convinced, must be the same guy who came up with the spork.

So, yes, the sno cone is just one step above bottled water as far as getting people to pay money for nothing.

But like most things at a county fair, the affection isn't about the object, per se, it's about pleasant associations.

My pleasant association is with my first fair. That was in my hometown of Olney, Illinois, population 9,000, which hosted a grand exposition each summer known as the Richland County Fair.

It pales in comparison to Pomona's fair, of course, but as a child, I thought the Richland County Fair was a big deal. I'd ride the kiddie rides, and look at the animals, and you'll never guess what else.

Eat a sno cone! (You guessed that? Aww, someone must have told you.)

Sno cones there came in several flavors. Cherry was a big one. Cola was another. Personally, I always opted for grape.

Grape was my flavor of choice for almost anything. Grape was my favorite Otter Pop. I liked grape gum. On TV, I watched *The Great Grape Ape*, a cartoon about a purple gorilla.

Grape was great.

When my grape sno cone was handed over, there at the fair, I rarely bothered with the straw with the scoop until the end.

No, I would just nibble happily at the crunchy purple ice rising over the rim of the paper cup. When that was gone, I would squeeze the cup to force the ice up, then nibble on that.

What can I say? I was easily amused.

The grape sno cone became my personal fair tradition. Every year, I would get at least one.

That's held true with the fairs I've attended in California as a grownup. Whether I'm there as a journalist or just there to have fun – although I'm usually there for both – it just doesn't feel like a fair unless I get a grape sno cone.

(Your own must-have fair treat might be barbecued corn on the cob, or lemonade, or ice cream, or something else entirely. Maybe it will be this year's novelty food, the deep-fried Snickers bar on a stick, although if you want a second one of those, I don't want to know you.)

Just to prove I can still grow and change as I age, I actually switched a couple of fairs ago from sno cones to shaved ice.

Shaved ice, I discovered, is a more perfect form of sno cone. Instead of crunchy crushed ice with a couple of squirts of flavoring, shaved ice is so fine it's almost like ice cream. There's flavoring in every bite. And it comes in a cup, not a cone.

The only L.A. County Fair stand that sells shaved ice offers at least 30 flavors, including exotic Hawaiian fruity stuff like mango and papaya. You can mix and match any combination of flavors.

One day last week at noontime, overheated and thirsty, I bought a shaved ice, then found – wonder of wonders – a shaded bench.

For a few happy minutes, I cooled down with my favorite fair treat, watched children ride the kiddie rides and thought back to my own childhood.

You might be wondering which exotic flavor I chose.

Do you really have to ask?

Healthy lifestyles, at the fair?

CONCERNED about health impacts on fairgoers from the deep-fried Snickers bar on a stick, I popped into the L.A. County Fair's First Aid center, notebook in hand, hoping to get an accurate count of fatalities.

Medical coordinator Dean Grose, who oversees the 25-bed health facility – conveniently located near a Fatburger stand – checked the log for me.

"I haven't had anybody in here for deep-fried Snickers on a stick," concluded Grose, who it should be pointed out is a trained medical professional.

What about injuries from foods-on-a-stick – for instance, someone walking with stick food, tripping and poking themselves?

"Not that I can recall," Grose told me.

His staff had, however, already seen 833 people "for Band-Aids, as-pirins and antacids."

Yes, antacids for fair food.

"If you eat something that doesn't agree with you," Grose said, "we can give you Rolaids, Alka-Seltzer or, if you need it, Pepto-Bismol."

Before you ask, no, Pepto-Bismol doesn't come on a stick.

When digestive problems arise at the fair, Grose explained, some-times it's the heat in combination with the food, and sometimes, as you'd expect, it's just the food.

Concessionaires get more creative every year, Grose said.

"Last year," he added, "they had deep-fried dill pickles."

I almost asked him for a Rolaids based on the name alone.

* * *

Besides deep-fried Snickers, the county fair has a second exciting innovation, the Healthy Lifestyles Building. Its existence can only be explained by some sort of equal-time law.

You enter Healthy Lifestyles by passing by – and hopefully not stopping at – the Hot Cinnamon Rolls stand. Among the, er, delights you'll find inside Healthy Lifestyles:

- Vitaballs, which are described as "vitamin gumballs."
- Scientologists.
- Wavy foam mattresses with moving footrests, called "spinal exercisers."
- "Tools for Expanding Human Consciousness"' videos.
- Bidets.
- A "natural energy stimulator" bearing the four words that act as a seal of approval for all your top medical devices: "as seen on TV."

In other words, this hall boasts the same high level of quality merchandise for which the fair is renowned.

And so, I highly recommend you visit the Healthy Lifestyles Building today – before the Federal Trade Commission shuts it down.

* * *

In the autograph area of the fair's Lights! Camera! Science! exhibit, I saw Rip Taylor chatting amiably with June Lockhart. Perhaps out of respect, he was not pelting her with handfuls of feathers.

* * *

First place in the fair's Spam cooking competition went to Cheryl Ankeney, whose winning recipe was for Creamy Spam Broccoli Pastry Shells.

Can I have that Rolaids now?

A DAY AT THE RACES (YAWN)

HAVING never been to a horse race, I thought I'd drop in at the L.A. County Fair's Grandstand, where they have real live horse racing right before your eyes – if you can manage to keep them open.

At the track Tuesday, I saw one race, lasting roughly one minute, followed by tractors watering the track and raking the dirt, lasting roughly 20 minutes.

Compared to horse racing, shuffleboard is packed with blazing-fast thrills.

Things certainly start off in a high-toned manner. At the 12:30 p.m. post time, a fellow in a top hat, frock coat, breeches and knee-high boots – what the well-dressed Pomonan is wearing this year – strides onto the track and blows "First Call" on his bugle.

Then the announcer comes on the P.A. system. Not one to let a bugler outclass him, he has, yes, a British accent. Is this Pomona – or Churchill Downs?

I didn't place any bets, mostly because I have no idea how horse racing works.

The fair's Media Guide didn't offer any clarity. Here's what it says under "Wagering":

"$1 exactas on all races; $2 quinella on all races; $1 trifecta on all races with six betting interests; $1 superfecta on the 3rd, 6th, 8th, 9th and last race with eight or more betting interests…"

So my betting interest had already dried up when the horses lined up for the first race.

Prince Charles, the announcer, says: "The hawses hahv nie ritched the stahting gyte."

Good for the hawses. A minute later, it's all over, and if you blinked, you missed the whole thing.

The winning hawses are certified and Prince Charles declares: "The exacta wid hahv pied tin dollahs and fawty cents."

With a payoff like that, you could afford lunch at the fair.

As you may have heard, the fair failed to dump racing this year but vowed to try again. That means this could very well be the last season you can see racing in Pomona.

So, if you have any interest, hustle over there.

Don't spare the hawses.

* * *

One thing I do have to say for the Grandstand: The seats offer a great view of the fire in the foothills.

Mingling with the crowd not far from my seat, the bugler goofed around by blowing a few bars of an old chestnut.

"Smoke Gets in Your Eyes."

I liked him.

* * *

Spotted at the fair: a food stand with the sign Baked Potatoe.

I eyeballed the employees, and no, Dan Quayle wasn't one of them.

* * *

More stick foods seen at the fair

- Cookie on a stick
- Egg roll on a stick
- Alligator on a stick

Shouldn't a health-oriented vendor counter with salad on a stick?

* * *

Today's fair tip: The Bean Spittin' Contest is at 5 p.m.

Winds are predicted to blow from the southeast, so position yourself accordingly.

A WALK ON THE QUIRKY SIDE

ATTENTION fairgoers: This is one tour of the Los Angeles County Fair that will NOT involve a tram.

And while Charles Phoenix's walking tour Saturday of the Pomona fairgrounds will focus on landmarks, the author and nostalgia lover's choices are more idiosyncratic than those pointed out on the fair's official tram tour.

One Phoenix favorite is the giant statue of a ranchero, an Old California landowner, carved in 1953 out of an unusual material: a redwood trunk. Fairgoers would interrupt sculptor John Svenson in mid-chisel to innocently ask: "Will it grow?"

He also loves the model garden railroad, which chugs through intricately detailed miniature scenes, including a citrus packing house, a mission and the Fox Theater, none much bigger than a shoebox. The exhibit began in 1924 and is, he said, "one of the most charming things at the fair."

Another must-see, in his eyes, is the quaint pedestrian bridge crossing a pond. The concrete railings are, folk art-style, fashioned to look like tree branches.

"There are just little treasures everywhere here," Phoenix said as he led a reporter and photographer on a preview of his tour.

The majority of the fair's public art, exhibit halls, food stands and other permanent attractions were built between 1926 and 1957, Phoenix said.

"My theory," he said, "is that the L.A. County Fair is a total treasure trove of vintage architecture, and a historic time warp."

An aficionado of 1950s style, Phoenix, 39, grew up in a '50s ranch home in Ontario and now lives in Los Angeles.

He's the author of *Southern California in the '50s* and *Cruising the*

Pomona Valley, both devoted to fun, quirky landmarks, and he puts on a show of old vacation slides with humorous commentary called "God Bless Americana."

His county fair tours – which are free – take place this Saturday only at 11 a.m., 1 p.m. and 3 p.m., beginning on the steps of the Millard Sheets Gallery, a few paces from the Clock Tower.

Phoenix pointed out that the gallery was designed by muralist Millard Sheets, its namesake, who went on to design Home Savings Bank branches.

The gallery "looks like a Home Savings Bank building," Phoenix said. "It's got the decorative trim on top, a mural over the door and a statue out front."

That statue, "A Horse and Young Farmers," was sculpted by Lawrence Tenney Stevens, whose followup commission was for the New York World's Fair of 1939.

Other points of interest on the tour include the Art Deco-style Food Court, the Flower and Garden Pavilion – whose sweeping arch is based on a church in Brazil, of all things – and the neon sign for Toad in the Hole, the fair's oldest restaurant .

Now known as Toad in the Hole Pizza, "it wasn't pizza originally," Phoenix explained. "It was a baked potato with a filet mignon in the middle. That's the toad in the hole. I guess it's a classic English dish."

Another stop is the Grandstand – but not for the horse racing.

Downstairs, Phoenix was delighted to find his personal Holy Grail: two of the vintage, Bob's Big Boy-like fiberglass figures of the fair's mascot, Thummer the pig.

Thummer was originally known as Porky until the cartoon pig of the same name forced a change in the 1950s.

Although Saturday's tours focus mostly on physical structures, Phoenix said he will also lead people to a few favorite exhibits, including the theatrical "slice-it, dice-it" cooking-gadget demonstrations. Vanished attractions such as the Jetsons-like monorail and the neon Fun Zone arch may also rate a mention.

Phoenix will also offer anecdotes and observations about the fair, which began in 1922 and was, culturally, a bigger deal when Los Angeles hadn't yet become a metropolis.

"What most people don't understand about the fair is that for many years, it was our Disneyland, it was our County Museum of Art – long before those places even existed," Phoenix said. "It was where we came to see the latest products, the latest developments. "

Frank Lloyd Wright was a guest in 1954 when *House Beautiful* sponsored a showcase of modern home interiors. The Sheets Gallery used to display works by Picasso, Renoir and Van Gogh.

"Can you imagine going in here and seeing a Van Gogh?" Phoenix asked in mock amazement.

Phoenix's secret is that while he genuinely reveres the fair, he doesn't take it too seriously.

As he passed the First Aid center with its charming block-lettered sign, Phoenix played his tour guide role to the hilt, intoning: "Hopefully you'll get a cut or scrape, because then you'll go into the historic First Aid building at the fair!"

Maybe the bent perspective is to be expected of a man whose earliest fair memory from childhood is of a huge cow, dyed purple, in Storybook Farm.

After adolescence, he thought he'd grown out of the fair. That was until the late 1990s, when he was researching *Cruising the Pomona Valley*.

Given access to the fair's archives, he said he came to appreciate it anew as "a pop-culture supermarket extravaganza" of the fascinating, quaint and bizarre.

Now Phoenix is a fan of the fair again. The tours are an outgrowth of his rekindled interest, a way to share his enthusiasm.

"I think a lot of people think they're too classy and the fair is beneath them," Phoenix said. "But they're really missing out."

His advice to cynics?

"Take it with tongue in cheek, but go. You'll have a great time. You're NOT above it."

IN SEARCH OF A SONG

MARK Warren, a member of the L.A. County Fair board, passes along a request of a historical – and musical – nature.

"We're looking for the L.A. County Fair song, more than likely written by Johnny Catron," says Warren, referring to the big band leader who often played the fair and was a staple of L.A. radio.

Lore has it that someone, probably Catron, wrote a song for the fair, but Warren said no one has been able to come up with evidence.

I'm wondering if people are thinking of "The Goddess of Fruits March," which was written for the fair in 1927 by A. DeCaprio, then the director of the local municipal band. Sadly, it has no lyrics.

On the other hand, maybe the fair should adopt folksinger and native son John Stewart's unofficial anthem "Back in Pomona." Among its lyrics: "All the racehorse crowd was always there/Back in Pomona at the county fair."

Anybody know if there's another county fair song?

OFFICIAL SONG NOT SO FAIR

THE L.A. County Fair's attempt to track down a forgotten "official fair song" from the 1950s had hit a dead end when I put out a call for information in a recent column.

The fair may be sorry I asked. Because reader Stephen Apple stepped forward with sheet music to a song so dreadful, I can't believe fair officials innocently forgot about it.

They must have repressed the memory.

Titled "Pomona's Queen of the Fair," this 1955 ode to a county fair beauty queen was the "official song of the Los Angeles County Fair," according to the sheet music. While I don't want to call the song a bomb, let's just say there would be a LOT of excitement had the United Nations found the sheet music in Iraq.

Reader Apple found "Pomona's Queen of the Fair" in his trove of sheet music from the era, and as he put a it after rereading the lyrics: "Something tells me Grammy wasn't waiting in the wings on this one."

But don't take our word for it. Maestro, let's take it from the top, in the moderate lilt suggested by the sheet music:

"I'm in love with a girl,
With a beautiful girl
Pomona's Queen of the Fair.
Her eyes softly shine
As they gaze into mine
And I light up like a flare.
She's all peaches and cream,
She's the dreamiest dream,
No other girl can compare.

With this lovely miss
And the bliss of her kiss
Pomona's Queen of the Fair.
I watch as she poses,
Her arms full of roses,
Most won'drous sight I've seen.
So sweetly vivacious,
So modest, so gracious,
She's ev'ry inch a queen.
I'm all puffed up and proud
Like a billowy cloud
I seem to float thru the air,
I can't realize,
That I've captured this prize
Pomona's Queen of the Fair."

They don't write 'em like they used to, eh? And thank goodness for that.

Blame for "Pomona's Queen of the Fair" should be split between tunesmith Dick Nethercott and lyricist Raleigh Borell, although their (ugh) handiwork was enabled by a vocal group named the Mellow Men. They reportedly recorded the song for Capitol Records. Proving that musical crimes do not pay, they were never heard from again.

Fair board member Mark Warren led the search for the long-lost official song, and it seems he can't realize he's captured this prize. In fact, his reaction to its discovery was akin to Geraldo Rivera's upon opening Capone's vault.

"After reading the words, I don't know if I want to tell the fair the song has been found," Warren admitted. "Nonetheless, thanks for your help. I'll be sure YOU get credit for locating it."

Sounds like no one's puffed up and proud like a billowy cloud over "Pomona's Queen of the Fair."

You know what they say: Be careful what you wish for – you might get it.

* * *

Second thought: If that musical travesty is the fair's official song, let's hope the unofficial songs don't surface.

* * *

Reader Mark Weis, meanwhile, tells me the fair used a memorable jingle in its radio ads a decade ago: "Eight dollars a day, to come and play, at the Los Angeles County Fair!"

Why, I'm about to light up like a flare.

WESTSIDE STYLE

IT'S no "Pomona's Queen of the Fair," and thank goodness for that. But Fairplex's Sharon Autry shared the 2002 fair's official radio jingle, which was sung to the tune of "Old MacDonald" and was clearly aimed at L.A.'s Westside crowd:

"L.A. County had a fair
Ee-i-ee-i-o
Weren't no implants anywhere
Ee-i-ee-i-o
No silicon here no collagen there
The animals all had their own hair
L.A. County had a fair
Ee-i-ee-i-o" ... whoa.

Fair is 17 days on a stick

Oh boy! Only two more days until the start of the L.A. County Fair – the exposition that from September 12 to 28 puts the culture in agriculture, and the pig in pigging out.

Gosh, I have so many unforgettable memories from last year's fair: There was the man demonstrating how to milk a camel, my colleague Will Matthews gagging on a deep-fried Snickers bar, and the family-run ice cream stand now owned by the founder's elderly granddaughter, who, when asked for the heartwarming story behind the 80-year-old stand, yelled at me to go away.

So it's easy to be sentimental. Thus, when a similarly wistful reader phoned with a hankering to see the lyrics to "Pomona's Queen of the Fair" again, how could I refuse?

This 1955 tune was once the fair's official song but was long forgotten. Forgotten, that is, until the sheet music turned up last year in the collection of reader Stephen Apple.

The lyrics were printed here last December and the world has never been the same. I'm not saying it's better, I'm not saying it's worse. I'm just saying.

* * *

In the widely accepted measurement of county fair quality known as FOSAC (Foods on Sticks Aggregate Count), Pomona's fair is bigger than ever. There are 33 skewered items this year, up two from last year, according to fair officials.

Among the debut items is Macaroni and Cheese on a Stick. To stay stuck to the stick, this item comes battered, and it can also be ordered with chunks of kielbasa inside.

Mmm-mmm! You'll make a noise very much like that as you go into cardiac arrest.

Also new this year is S'mores on a Stick – campfire not included –

and, in answer to a pressing culinary need, Key Lime Pie on a Stick.

Is the key lime pie authentic? Well, according to a press release from the fair, this item comes "shaped like a piece of pie," and that should be close enough.

Finally, if at any point during the fair you are tempted to indulge in foods you shouldn't, your appetite will go away if you ponder this item available on the fair's Aloha Fridays: Spam on a Stick.

'Nuff (urp) said.

WHICH KNIFE FOR CUTTING REMARKS?

THE L.A. County Fair has a contest for elaborately presented dinner settings, but if you're expecting high-society entries, consider these:

- A tribute to Harley-Davidson's 100th anniversary done up in orange and black, including a faux-leather tablecloth.
- A *Chicago* table with twin feather boas down the center and a gun partly hidden under a handbag.
- A military table set for four, using mess hall-style metal trays with compartments, a camouflage-print tablecloth and place cards for distinguished armed-forces guests: General Anxiety, Colonel Corn, Sergeant Pepper and Captain Crunch.

Clearly this is beyond anything envisioned by Emily Post.

"We get a lot of creativity," said Linda Keagle, who judges each year with Maura Graber. "Some people who enter every year really push it to the Nth degree."

On Thursday, I joined Keagle, a restaurant owner, and Graber, an etiquette consultant, as they made their critiques. As expected from reading their biting comments on the judges' cards in the past, it was a spirited affair.

(A documentary on the 2001 judging was recently completed by acclaimed LA. artist Judy Fiskin, who told me: "There wouldn't have been a documentary if Linda and Maura didn't have such strong personalities.")

At a formal Valentine's Day table, the homemade placemats are edged with real flower petals, a nice touch. Everything was deemed perfect. Except for one oddity.

"What's with the cherub?" Graber asked, referring to the centerpiece angel figure with an unusually pained expression.

"That's an ugly cherub," Keagle agreed.

"It looks like it's in agony," Graber said.

Keagle shrugged and said: "Maybe her grandmother gave it to her."

Valentine's Day is one of six themes this year. Another is *Chicago*, the musical set in the 1920s.

One *Chicago* table is made up like the booth of a speakeasy and won best in show. At another, each corner of the tablecloth is cinched with handcuffs.

People learn the themes in the spring and spend months getting ready, but they have just two hours to set up on the 40-by-60-inch tables provided by the fair.

Besides holidays, which are big, past themes have included *The Lion King*, the Titanic, favorite TV programs – "you should've seen the *Star Trek* tables," Graber told me – and the 100th anniversary of Crayola.

This year's century-old-product theme is Harley-Davidson. One entry has a dotted white line down the middle and a plush pig doll in biker garb as the centerpiece. The menu, displayed within a license-plate frame, includes bull testicles.

It's described as a formal table. So that's how it was judged.

"Butter knives are turned incorrectly," Graber told Keagle, who had the scoring sheet.

Neither was sure which fork to use for the testicles.

They judge on interpretation of theme and overall look, which are somewhat subjective, and correctness. If the table's menu calls for soup but there's no soup spoon, for example, points are deducted.

Graber fields a half-dozen objections each year, usually over the correctness scores. "We had lawsuits threatened a couple of years ago," she said.

Some creative choices are plain wrong, with no subjectivity about it.

Two years ago, a Christmas table decorated in Western style featured a bleached cow skull.

As Graber put it, "Nothing says Christmas like a cow's skull."

IT'S THE GOLDEN ANNIVERSARY FOR THE COUNTY FAIR'S REDWOOD

AN unheralded 50th anniversary at the L.A. County Fair: It's 50 years since sculptor John Svenson began carving his statue, Ranchero, from a redwood log in front of curious fairgoers.

Svenson stripped off the bark on the fair's opening day in 1953 and spent the next 17 days carving under the public's watchful eye, according to a placard in the Court of the Redwoods area.

Lore has it that fairgoers had one main question for Svenson regarding his redwood figure: "Will it grow?"

Some were so impressed by the work, they asked Svenson to autograph a wood chip for them as a souvenir.

Debuting at the 1954 fair, Ranchero still stands today – at its original height – outside the Millard Sheets Gallery, rising nobly, if a bit incongruously, behind a row of coin-operated foot massagers.

To quote the placard, the sculpture shows "a determined ranchero surveying his newly acquired Spanish land grant."

Based on his line of sight, today he determinedly surveys a Ferris wheel.

* * *

Rather than giving you a number with your order, the Pink's Hot Dogs stand at the fair gives you a movie star's name.

After taking my order, the clerk told me: "I'll call Mel Gibson."

What if the real Mel Gibson shows up to claim my chili dog, I asked.

The female clerk assured me the hunky actor wouldn't get away with it.

"I'll tackle him for you," she vowed. "Repeatedly."

* * *

There was confusion anyway. Another clerk called a name that might have been Mel Gibson. I stepped forward.

"Are you Kate Hudson?" she asked.

I felt like saying: "Do I look like Kate Hudson?" But then I couldn't claim a close resemblance to Mel Gibson either.

MILES OF SMILES AT THE COUNTY FAIR; YOUR MILEAGE MAY VARY

THINGS that made me smile at the L.A. County Fair, which ends Sunday:

- On an outdoor stage, a performer named Mad Chad taking bites out of the apple he's juggling while also juggling two knives – and no doubt praying he doesn't get out of sync.
- A tent whose sign promises: "Come Face to Face With a 16-Foot Great White Shark."
- Wondering if the Great White Shark people ever said in awe, "We're going to need a bigger tent."
- The perennially misspelled Baked Potatoe food stand sign. It's so wrong, I know. But rolling my eyes at it each year feels so right.
- In the display cases in the crafts hall, a homemade toy train made almost entirely of Caffeine Free Diet Coke cans.
- Likewise, a gingerbread haunted house whose roof is tiled with Golden Grahams cereal; an intricately carved wooden clock resembling a three-story European cathedral; and the Postal Service's Elvis stamp reproduced in needlepoint.
- The inspiring sight of thousands of happy people of every race, creed, color, nationality – and size.
- Speaking of cross-sections, the giant Sequoia, 16 feet in diameter, with a timeline of the tree's life from Caesar's reign (44 B.C.) to JFK's (1961).
- Knowing the tree is named Doris.
- In the Shopping Place, sales people trying to move such unlikely products as sneaker polish, the "original" vacuum mop – accept no cheesy substitutes when you can have the cheesy original! – and a "hair removal system."

- A booth whose filterless air purifiers are touted with a curious banner reading: "Raved By Radio Hosts and the Pentagon." Uh, OK. But is it seen on TV?
- Huge groups of tiny children on field trips, walking in a line, sometimes holding hands. Awww.
- A stand named, with typical fair hyperbole, Mile Long Hot Dog. As they say, your mileage may vary.
- The restored Clock Tower.
- Wondering if any women have stopped at the Sunset Cabana food court, formerly known as the Super Diner, to ask about cabana boys.
- How cool the Flower and Garden Pavilion always is. Literally cool.
- Jamaican musicians getting a steel drum groove on in an old-fashioned gazebo near the Pie A La Mode stand – a long way from the islands, mon.
- A new fair first: an Oxygen Bar. Now that puts the "L.A." in the L.A. County Fair.
- The fact that I kept my appetite even after seeing a sign reading "Custom Fit Toe Rings."
- Two child-size Hummer miniatures, displayed to promote a giveaway of the real vehicle. At last viewing, the waist-high Hummers had escaped vandalism by that wacko ELF group.
- In the "100 Years of Flight" exhibit, a room supplied with sheets of paper for kids to make paper airplanes.
- Outside, the nice man who told youngsters to keep an eye on their teacher: "She looks like she misbehaves."
- The nice woman at the Dr. Bob's ice cream stand who sold me a cone and gave me a 2-for-1 coupon. See, at least one ice cream woman at the fair doesn't yell at me.
- The art gallery's replica of the *Brady Bunch* staircase. It's so un-canny, I wanted to run upstairs and see if the Brady boys and girls were still dividing the floor space with tape.
- The thought of seeing Willie Nelson tonight!
- Feeling like a kid at the fair – and drawing an adult paycheck for doing it.

IN TWO HOURS, WILLIE GAVE THE FAIR CROWD A FULL NELSON

A S an impressed friend put it, "Nobody told Willie Nelson he was playing a county fair." Performing at Pomona's fair on Friday, Nelson played a lively set that ran two hours – a half-hour longer than the fair's other, younger music acts.

Now you'd think that at age 70, Nelson would want to avoid taxing himself. Especially with his tax problems. But it was made clear in advance by Nelson's reps that he always performs for two hours, and fair officials didn't argue.

Besides, who's going to tell an outlaw to please stick to the schedule?

All told, according to my notes, the Red-Headed Stranger ran through a whopping 41 songs. Or, technically, 39 songs, because two of them went over so well he played them twice.

To save time, he didn't even leave the stage before his encore. He simply said, "Oh, I've got time for a couple more" and then sang four. (Funny how time slips away.)

One of his earlier numbers was "If You've Got the Money, I've Got the Time," and I guess he meant it.

* * *

Nelson's trademark red braids fell to the middle of his chest, where they were tied together in a loop, like a lasso.

I wonder, does the hirsute singer braid and tie his own locks, or does his entourage include a hair wrangler?

* * *

It was a blast to see Nelson play his famously battered guitar,

Trigger. He's often said that if his guitar ever goes, he'll retire. Close-ups of Trigger on the Jumbotron screens made the end look imminent. It has a gaping gash and a weathered face rivaling Nelson's own.

Paying no heed, the singer plucked, strummed and flailed away at the delicate instrument. At the show's close, he brandished Trigger over his head and waved it twice to the audience. Then Nelson's roadies carried Trigger offstage as gingerly as a Fabergé egg.

* * *

Here's an illustration of changing attitudes toward smoking. Not long ago, when the fair's concert announcer, Sid Robinson, would say "There will be no smoking in the grandstand," people would boo.

When he mentioned the smoking ban at Willie Nelson's show, people applauded.

THERE'S BIG FUN AT THIS DRIVE-IN THEATER – IF YOU'RE REALLY SMALL

YOU probably know about Montclair's Mission Drive-In, hailed as the last drive-in theater in the area. But do you know about the Sunset Drive-In in Pomona? If you're hazy on the location, the Sunset's screen looks an awful lot like an old console television and it's adjacent to a railroad track.

Well, a toy railroad track.

Yes, the "theater" is actually a setpiece within the L.A. County Fair's beloved Fairplex Garden Railroad, said to be the oldest and largest miniature outdoor railway in the nation.

While the oldest known photo is from 1952, I'm pleased to report the theater is still part of the railway more than 50 years later. (Presumably the movie has changed.)

That image is from a new book, *Southern Californialand: Mid-Century Culture in Kodachrome*. Author Charles Phoenix compiled other people's slides from the 1940s, '50s and '60s, all rescued from thrift stores and swap meets.

If we popped the trunk of one of those miniature cars, do you think four teenagers would be hiding inside, sneaking into the drive-in for free?

FAIR '04: THE DUKE IN OILS, ELVIS IN B&W AND A TASTE OF GRAPE

THINGS I like about the 2004 Los Angeles County Fair:

- The low-carb craze hasn't affected the Ten Pound Buns stand.
- The real-life Van de Kamp's in Pomona was bulldozed recently, but a tiny replica, complete with windmill, still exists in the fair's outdoor garden railroad.
- In the amateur art show, an oil portrait of John Wayne won first place. Disturbing note: As pictured, the Duke has tiny teeth like kernels of corn.
- For $3, fairgoers can be photographed with a monster truck bigger than a tank. Its name: Ecology's Eliminator. It doesn't appear to be meant ironically,
- A vendor's banner in a booth selling sharp blades asks the provocative question: "Tired of pounding that whacker?"
- Among the miracle-product come-ons that furrowed my brow: cooking "without water," a cleaning product touted as being "made in Germany" and the promise that you can "clamp anything, any size, anywhere ... with wire!"
- Another booth sells brassieres. For all I know, they may also be clamped with wire.
- In the America's Kids hall, a fourth-grader's tabletop replica of Mission San Luis Obispo is constructed out of beans.
- The centerpiece of the majestic, tree-shaded Court of the Redwoods is a picnic bench made of plastic. On the bright side, no trees were harmed to make it, right?
- Shout-outs to Rose's Mexican Food, celebrating its 20th year at the fair, and to Avalon, the remodeled Anthony's at the fair, a surprisingly snazzy building in Art Deco style.

- The "Cars of the Hollywood Stars" display includes a 1953 Cadillac Coupe once owned by actress Rita Hayworth. Nice chassis.
- My childhood love of the grape sno cone has been well-documented in this space. Well, this year there's a stand that not only has shaved ice – a cut above the coarse ice in the traditional sno cone – but also allows customers the unheard-of luxury of choosing and pumping their own flavors. A dozen to pick from!
- After careful consideration, I chose grape.
- On display in the Millard Sheets Gallery: a painting by Impressionist Mary Cassatt (1845-1926). No, it's not of John Wayne.
- In the Tapestry of Tradition hall, a cake baked in tribute to 9/11 is frosted in red, white and blue. Rising vertically from the cake's surface are six-inch-tall World Trade Center towers in chocolate. It's oddly touching.
- Anticipation for Jackson Browne's concert Saturday has me running on empty.
- In "The Beat Goes On," an exhibit on the history of rock, you can see a 1956 photo of rising star Elvis Presley standing in line at a food cart for a hot dog like any other schmo. Think he ordered his dog with peanut butter?
- "Colors of Mexico" is the theme in the Flower and Garden Pavilion. It was a bright idea. Very bright.
- Blue-ribbon-worthy spelling mistakes at the fair: "Everlasting Photo's," "Australian's," "Louisiana Cooking at it's Best" and the fair perennial, "Baked Potatoe."
- In one Fairview Farms livestock pen, goat kids and human kids get familiar. I smiled as a girl about 3 years old stooped, gave a young goat two firm pats on the top of its head, pat pat, and tottered off.
- I'm pleased to see that despite high gas prices, Willie Nelson, who closes the fair Sunday, is on the road again.
- In the Pirates Cove area, a steel-drum band plays lilting Caribbean music. Its neighbor is a business selling artificial grass. No reggae fans were observed trying to smoke it.
- There's so many things I haven't done this year. But my philosophy is: Always leave a few for next year.

MARK YOUR CALENDARS FOR A HOT TIME IN THE INLAND EMPIRE

IN his lively show Saturday at the L.A. County Fair, singer-song-writer Jackson Browne offered up several local references between songs:

- "Last time I was at the fair I was 10 years old... My whole view of the L.A. Fair is through a glass darkly."
- Introducing his song "Culver Moon": "I thought somebody should write a song about Culver City. They got songs about Fontana. (pause) Don't they?"
- "How many people are from the Inland Empire?" (loud applause) "So this is like a local gig for you, right?"

Well, we didn't drive to the fair from Culver City, pal.

* * *

Browne, who had played a show in Reno the night before, also commented on his flight. "I had to think, have I flown into Ontario before? Not that I would have had a reason to come here. Ontario is where they reroute you if you're fogged in at LAX," he cracked.

Browne introduced his last song by mocking the view that people in L.A. are jaded, saying: "Maybe they are in Ontario."

And during that song, "The Load-Out," he playfully altered the line "We've got to drive all night and do a show in Chicago" to "We've got to drive all night and do a show in Ontario."

Cute. But you had to wonder: Was the quintessential L.A. singer-songwriter unaware he was in Pomona?

* * *

For anyone keeping track, Browne has played Ontario. He was at the old Ontario Motor Speedway for 1974's California Jam festival, sitting in with the Eagles, singing "Take It Easy," which he co-wrote. Guess he didn't fly in for that show.

* * *

Willie Nelson closed out the fair on Sunday and packed the place, just like last year.

And once again, Nelson and his band put on an entertaining show. It was an honor to be in the same space as him. Not everyone saw it that way. Near me, a boy about 7 grew restless and shifted frequently in his seat.

His mother took the long view: "You'll thank me when you get older."

THESE TEMPS ARE TEMPORARY

THE weather has cooled off a bit in recent days, but if any new-comers to the valley think fall is here, let me clue you in to something.

The L.A. County Fair in Pomona is still ahead of us September 9 to October 2. Fairgoers know what that means: Despite this brief respite, temperatures will soon soar into the upper 90s again – guaranteed.

STANDBYS ASIDE, EVENT STILL WILL BE FAIR-LY FRESH

YIPPEE! My favorite event of the year starts today. No, not a new season of *The O.C.* – that began Thursday – but rather the good ol' L.A. County Fair.

Jaded types think the fair is the same every year. As if! Why, this fair won't resemble previous fairs in the slightest.

OK, except for the food, the animals, the rides, the withering heat and the smells. And except for the band War, which has played opening night at the fair since approximately 1949 (or maybe it just seems that way).

But there are new things. Among them:

- "SportsFest" is the big exhibit, with SoCal sports memorabilia, historical displays and interactive skills challenges. Note: Steroids not included with fair admission.
- This fair brings a chance to see a zonkey (a cross between a zebra and a donkey) and a giant alligator, Big Al.
- On the menu this year: deep-fried avocados, deep-fried tomatoes and deep-fried apples. At the L.A. County Fair, even fruit can kill you.
- After your fill of the fried stuff, try a light, healthy snack: a chocolate-filled churro.
- In the Flower and Garden Pavilion: "Treasures of Polynesia." Yes, the theme is Tahiti! I believe the feature attraction will be a 30-by-20-foot replica, in flowers, of the late Marlon Brando (in other words, life-sized).
- Amazing new products for sale: hanging fish aquariums, a "lip plumper" – demonstrated by Angelina Jolie? – and a wax coating to preserve your teddy bear. Seriously.

Imagine if Calvin had dipped his tiger, Hobbes, in wax.

- Also new: a poker tournament. Yes, poker at the fair!
  I believe the poker chips will be deep-fried.
- Parking is still awful, but the names of the levels have changed.
  "Last year it was 'Good,' 'Better,' 'Best.' Now it's back to 'General,'
  Preferred' and 'VIP,'" spokeswoman Wendy Talarico said. She
  quipped: "It wasn't resonating."
- The biggest change: the schedule.

For the first time, the fair will be closed – yes, closed – each
Monday and Tuesday. Coupled with the addition of one day, for a
total of 18, the fair is able to sprawl over four weekends, not the
usual three.

For many fairgoers, "weekends are a more convenient time," Talarico said.

Fine, but I do foresee one problem.

What if you absolutely MUST have your teddy bear waxed on a
Monday?

Dept. of dept. heads dept.

ODAY is "L.A. County Day" at the L.A. County Fair, offering the thrill of seeing various county department heads – sheriff, fire, library, weights and measures, etc. – riding in a parade.

Sudden thought based on recent headlines: Do you think the head of King/Drew Medical Center will ride in a hearse?

* * *

Science says dinosaurs didn't exist in the same era as humans. So how does science explain Crosby, Stills and Nash lumbering into the L.A. County Fair tonight?

NOT ALL THE FAIR'S FARE WILL KILL YOU

WITH all the blather about deep-fried avocados, this year's L.A. County Fair is shaping up as another nutritional train wreck – not that fairgoers would have it any other way.

The fair's only once a year, the argument goes, so why not stuff your face?

Fine, but as the portly people waddling along the Pomona asphalt prove, for much of America, it's fair time 365 days a year.

Hey, I indulge at the fair myself. I draw the line at the deep-fried goop, but a Pink's chili dog is a must.

Call me a rebel, but I began to wonder: Is it possible to eat healthfully at the fair? At lunchtime Wednesday, I resolved to give it a shot.

Entering at the Red Gate and heading toward the rides, the fare was meat, meat and more meat. One stand was selling artichoke hearts, mushrooms and zucchini – all deep-fried. No vegetable makes it into the fair unscathed.

Past the battered potatoes and fudge, a woman was selling smoothies from a cart. She was reading a book because she had no customers. In retrospect, I should have stopped for sustenance, but I figured I'd press on. This proved to be a mistake.

Some of the vendor signs:

- Full Breakfast Bacon Sausage Ham Pork Chops
- Smoked Meats
- Chili Cheese Pigglys
- Fried Oreo Cookies
- Ten Pound Buns

Playing off the old name for its midway, the fair should call this cuisine the Fun Zone Diet.

The only thing more popular than bad food is big bad food: Giant Turkey Legs. Jumbo Corn Dog. Giant Western Sausage. Mile Long Hot Dog.

I'd been at the fair a half-hour and had yet to find anything that wasn't lethal. How about a Mile Long Salad Bar?

Thankfully, in Heritage Square I found Cafe Deli, which has Caesar salads, with or without chicken.

"The salads are doing OK," manager Teresa Acosta said. Not as well as the deli sandwiches or the Nachos Grande, though.

Maybe it's marketing.

"What about a deep-fried salad?" I asked. "Could you do that on a stick?"

Acosta was doubtful, so I continued on to the Shopping Place and found – *mon dieu!* – the Crepe Connection.

I paid for a turkey wrap, then chatted with the proprietor.

"People say they like to come here because our food isn't fried and it's not on a stick," vendor Veda Maples said.

Then came bad news from the kitchen. "We're out of lettuce," Maples informed me. "Would you like something else?"

Sigh. I got a chicken fiesta crepe. It has melted cheese and sour cream, so health-wise it's a little questionable. But it was light and, by fair standards, practically constituted bran.

In fact, I'd struck paydirt.

Across the pathway was That's a Wrap, which has wraps, salads and veggie burgers. And a few steps away, inside Building 6, was Wolfe's Market with salads, deli sandwiches and fruit cups.

"The vendors love it, they've been here every day," Tom Wolfe told me. "Anybody health-conscious does."

At that moment, he had no customers.

Wolfe sold me a premium pineapple cup, which was good stuff indeed – and would have to do for my dessert.

At That's a Wrap, vendor Marie Giddenis was between customers, too. Then Linda Sirkin, of Claremont, ordered a chicken club wrap.

Sirkin, who was carrying a water bottle, said she's avoided sugar and grease the past two years and is the better for it.

As for sticking to a diet at the fair, Sirkin said: "If you have the willpower, you can do it."

I left the fair, willpower triumphant.

But next time, clear a path between me and Pink's.

CORTEZ NOT ONE FOR PORK POLITICS

WHEN I met Eddie Cortez, the mayor of the fifth-largest city in L.A. County was in a ring at the fair, calling hogs.

His competition in that 1999 hog-calling contest included Claremont's mayor, an Elvis impersonator and three children, none of whom could get a hog to budge.

Cortez, however, emitted a series of high-pitched squeals that caused two hogs to bolt directly toward him.

"Let's hear it for Pomona," Cortez proclaimed.

Yes, that quaint farming village of Pomona.

Cortez told me he had slopped hogs and called them to dinner plenty of times as the son of a migrant farm worker, giving him a crucial edge over his cityslicker opponents.

Sadly, Cortez, 64, died early Tuesday of cancer after several months of declining health. What a shame.

My post-hog encounters with Cortez were never as colorful, or as pungent. But he was always a delight.

A faithful reader of this column, Cortez once phoned me to explain his absence from a council meeting I'd attended. The mayor wanted me to know that he'd been in Sacramento on city business.

What could I say? I excused his absence.

Cortez was a regular-guy mayor who owned an auto repair shop, Cortez Automotive. If you called, he picked up.

Good thing, because he didn't carry a cell phone. He liked peace and quiet.

When it came to making or returning calls, "he'd get to it when he could," Councilman Dan Rodriguez told me.

No cell phone? I knew there was a reason I liked the guy.

Said to be Pomona's first Latino mayor, Cortez didn't fit any stereotypes.

He was a Republican, a middle of the road fella, a Mormon.

Whatever, he clicked with voters. Come election time, he crushed the competition, as recently as last November.

Despite his tenure as mayor, he never seemed jaded.

Reflecting on his beginnings, he sometimes marveled at the opportunities he'd had, Councilwoman Paula Lantz said.

Instead of slopping hogs, he was setting sewer rates. And he was meeting President Bush and Governor Arnold Schwarzenegger, at their invitation.

"He felt like he wanted to pinch himself, that he was sitting in this room, with this person, who invited him. ... It wasn't him trying to get an audience," Lantz said. "He never lost his humility."

The public face of Pomona, Cortez was a genial figure, often showing up at events to smile shyly and say a few words.

Last September, for instance, he spoke at the dedication of a wall-sized mural downtown in the Thomas Street Plaza.

He admitted he was no arts sophisticate – he made his living with his hands, fixing cars. He wished he had artistic talent, but he didn't. So he applauded the artists for being able to do what he couldn't, and do it so well.

Refreshing and classy.

Cortez wasn't one to lose his temper, at least not in public. Quiet, composed, he could be hard to read.

"When things didn't go his way, he smiled," Rodriguez said. "That was dangerous. You didn't know what it meant until you could sit down and have a heart to heart."

Let's not make Cortez something he wasn't. He wasn't a visionary, he wasn't charismatic, he wasn't leading Pomona to greatness.

But let's not overlook what was so good about him.

He was competent – no small thing in a city as troubled as

Pomona – and compassionate.

Call him a steady hand on the tiller. When outraged citizens packed the Council Chambers, he calmed the waters.

Perhaps he was just what Pomona needed.

"It's something that's hard to quantify," Lantz mused of Cortez's brand of quiet, dignified leadership.

"I probably took it for granted because it was always there," Lantz continued. "Like a lot of things, you don't know what you've got until you don't have it anymore."

A lot of qualities about Eddie Cortez will be missed now that we don't have him anymore. He was a decent, likable guy. Even hogs liked him.

IS HE REAL? FAIR'S GIANT ALLIGATOR CERTAINLY IS NO CROCK

H E'S Pomona's answer to Reggie, the Lake Machado alligator who has caught L.A.'s attention while eluding capture himself.

The L.A. County Fair gator's name is Big Al. At 13 1/2 feet, he's nearly twice as long as Reggie, and weighs 1,200 pounds.

Big Al is one of the weirder attractions at this year's fair. Housed within a small tent – did you think the alligator would be in the petting zoo? – he can be seen for a fee, like a bearded lady or dog-faced boy from the old freak shows.

Yes, folks, for just $1 – 10 thin dimes, ten-tenths of a dollar – you too can regard this remarkable reptile.

Most passers-by are taking a pass.

"It's not Reggie, it's Big Al," a woman said with amusement Wednesday. Reading the sign, as I was doing, she said incredulously: "He's 65 years old?"

Her husband cracked: "Reggie'll get to be 65, too, with the luck they're having catching him."

David Harrell, who works for Bradenton, Florida-based Outdoor Exhibits, Big Al's owner, said Reggie is a big topic of conversation with his customers.

Would 7-foot Reggie attract attention in Florida?

"Normal. Typical. It's like watching a dog walking across the road," Harrell said dismissively. "You see a lot of ones that size down there."

American alligators can reach 15 feet in length, so at 13 1/2 feet, Big Al isn't the biggest. Don't get me wrong, though: He's plenty big.

In fact, he's awfully impressive! Wow, what a beast!

(Sure, he's big, but what if he's insecure?)

Outdoor Exhibits has owned Big Al for more than 16 years, snapping him up, so to speak, from another exhibitor. He is taken from fair to fair in the western states during summertime.

Like a lot of 65-year-olds, he winters in Florida.

Unsure what to expect, I went inside the tent. Instant disappointment: Big Al is housed in an ordinary trailer. You gape through the small windows crisscrossed with iron bars.

Inside, Big Al just lies there, his chin resting on a wheel well, unmoving. Not that he could turn around anyway.

Once past that, you have to admit he's one gi-normous gator.

"It's awesome. It's great," enthused Carlos Bohl, who was there with his girlfriend, Bebe Hart.

"It's definitely worth the buck," Bohl added. "I'd have paid $2." Twenty thin dimes, twenty-tenths of a dollar ... nah.

"I've never seen anything this big, this close," marveled Dee Woodson, who presumably never met Barry White.

"Is he real?" Woodson asked me, thinking I worked there. (Harrell had told me, with a grimace, that "Is he real?" is the No. 1 question.)

Her friend Leslie Williams snapped a photo. The flash went off. Big Al's big eye blinked, and Williams squealed.

"Now you know! Now you know he's alive!" she cried.

Nicholas Granlund, 6, wasn't nearly as excited.

"Why isn't he moving?" Nicholas asked his dad, John.

"He's just hanging out waiting for a little boy to go in there," John teased him. "He's a big fat guy. I bet he's eaten lots of little kids."

In truth, Big Al eats "ribs, fish and chicken," Harrell said.

Ribs, fish and chicken? Toss in deep-fried avocado and there's your Pomona fair diet.

But not so fast – Big Al rarely eats unless it's winter.

And he hardly moves unless he's eating. This isn't *When Animals*

Attack.

"People watch too much TV," Harrell said with some disgust. "They're pretty dormant, docile animals."

The couch potatoes or the alligators?

* * *

I hope it was merely a broken water pipe rather than a hurricane. Fairgoers on Wednesday saw sandbags at the Leigh Adams TV tent and this sign: "Flooded Out!"

A RECONCILIATION WITH HALL & OATES HISTORY

As Daryl Hall and John Oates ran through their string of bouncy hit songs for an adoring crowd at the L.A. County Fair on Friday night, I couldn't help reflecting on how much I hate them.

Or at least, how much I used to hate them. When I was growing up, the radio was clogged with Hall & Oates songs.

There was the wispy "Sara Smile," in which Hall gives the word "forever" something like nine syllables.

And "Rich Girl," which contains a naughty word rhyming with "rich." Hearing this on the airwaves at age 11 was funny, in a kind of nervous way. (It still is, actually.)

Five years after "Rich Girl," there was the unnecessary "You've Lost That Lovin' Feeling," a remake as exciting as a flat Pepsi.

The duo followed this with a torrent of hits, one after another, all inescapable: "You Make My Dreams," "One on One," "Say It Isn't So," "Did It in a Minute," etc.

Some of them weren't bad, and I actively enjoyed "Kiss on My List." But week after week of hearing them on "Casey Kasem's American Top 40" made me sick of this faux soul.

As a music snob, I never stooped to buying a Hall & Oates record. But I did tape a college roommate's copy of their greatest-hits LP, *Rock 'n' Soul Part 1*, mostly to possess "Kiss on My List."

This tape was pretty much forgotten until August. Playing all my old mix tapes again, with the goal of tossing most of them, I heard the Hall & Oates stuff fresh after two decades and thought, oh, maybe I should buy a best-of CD.

My college self cried: "Say it isn't so. Oh oh oh."

This mysterious urge led me to *The Very Best of Daryl Hall/John*

Oates, an ampersand-challenged 18-track collection.

I furtively purchased this at Best Buy. That way, I didn't have to face the shame of buying a Hall & Oates CD at a real record shop, where a hip clerk might silently, but devastatingly, arch an eyebrow.

I liked the CD more than I'd expected. True, the songs aren't deep. Judging by their carefully coiffed manes in the booklet's vintage photos, Hall & Oates spent more time on their hair than their lyrics.

And some of the songs today sound WAY too 1980s. But most remain catchy. What bugs me is that *The Very Best* unconscionably fails to include their very best song, the sublime "She's Gone."

Will I now have to buy a second Hall & Oates CD? Say it isn't so! Oh oh oh!

It wasn't but a couple of weeks after all this that the fair's concert lineup was announced. Among the acts: Hall & Oates. Was this fate?

It's free, I mused. This is my chance to reappraise them, in person, after all these years. Perhaps what I need is an adult education.

So there we all were Friday night. Hall & Oates came out, launched into "Maneater" and continued with enough other hits to make Hoobastank tearfully pack it in.

Dressed casually in jeans, Hall & Oates looked trim even as they near 60. You'll be relieved to hear they still have great hair. (Hall's shoulder-length 'do is definitely real; I can't vouch for Oates' shaggy mop.)

Oates, thankfully, has ditched his stuck-in-the-'70s mustache, while Hall has added a goatee.

The audience was full of nostalgics, recalling their own youth, or in some cases – such as state Senator Nell Soto, who was a couple of rows behind me – their own middle age.

What surprised me were all the young women dancing in the aisles for "I Can't Go For That" and "Out of Touch." They couldn't have been born when those came out.

The songs must have staying power. After the second encore, with "Rich Girl" and "Kiss on My List" – yes! – fans who hadn't had enough got in line to buy instant CDs of the concert, a neat innovation.

I counted 90 people and growing for CDs selling at 25 bucks a pop. (You can rely on the old fans' money?)

While I have newfound, if grudging, respect for Hall & Oates, this literal did-it-in-a-minute disc wasn't for me. I couldn't go for that. No can-do.

Even if they did sing a good version of "She's Gone."

Fair '05: Big savings, little ships and a zonkey

NOTEWORTHY things observed – but not on Mondays or Tuesdays – at the 2005 L.A. County Fair, which ends Sunday:

- The Rock Waterfall Pools booth with its sign that boasts: "Only $11,995. Biggest Savings of the Year!"
- Proving the sign accurate, I walked on, saving $11,995.
- Who says youngsters today have no ambition? In the America's Kids hall, a 7-year-old from Chino named James built a scale model of the Queen Elizabeth I ocean liner – out of Legos. Nice job, James.
- Nearby, a fifth-grade feminist created a poster illustrating the importance of equal rights for women. I'm impressed by her zeal.
- In an unfortunate typo, however, her piece ends: "I am proud to be a women."
- In Fairview Farms: The zonkey, a cross between a zebra and a donkey, with black and white striped legs. Although I was disappointed a zonkey isn't a cross between a zebra and a monkey.
- To lure *Napoleon Dynamite* fans, maybe next year the fair can get a liger.
- Decorated cakes in the Tapestry of Tradition hall are a must-see. One cake depicts a jungle island complete with volcano and the message "Have a Wild Birthday." Perhaps too wild – by my visit, the cake volcano had toppled over.
- Inside, outside, it didn't matter – people on electric carts were always careening toward me. Yikes! This was even more alarming than the five-day-a-week schedule.
  Prediction: It's only a matter of time before the fair sponsors an electric cart race.
- Also in Tapestry of Tradition, handmade cloth dolls of the 1960s

cartoon character Super Chicken ("Bukack!"), accompanied by his valet, Fred the Lion. Let's raise a toast of Super Sauce to Ernie Garcia of Claremont.

- On the midway, one food stand fills every man's need. Its name: Chili Bowl and Beer.
- Another stand is named Fresh Frys. This is just me, but I like to silently pronounce it "Friss."
- At the Millard Sheets Gallery, a favorite work is Joe Bravo's unique twin portraits of Frida Kahlo and Emiliano Zapata. The medium, as described on the exhibit card, says it all: "Acrylic on Flour Tortilla."
- That Latino art show, incidentally, is one of the best exhibits I've seen at Sheets. Fun, colorful and even militant. Check it out.
- 2005 marks 50 years since entrepreneur Fred Morrison sold flying platters at the fair. The fledgling Wham-O company bought the rights two years later and marketed the disks as – you guessed it – the Slip 'n Slide. I mean: the Frisbee.
- My big discovery this year is a stand selling shaved ice for a mere $1. Aside from those coin-operated foot massagers, this might be the cheapest thing at the fair.
- Scale models in the Garden Railway of two downtown Pomona icons, the Mayfair Hotel and Fox Theatre. Both models are bustling with tiny figures and cars coming and going. If only the real buildings were like this.
- Where else in 2005 but a free stage at the fair can you see a guy juggling pins and spinning plates?
- I walked up to the Pink's stand, ordered a chili dog and was served in five minutes. If you've ever waited an hour at the L.A. location, you'll understand.
- As I ate an apple crisp a la mode at the pink-roofed Gingerbread Shop, a fellow customer jovially told me I'd made a huge mistake by not getting the strawberry shortcake.

OK. But shouldn't we both be trying the Gingerbread Shop's gingerbread?

Well, there's always next year.

THIS YEAR, FAIR WEATHER DIDN'T DEEP-FRY FAIRGOERS

THIS was the coolest L.A. County Fair in recent memory, and I'm not just talking about the zonkey.

While the September fair typically coincides with temperatures in the 90s and a heavy curtain of smog, this fair, which ended Sunday, was often downright brisk.

It even rained once!

"It was great. I think the average temperature was in the 80s," fair spokeswoman Wendy Talarico enthused. "It was really pleasant."

Fair weather "pleasant"? There's a phrase you never thought you'd hear.

The temperature hit 90 just five days this year, compared with eight last year, according to statistics compiled by Sharon Autry, another fair spokeswoman.

One Saturday this year, the noon temperature was 69, well under last year's 92. Lows were in the lower 60s some days.

No wonder yours truly wore long-sleeved shirts for a couple of visits. It was like attending a county fair in Minnesota.

Meanwhile, Talarico said the first-time closure on Mondays and Tuesdays appeared to be well-received by fairgoers and vendors. The 2006 fair is likely to repeat that schedule.

Perhaps fair officials can ask for a repeat of the mild weather, too.

* * *

Observant fairgoers may have wondered: What happened to the Clock Tower?

The 50-foot tower was gone, replaced by a temporary clock in the same location atop four steel legs, resembling scaffolding.

Here's the story: One week prior to the fair's opening, a planned repair to the Guest Services booth at the tower's base revealed serious rot, Talarico said.

Because she said "it was structurally unsafe," the tower, built in 1952, was – gasp – immediately taken down.

Yes, time ran out for the Clock Tower.

Knowing that many people use it as a handy meeting place – "Meet me at the Clock Tower" – and a point of reference, fair officials hastily threw up a skeletal tower with the original clock faces on top.

Fair officials will take a fresh look at how to best use that area. A new Clock Tower is almost inevitable, "but I don't know what form it will take," Talarico said.

Let's hope they bring something Clock Tower-ish back for 2006. Somehow, "Meet me at Building 7A" doesn't have the same ring.

L.A. FAIR MAKES LOVE, NOT WAR – OR TOWER OF POWER

FACE the music: The L.A. County Fair is headed our way September 8 to October 1, and the concert schedule, as usual, is chock-full of 1970s acts doing the faded-glory thing. We've got Heart, Pat Benatar, Creedence Clearwater Revisited, Grand Funk Railroad paired with the Doobie Brothers, and, on the last night, Donna Summer.

For fair-watchers, the big surprise from the lineup is who isn't performing: War and Tower of Power.

Both bands have played the fair each fall since 2000. That's six straight appearances – until this year.

I expect 'Power partisans will shout in frustration at the fair's concert bookers: "What is hip?"

War fans, meanwhile, may take a more conciliatory approach, asking bookers wistfully: "Why can't we be friends?"

(Those are the titles of the bands' best-known songs. Try to keep up.)

Fair officials say they did want the bands back for a seventh year but conflicting gigs scotched the effort.

"Every group has radius clauses where they can't play another venue within a certain area within a certain period of time," spokeswoman Wendy Talarico told me Thursday. "And unfortunately, the timing of it didn't work out.

"It doesn't mean we won't see (either band) again next year or the year after that," Talarico added. "They continue to draw a great crowd each year. Guests love 'em."

Fair enough. Personally, I'm glad the concert schedule was shaken out of its rut.

In fact, I wish we could get as diverse a lineup as our country cousins to the south, the Orange County Fair, which is hosting, among others, Paul Simon, X, Henry Rollins, Cyndi Lauper, Steppenwolf and Gnarls Barkley.

But at least we get Donna Summer.

THIS YEAR'S L.A. COUNTY FAIR IS COOLER THAN EVER

PARDON my delay in writing about the L.A. County Fair, which began way back on September 8. I blame the weather.

In a typical Inland Valley summer, the pattern is this: Weeks of intense heat, followed by a brief cooling trend that seems to promise fall. Then summer returns with a roar, blasting us with withering, soul-sapping, asphalt-softening heat.

Ahhh … must be fair time. You could set your calendar by it.

This year, though, temperatures have been so mild I've been digging into my fall wardrobe. What's that you say? The fair has been under way for more than a week?

Seems impossible, but I headed west just in case.

Surprisingly, the fair is indeed back, each Wednesday through Sunday through October 1. Good news, because the fair is my favorite place to be as summer gives way to autumn.

(Granted, the fair has slipped to No. 2 on my list of favorite Pomona entertainment activities, but it's hardly the fair's fault the City Council is so reliably nutty.)

I entered the fairgrounds shortly before noon. Within two minutes, I was confronted with a shaved ice stand.

Longtime readers may recall my irrational love of grape sno cones. I wavered, but I kept walking. No point in peaking early.

I did, however, indulge all my other perennial cravings: a chili dog from Pink's, a lemonade from Hot Dog on a Stick and an ice cream from Dr. Bob's.

At Dr. Bob's, where the ice cream is made by hand, the woman behind the counter handed me my peach cone and said the $3.75 item, for which I'd already extracted a $5 bill, was $4.06 with tax.

I fished into my pocket with my one free hand and pulled out a fistful of coins. Just as I was about to hand back the cone to free up my coin-pickin' hand, the nice counter woman asked, "Would you like me to find six cents?"

She plucked six pennies from my outstretched palm. I felt like a tourist in a strange land, offering unfamiliar money and trusting in a storekeeper's honesty.

From there it was on to the Winter Wonderland building, one of this year's signature attractions. It promotes a sort of "Christmas in September" theme.

Half of the interior is devoted to vendors selling stuff, but the fun is in the other half. There, you'll find an indoor ice rink and a "snow" play area, complete with a small incline for sledding.

That's our fair – always full of surprises.

The ice rink is 40 feet by 72 feet, surrounded by a wooden railing. It's real ice, albeit no more than 3 inches thick.

I leaned against the railing for a while, watching skaters glide by and cooling off. While the outdoors had been warm, not hot, being near that much ice was refreshing.

Consider that a tip: The Flower and Garden Pavilion is now demoted to the second-coolest place to take a break at the fair.

It finally struck me that the Winter Wonderland building combines snow with a beach town look. A lifeguard station overlooks the rink, for instance. A Zamboni was parked next to three potted palms.

"The concept is, this is the beach where Santa has his summer vacation and there was a freak snowstorm, so it became Frostbite Beach," explained Michael Converse, the fair employee who runs the building.

Every hour on the hour, the lights dim, music is piped in and snow falls from the ceiling. Not the real stuff but soap bubbles, the same way they make snow in the movies.

It's a fun effect. Small children who had been playing in the ice play area – where ground-up ice resembles snow – look up. Some shriek in delight. Catching soap bubbles on your tongue, however, is perhaps not a good idea.

Credit Lisa Girolami, the fair's creative director. The snowstorm was her brainstorm, as was the rest of Winter Wonderland.

"If people were looking at a map, what would they want to see – other than pig races?" she said, explaining her thought process.

"What if it were snowing inside of a building," Girolami continued with enthusiasm, "a freak snowstorm, and it's 100 degrees outside? People would want to see that."

And I believe they will.

Even if it's only 70 degrees outside.

Tracking down the origins of the Garden Railroad

As they've done since Depression days, model trains chug around a nearly two-mile track outdoors at the L.A. County Fair. With dozens of scenes – from a Gold Rush mining camp to a sci-fi city – and real trees, the Fairplex Garden Railroad is a backyard hobbyist's dream layout and one of the fair's most charming features.

How did this railroad begin? Readers, I give you Paul Hull.

Hull, 88, wasn't there at the beginning, but he was there awfully close to the beginning.

I met Hull, a 1936 Pomona High graduate, in May at his class's 70th reunion and was excited to learn he had known the railroad's builders. He had even done some of the railroad work himself.

Last week I called Hull at his home in Utah for the full story.

Credit belongs to Herman and Homer Howard. The Pomona brothers combined their passion for electronics and trains to create what was then known as the Miniature Railroad.

"It was fascinating back in those days because nobody ever saw anything like that before," Hull explained. "It functioned just like a railroad. They made it as realistic as possible."

Herman and Homer loved building things from scratch, like a radio-controlled boat they made years before anyone sold commercial plans for such a thing. Cousins of Walt Disney, they built a miniature train for Disney's backyard in Toluca Lake.

Their Pomona train began modestly in 1924 as part of a diorama and expanded to a 100-by-300-foot outdoor site in 1935.

Herman built the cars and engines by hand, observing trains

that pulled into Pomona and duplicating them at home in miniature using sheet metal. Homer, meanwhile, designed the electrical system.

Hull knew the brothers through their Pomona Hobby Club for boys. An electrical buff, Hull said Homer's plans were complex. The plans were spread across the clubhouse's Ping-Pong table for quick consultation when problems arose.

Model trains of that era ran on DC power. But when trains stopped as they pulled into a station, the lights and engine would go off as well.

Homer's system would switch to AC power at that point, keeping the lights and engine going. Hobbyists were reportedly astounded.

"In its day, it was unique. The guy who wanted to know how it was done never got an answer to it. They kept the secret to themselves," Hull said.

"I never told anyone what I just told you," Hull added, "because I promised Herman I wouldn't."

Herman and Homer kept adding stations, houses and commercial buildings as the years went on. Homer, who was always in poor health, died first. Herman sold the railroad in 1958 to a man named Herman Templin.

In a freak accident 10 years later, Templin was electrocuted while working on the trains.

His assistant, John Huie, took over and continued running the exhibit until 1996. With the railroad growing decrepit, a group of volunteers was contracted to completely overhaul it. The electrical system has been replaced, as has the original half-inch track, which is now G-gauge, able to run commercially available trains.

Some of Herman's impressively large handmade train cars, up to two feet long, are displayed in a Garden Railroad building.

I thanked Hull, who remains handy with mechanical objects, for his help in illuminating the railroad's early days.

"I don't think anybody else could've told you that story," Hull remarked. "I'm probably the last one alive."

The last time he saw the train was during the John Huie era, before the upgrades.

"The guy who was there when I saw it didn't know anything about electricity," Hull said. "I explained how the system worked and asked if he understood it, and he said no. He just replaced the lights when they burned out."

FAIR TOUR RANGES OVER WIDE TERRITORY

As Walt Whitman wrote of himself, the L.A. County Fair is large, it contains multitudes. There are probably as many perspectives on the fair as there are fairgoers.

You may go mainly for food, carnival rides, cake baking contests, flowers, horse racing, paintings, sheep – or stay away for just as many reasons: crowds, prices, parking, general disgust. You may embrace the fair wholeheartedly or keep it at arm's-length.

Then there is the tour by the Los Angeles Urban Rangers.

A Ph.D. candidate from UCLA named Emily Scott dresses in park ranger garb – a tan shirt, green tie and shorts, hiking boots and a felt hat – and leads free tours of the fair as if it were a forest.

Claire Stover, who loved retro author Charles Phoenix's tour of kitsch landmarks at the fair a couple of years ago, tipped me off to Scott's unusual ranger tour, which takes place each Sunday at noon in front of the Millard Sheets Gallery.

So last Sunday I lined up with about 35 others. Most were USC students in public arts studies, a class taught by another Urban Ranger, Sara Daleiden. Only a bare handful of us had ever ventured to Pomona's fair before.

The tour, Scott explained, is about exploring the fair in new ways. She said the Urban Rangers' goal is to "facilitate a meaningful connection to place."

(Embarrassingly, my own personal goal is to find the perfect tuna melt. Maybe I should aim higher.)

"We're going to be doing a one-way hike today between the gallery and the grandstand," Scott announced. She suggested we bring water to combat the rigors of the hike.

"Dehydration is a major concern at the L.A. County Fair," Scott cautioned. "Other things you'll want to be concerned about are caloric intake, overspending and wandering off from the group."

Specimen bottles and petri dishes were distributed in case we wished to collect field samples during our hike. Yes, it's a tongue-in-cheek tour.

Our stops included the Sheets Gallery, the Court of the Redwoods and Fairplex 4, once known as the Palace of Agriculture. At its debut in 1930, the building was called the largest exhibit space in the world. Now it's home to vendors hawking odd and delightful products.

"You may find yourself pulled by the many seductive products on display," Scott warned as we entered.

We learned that the fair began on a 43-acre beet and barley field, in an era when there was little but farmland between downtown L.A. and Pomona.

Today the fair is 543 acres, about half of which is devoted to parking. The fair can park an impressive 30,000 vehicles. It really does contain multitudes.

Our next stop was an unlikely one: a row of portable toilets near the Garden Railroad.

While the fair has permanent bathrooms, so many people visit that portable toilets are a necessity.

In addition, some 150 tons of trash a week are exported from the fair to a waste-sorting center in Fontana. Non-recyclables are taken to a landfill.

"There's a lot of consumption and waste production at the L.A. County Fair," Scott noted.

Outside Avalon, a sit-down restaurant, we were told the fair sells 3,000 food items.

While the fair began in 1922 as an agricultural exhibition, only one food item, Scott said, is now produced here from scratch: milk from fair cows that is sold at the fair's Moo Market.

Otherwise, fair food is "heavily processed" from items probably not even grown within L.A. County, Scott said.

"There's certainly a tension," she observed, "between the county fair as a place to see healthy, locally grown produce and animals, and the kind of food you can buy here now."

Inside the Tapestry of Tradition building, our group discussed the displays of baked goods in objective fashion.

We decided it is a largely uncommercial space, one in which food is behind glass, inaccessible, almost on a pedestal. At a small-town fair, the display cards may prompt a smile as you recognize the name of a neighbor. Here, the cards often show a remote address, such as Baldwin Park or Van Nuys.

Those are some of the highlights, but there were more. I recommend the tour, as it gives a new perspective on the familiar. If nothing else, pick up the Rangers' sly map for a self-guided tour, available in the Sheets Gallery.

Yet there was something detached about it all. And I imagine the USC students on their field trip to Pomona peered at us as would anthropologists, cataloging us as fascinating specimens of *fairus bumpkinus* before retreating westward, never to return.

Oh well. As I said, the fair is so sprawling, so impossible to get your arms around, that it's open to all sorts of interpretations, from the innocent to the ironic. The L.A. County Fair is bigger than all of us. All analyses are valid, all ultimately futile.

Not least of which is invoking America's greatest poet to describe a county fair.

L.A. County Fair: Calories, cable cars, canines and cozies

HIGHLIGHTS and lowlights at the 2006 edition of the L.A. County Fair, which ends tonight:

- If the idea of a chicken patty fried and stuffed inside a sliced Krispy Kreme doughnut is too extreme, its originator, the Chicken Charlie's stand, counters with the comforting "Fresh Veggie Combo."
- This combo consists of zucchini, asparagus, artichoke hearts and mushrooms – all battered and deep-fried. The non-healthy alternative!
- In the Big Red Barn, seven newborn piglets suckled from their mother, who was lying on her side. It was fascinating and charming to watch as the children jostled each other, climbing over and under, to change position against their prone mother.
- Several women stood nearby, watching expressionlessly. I wondered what thoughts were going through their heads.
- One popular toy: Plastic "guns" that shoot a steady stream of soap bubbles. Although the vendors demonstrating the bubble guns looked incongruously glum, I was thrilled by the innovation. Finally, an end to the antiquated process of blowing bubbles manually!
- Avoiding an hour-long drive to L.A. and another hour-long wait in line, I walked up to the Pink's booth, ordered a chili dog and received it within one minute. The county fair is so awesome.
- Overheard: "Want to ride in the cable cars?" a man asked his date, pointing, not to San Francisco, but overhead to the ski lift-style Sky Ride.
- The Chuck Wagon stand has an Old West theme, a rail-fence

ambience and an array of smoked meat items, including chicken sandwiches. Believe it or not, the chicken is – how 19th century – served on buns, not doughnuts.

- Captivating come-ons on vendor signs in the wacky-product buildings: "Unleash the Power of Mangosteen," "WonderVase: The Amazing Vase You Can Shape!", "Home Soda Maker" and "Experience the Difference of Emu Oil."
- Also for sale: individual steam rooms. Slogan: "Burn 300 to 900 calories in just 30 minutes!"
- Might be a nice addition to the Chicken Charlie's booth.
- A display in the foyer of the Millard Sheets Gallery details the art gallery's history. In the glory years of 1950-'53, Sheets, the curator, obtained loans of art from the Louvre, the British Museum and the Metropolitan Museum of Art. Artists represented in those years included Picasso, Van Gogh and Cezanne.
- This year, gallery patrons were treated to the work of L.A. artists, who gave us a real palm frond painted silver, rolls of toilet paper with stenciled butterflies and a huge expanse of empty gallery space. I found the empty space soothing.
- As usual, one of the fair's highlights is the lovely, colorful Flower and Garden Pavilion. This year's theme: "Magical, Mystical Morocco." Well, it beats magical, mystical Montclair.
- Outside the "K9's in Flight" tent, a dog named Sport ran, leaped, even somersaulted to catch a yellow Frisbee. Sport missed one Frisbee but caught it on the first bounce. "We planned that," the trainer joked.
- Among the tiny settings in the always delightful Fairplex Garden Railroad: an industrial, *Metropolis*-style cityscape called Futuropolis, an octopus and mermaid riding a train on a pier, an Old West town with its own Boot Hill, a drive-in movie theater and, in a preview of next year, a miniature sign on bare dirt reading "Future Landfill Site."
- Covering its bases in lieu of simply using a dictionary, one food stand's sign advertises, in large letters, both "Teriyaki" and "Terriyaki."
- On display in the Tapestry of Tradition home crafts building: a

Last Supper in white lace, a series of Warhol-like silkscreened images of singer Alice Cooper, a cross-stitch of the Teenage Mutant Ninja Turtles and a quilt depicting album covers by Led Zeppelin, Iron Maiden and Queensryche.

- Did I mention the Elvis-themed knitted Kleenex cozy?
- Overheard in the men's room, a small boy inside a stall: "Daddy, where are we?"
  Father, waiting outside the stall: "The Pomona fair."
  Boy: "I like it."
- The kid's got a poor sense of direction, but great taste.

IN POMONA, TINY OUTDOOR RAILROAD'S HISTORY GROWS EVEN LONGER

RAILROAD job: Here's a bit more on the Fairplex Garden Railroad, the subject of a column here last month.

Several readers responded with intriguing details about the L.A. County Fair attraction, often referred to as the oldest and possibly largest outdoor model railroad in existence.

The railroad was the handiwork of Pomona High auto shop teacher Herman Howard, as I wrote.

Two of his former students contacted me.

"Mr. Howard built the train set in the late '20s in his backyard on East Jefferson," reader William Hartley told me. "That's where I first saw it in 1930, when I came to California."

I doff my railroad conductor's cap to Hartley. Isn't it amazing that we can still get first-hand information on stuff that happened 80 years ago?

Likewise, Leroy Amos, who also had Howard as a teacher in the 1930s, recalls him as an excellent teacher and human being.

Every month, Howard would borrow a car or two from one of Pomona's 26 dealerships and treat his auto shop students to "a ride in a new car," Amos said. He laughed. "I know we were supposed to go home and nag our parents to buy one."

But back to the tiny railroad. Herman Howard sold the display in 1958 to Herman Templin, apparently wishing to keep it among men named Herman.

Templin had figured the railroad would be a good retirement project, but as reader Warren Weiss tells me, Southern Pacific soon dropped its sponsorship, turning the layout into "a losing business."

As I wrote, Templin was electrocuted and died while preparing the display for the 1968 fair.

In stepped John Huie, who volunteered to help Templin's widow keep the trains running on time. In 1970, the fair bought the display, allowing her to recoup some of her investment, and hired Huie to manage the railroad, Weiss said.

Weiss credits Huie with countless hours of labor to rebuild and improve the display in keeping with Howard's "original vision and concept."

It sounds as though he was workin' on the railroad all the live-long day, he was workin' on the railroad just to pass the time away. (Sorry.)

Anyway, Huie and the fair had some sort of dispute over the train in the mid-1990s and new volunteers took it over, converting everything from Howard's original half-inch scale to G-scale, a smaller, more standard size for ease of replacement parts.

Hey, I don't want to get into adjudicating a decade-old dispute, And no matter what size the equipment, the Garden Railroad remains one of the fair's most charming features.

Even though the fair is over, the railroad can be viewed, for free, the second Sunday of each month from 11 a.m. to 4 p.m.

Kudos to the volunteers who keep the trains running. And let's give credit to John Huie for almost three decades of work, too.

"Were it not for John Huie," Weiss said, "the magnificent, one-of-a-kind layout would no doubt be the location of a kiddie ride or some snack stands."

And that's no hooey.

Huie himself told me Herman Howard's original trains, all built in his own machine shop, were a "real piece of Americana," as well as a marvel of detail.

"One dining car had place settings," Huie said. "Another car had a pressurized tank for a working shower."

Isn't that something?

If Howard's trains had working toilets, though, I don't want to know about it.

L.A. COUNTY QUILTER
GOES UNDERCOVER

CONTINUING my intensive coverage of the vacationing Pomona City Council, I attended the L.A. County Fair's opening ceremonies Friday to see which bigwigs would show up.

A council quorum – Norma Torres, George Hunter, Paula Lantz and Freddie Rodriguez – convened, and even though they haven't met formally since August 6, and won't meet again until September 17, they say they're keeping busy.

"It's not a holiday. We just aren't meeting," Lantz explained.

Speaking of bigwigs, Gloria Molina was introduced not only as a county supervisor but as an avid quilter. Who knew? She was said to enter the fair's quilting competitions each year under an assumed name, so the judges won't be influenced.

Really?

"I use a different name each year, and I'm from a different place," Molina told me cheerfully. "I've won a couple of times. I'm not going to win this year. I entered only a couple of small pieces."

Maybe she needs a really killer pseudonym. In any event, I'm happy the fair is back. It'll help me kill time until September 17.

BUGGING OUT AT FAIR'S CREEPIEST EXHIBIT

A T Mrs. Millipede's Insect Barn at the L.A. County Fair, employees hold African emperor scorpions and giant African millipedes and ask if you'd like to (blecchh) hold the insects too.

Most people react as if, um, snakebit.

"The little boys seem to like them, the little girls tend to shy away. And I'm up to 14 screams today," quipped Kender MacGowan, who was cradling a foot-long black millipede when we spoke Thursday.

Patti Cota, meanwhile, was showing off a scorpion to anyone who could bear to look. About five inches long, this scorpion is creepy-looking but docile.

Cota assured me African emperor scorpions are all bluff.

"They're like those 300-pound, really tall guys who are actually pussycats," Cota said.

Cota and MacGowan work for Pacific Animal Productions, which also has hedgehogs, bearded dragons and tortoises at the fair and takes its educational exhibits to classrooms.

The pair got their jobs through Craigslist, the classifieds and social-networking website.

"They advertised the job under 'Everything Else,'" MacGowan noted.

"My son is real excited about me working here," said Cota, who has a millipede and other crawling things at home. "He thinks it's the greatest job ever."

Solely for the benefit of you, the inquiring reader, your squeamish columnist held the (ugh) scorpion. It sat on my palm, unmoving – thankfully.

More happily, the millipede's estimated 200 to 400 tiny legs offered my hand a pleasant massage as it walked.

Perhaps the millipede and I bonded because we have certain characteristics in common. As the display card over its enclosure says: "Their main line of defense is to curl into a tight ball." Hey, me too!

Fair tidbits: BBQ, pigs, art and a good deed

S IGHTS, sounds, but thankfully no smells, from the 2007 L.A. County Fair, which ends Sunday:

- In the Shopping Place, a vendor sells a product with an evocative name: The Rodman Nibbler. It's a drill bit and not, as I feared, the offspring of an unholy union between Dennis Rodman and Mike Tyson.
- I heard the guy behind the Vita-Mix blender make this unusual claim: "I can make a four-course meal here faster than you can go to Wendy's and come back." Hard to argue, as the nearest Wendy's is miles away.
- In perhaps the fair's biggest surprise, the Baked Potatoe stand, after years of inspiring snickers over its spelling, became the Baked Potato stand. You can see the white paint that covers the unnecessary E. Upsides: Better English and an example to our young people.
Downside: No more Dan Quayle cracks.
- Proving that nature finds a balance, a nearby vendor selling toy copters has a sign that reads "Helicopter Flys Real High." And outside, a longtime food booth still claims to sell "Frys."
- As a sow gave birth, slowly, in the animal barn, some 100 of us gathered around. Inside the pig's pen, an avuncular commentator, who was eating a hurried lunch on a stick, quipped: "I hope you'll help me disguise the fact that I'm eating a pork chop right now."
- He also said, during the long wait, that the TV network Animal Planet is not always accurate in its depiction of birthing: "You'll see them in the pen, turning the animal, stroking her, comforting her. We don't do that. You try to comfort one of those cows over there, she will hurt you."
- In line at Hot Dog on a Stick for a lemonade, I saw a paper

basket blow off the counter. I picked it up, walked it to a trash can, tossed it in and got back in line.

After handing me my drink, the guy behind the counter refused my $3.50, saying: "It's on us. Most people would have walked past the trash or stepped on it. Thanks for picking up our trash for us."

Very nice of him, especially since doing the right thing had already given me a self-satisfied glow. That said, I was on the alert for more good-deed possibilities every time I walked past.

- At Mrs. Millipede's Insect Barn, as an employee held an African Emperor scorpion in her hand, a man walked by and said dismissively, "It's plastic." As one who held the (ugh) scorpion myself, let me say: No, it wasn't.

- Wednesday evening, passers-by gathered around the giant TV at the Leigh Adams tent to watch *Dancing With the Stars*, despite the sound being turned off.

- In the Flower and Garden Pavilion, where this year's theme is Italy, rainbow-colored Italian Tapestry roses are on display. The card reads: "This beautiful and exotic rose is hand-dyed in The Netherlands and shipped overnight to the L.A. County Fair." How about that!

- The Millard Sheets Gallery this year has a welcome theme: Millard Sheets. Work from 1926 to 1988 by the late artist is on view, and it's great stuff.

- The Tapestry of Tradition home-craft exhibits are always a high point for me. I admired a first-place farm scene (by Susan Smith of Ontario) constructed entirely out of food, including trees made of popcorn and a farmhouse roof shingled with Golden Grahams. And don't miss the cake in the shape of a peace symbol, "tie-dyed" with food coloring.

- The sewing area includes a hand-embroidered pillow featuring a most unusual version of the Tooth Fairy: a full-sized man with wings who relaxes on a tree branch in a forest near a raccoon and a bear.

- I also marveled at a version of the God-touches-Adam's-finger scene from the Sistine Chapel, rendered faithfully in cross-stitch.

It's actually quite impressive.

- A huge quilt has panels drawn in crayon by siblings named Albert and Deana and is titled "August 1990 Vacation Time at Grandpa's and Grandma's."

The panels take the youngsters from the airport to a barbecue, a theme park, a parade, berry picking, two games of checkers and back to the airport. It wasn't all fun. "Albert and Deana Bring Up the Grocery," as one panel is labeled, shows the two in profile, with sad faces, carrying bags of groceries up the stairs.

The whole thing is hilarious and sweet.

- Barbecue stands are everywhere at the fair. Which to try? One stand seems to present an overview: Its sign advertises "Texas style BBQ brisket/St. Louis style ribs/Santa Maria style tri-tip." But no baked potatoe.

TOAD IN THE HOLE CROAKS

TOAD in the Hole, the L.A. County Fair restaurant with the curious name, won't be hopping during fairtime next month. The structure dating to 1933 has been bullfrogged – I mean, bulldozed. A booth selling pizza will replace it.

The restaurant was named for its original specialty, but what toad in the hole meant in Pomona is unclear.

Was it "filet mignon tucked inside a baked potato," as Charles Phoenix says in his book *Cruising the Pomona Valley*? Or was it "a piece of toast with an egg fried inside it," as fair spokeswoman Sharon Autry recalls?

Maybe they're both right, and the restaurant's version of the dish morphed over time. After all, the neon sign out front advertised the signature item as "Aristocrat of Foods," which strikes me as more applicable to steak than a fried egg.

Perhaps you fairgoers can settle this point.

In any event, beginning in 1998 the Toad became a pizza parlor. The neon sign was altered slightly to read "Toad in the Hole Pizza, Aristocrat of Foods."

Which must have only confused everyone even more.

County Fair sign
RETURNS

I TOOK a drive on Arrow Highway the other day to check out the new/old L.A. County Fair sign. It stands a few yards west of White Avenue in La Verne at Fairplex Gate 15.

The sign originally stood at Foothill and White near the Mount Baldy Drive-In sign, which featured three images of a skier on the slopes; when the neon blinked, the skier appeared to be in motion.

The drive-in was in existence from 1960 to 1984, according to Charles Phoenix's *Cruising the Pomona Valley* guidebook. The fair sign was there in approximately the same span and, after being taken down, was preserved in a Fairplex warehouse until its recent restoration.

"That was a little miracle they found it," Phoenix told me. He was pleased to know it was restored, and by the same company that made it originally, Pomona-based Williams Sign Co.

It looks pretty sharp, and I'm looking forward to driving past there at night to see the neon.

MIDLIFE GRRRL POWER

A N L.A. County Fair audience was bewitched, bangled and berlin'd last Friday by a concert lineup of female-led 1980s pop bands: the Motels, the Bangles and Berlin.

All the bands' frontwomen are now in their 40s and 50s and had their heyday 20 years ago. That may have accounted for the Bangles' opening song, "Hazy Shade of Winter," whose first line is: "Time, time, time, see what's become of me."

But age was dealt with more directly by Berlin singer Terri Nunn.

"How do you like this old-woman bill tonight?" Nunn cracked after belting out "No More Words." Her joke drew a roar of approval. Nunn, 47, added: "I love it!"

Me too. Note to the fair: Can we get the Pretenders next year?

The Motels were in fine form. The Bangles, who played last, were actually kind of a letdown. It didn't help that guitarist Vicki Peterson at one point declared: "It's great to be here at the California State Fair."

The evening's peak was unquestionably, if surprisingly, Berlin.

Nunn commanded the stage and sang her lungs out. Before the final song, she said we'd made her dreams come true that night – she actually seemed to mean it – and then gave back in startling fashion.

She climbed on a roadie's shoulders and he walked her into the audience as she sang the ballad "Take My Breath Away." They went through the VIP area, the box seats and partway into the free grandstand seats (but not as far up as yours truly sat), shaking hands and singing all the while. I'd never seen anything like it.

Take our breath away indeed.

* * *

Female-led bands have more obstacles than I knew. My spellcheck suggests that "frontwomen," above, be replaced by "frontmen."

HOLE IN TOAD LORE FILLED

NOT that anyone appeared to care, since I didn't receive a single comment. But the minor mystery of the foodstuff specialty of Toad in the Hole, the L.A. County Fair restaurant that was bulldozed recently after more than 70 years, has been solved.

Was it a filet mignon inside a baked potato, as author and unofficial fair historian Charles Phoenix said? Or an egg tucked inside a piece of toast, as fair spokeswoman Sharon Autry suggested?

Autry tracked down a longtime horse racing employee – tracked, get it? – who told her a Pomona toad in the hole "was indeed the biggest baked potato he said he ever saw, with filet mignon inside, served with vegetables on the side.

"People lined up to get in and it was excellent," Autry reported.

She graciously admitted her error.

"Thank goodness for wonderful people like Charles Phoenix who love the fair, and people who attend and share their memories," Autry said. "That's what it's all about, people and creating memories."

Phoenix was happy to hear he'd been vindicated but he expressed dismay at the demise of the restaurant. Erasing memories, not creating them, seems to be the fair's modern approach, he griped.

"On average they tear down one historic building every year," Phoenix told me. "Fifteen or 17 years from now, we can pretty much count on the whole thing being leveled. They're going to raze part of what they had to offer, which is sad."

On the bright side, at least I can count on 15 or 17 future columns.

Like its specialty, the quirky Toad in the Hole neon sign is now tucked inside a Fairplex warehouse. The sign rejoins its former next-door neighbor, the Ernie's BBQ sign, which was removed prior to the 2007 fair.

The Ernie's sign depicts a pig in a chef's hat holding a plate of ribs and looking strangely happy about it.

DID THEY DEEP-FRY IN 1911?

As all schoolchildren know, the L.A. County Fair (which runs today through September 28) began in 1922 and, except for an interruption for World War II, has continued annually ever since.

But did you know Pomona had a fair-like event from 1911 to 1921? Probably not, unless you're incredibly old.

Or unless you're Betty Peters, an intrepid researcher who's a mere child of 85.

Peters, a volunteer at the Pomona Public Library and an authority on the nooks and crannies of local history, recently turned up a mention of a Pomona Valley Fair. Curious, she dug into the topic.

She directed me to microfilm of 1911 editions of the Pomona Progress, where I learned that the first Valley Fair took place from September 13 to 16 in tents set up near City Hall.

That Valley Fair included livestock judging, home arts, parades, an aerial show with a biplane, a queen of the fair, a circus, "huge African lions" and an "Orang-outang," a grand ball and seven carnival rides.

Among the rides: a merry-go-round. Ooooh, scary.

If there was a concert, I imagine the singer was some has-been from the 1890s.

"All the cities from Glendora through Cucamonga were invited," Peters said. According to her research, the Valley Fair occurred every September until supplanted by the county fair.

One question remains unanswered.

Did the Valley Fair sell any food items on sticks?

You hate the Fair? 'Baaaaa'

SIGHTS, sounds and smells from the 81st Edition of the L.A. County Fair, which ends Sunday:

- A recorded voice at a barbecue stand says in a masculine drawl: "If your belly button is gnawin' at your backbone, come to Juicy's."

- I kept on walking to Pink's for my annual chili dog with onions. Yes, it was $5.50, which seems outrageous. The same dog is only $2.85 in L.A.

  Of course, to get to L.A. requires, oh, $12 in gas. And, at Pink's, an hour's wait in line, compared to no line in Pomona.

  Also, in Pomona, there's an added bonus: They'll give you a celebrity name and call it when your order is ready. "Your name is Tom Hanks," the clerk informed me.

  OK, Pomona wins. Even if the Tom Hanks reference is stale.

- If I were 8 years old, I would never want to leave the "A Pirate's Life" area with its swashbuckling aerialists, mock pirate ship and pirate academy.

  As an adult, of course, you notice things. It's barely possible the area isn't 100 percent historically accurate. For instance, what appears to be a ship's cannon actually discharges a cool, refreshing mist.

  Also, while my research is inconclusive on this point, I'm aware of no other buccaneer ships with a sign reading "Pirate Slide $3."

- In the Flower and Garden Pavilion, themed "Escape to Hawaii," there's an enchanting array of blooms alongside replica surfboards and fruit crate labels. Very nice, as always.

  And an "underwater" scene has this sign: "And the Humuhumunukunukuaptia'a go swimming by."

  I *thought* that's what they were.

- Biggest disappointment: White Castle hamburgers were indeed on the menu this year, but only in the fair's preferred mode of food presentation.
  To quote the sign: "Deep Fried Cheeseburgers."
- The Tapestry of Tradition building continues to be among my favorite attractions.
  Where else can you see not one but two crocheted pillows featuring Snoopy atop his doghouse? Or a "machine-knit gingerbread house" standing three feet high? Or cakes shaped like 1) a 1930s radio, 2) a plate of spaghetti and meatballs or 3) a Dodgers cap?
- Among the amateur art on display is a five-foot-high pedestal bearing a globe covered in metal shavings. Symbol-laden title: "Ball of Confusion on the Pillar of Civilization."
  Heavy, man.
- In slightly less profound art, the Millard Sheets Gallery is devoted to the horse through history, from cave paintings and the migration across the continents to the Old West and horse racing.
  Good stuff, and educational too. I overheard a woman say to her husband: "We must be the only country with an aversion to eating horse. China, Africa, everywhere else eats horse."
  Perhaps the fair could sell deep-fried horse on a stick.
- In Thunder Alley near the Sheets Gallery's "Hoofprints" exhibit, more than two dozen vintage cars are on display. A different kind of horsepower!
- Biggest worry: Doris, the giant sequoia cross-section dating to 44 B.C. and standing at the fair since 1961, has been stripped of its timeline markers. Uh-oh.
- Biggest ripoff: a $3.50 bottle of water.
  You expect to get hosed at the fair, and you adjust your standards accordingly, but you rarely feel as gouged as when you know $3.45 of your $3.50 purchase is pure profit.
- In the America's Kids building, 31 ant farms are linked in a row. That's ants, ants, ants, crawling through plastic for something like 24 feet. You can't tell me that's not worth a visit.

- The Garden Railway continues steaming along with model trains wending their way past delightful dioramas. One change: the drive-in theater screen is no longer a disguised TV but a more realistic version.
  In an example of unreality, the miniature Fox Theater still has a rooftop sign and marquee, and no construction crew.
- I defy you – yes, I defy you – to find anything at the fair cuter than newborn piglets.
  Unless it's the sheep going "baaaaa" and, in response, small children going "baaaaa" right back.
- At a booth with the unlikely name (and product) Yarn Marionettes, the sign promises: "Pure Fun for Kids 3 to 103."
  Yarn marionettes? Maybe 3 AND 103.
  Unlike the fair, which hits the full age range.

Beep! Beep! Congestion
dooms county fair
trams

AND you thought traffic on the freeways was bad. Trams that traverse the L.A. County Fair carrying weary or lazy fairgoers often come to a standstill because so many pedestrians are crossing their path.

Idling trams won't be a problem any longer. Putting the brakes on a decades-long tradition, the fair is ending tram service.

I hope you were properly seated for that jolt.

"Because of the size of our crowds, the trams have been very ineffective," fair spokeswoman Wendy Talarico told me Tuesday. "They can't get around. They end up stopping for long periods of time."

Maybe the fairgrounds needs a trampool lane.

Trams have been (slowly) plying the fairgrounds since 1948. That year, four "elephant trams" were purchased from San Francisco's Golden Gate International Exposition, according to Charles Phoenix's book *Cruising the Pomona Valley*.

Those trams, which resembled elephants, cost a quarter per trip – slogan: "Tour the Fairgrounds for 25 cents" – and were retired in the mid-1980s. In recent years, rides on more modern trams were free.

There were two routes, both departing from the Administration Building and going either to Fairview Farms or the Yellow Gate.

Tram drivers would offer comments about sights and trivia, although there was a brief experiment with recorded narration.

With more than 1.3 million visitors milling around during the 2008 fair, Talarico said the trams were proving an ineffective way to move people.

Likewise, she's stopped using the fair's employee golf carts because of the congestion.

"I've found it's faster to walk almost anywhere on the grounds," Talarico said. "The majority of fair guests are walking."

Well, you've gotta burn off those deep-fried calories somehow.

And before you ask, the decision has nothing to do with money, fair officials say, because the trams are being transferred to the parking lots to get people to or from their cars faster.

OK, but isn't there congestion in the parking lots?

*   *   *

More fair: The 82nd edition of the fair runs September 5 to October 4. Those dates mean the fair will be open Labor Day weekend for the first time, with fair officials hoping to lure staycationers in a troubled economy.

In all, this year's fair will be open 23 days compared to the usual 18.

"We added five days. Five more days of fun," said Sharon Autry, another fair spokeswoman.

Can't wait.

WOMAN GIVES SERVICE WITH A SMILE AT THE FAIR

WHEN you enter the glorious cacophony that is the L.A. County Fair, or when you leave, drooping from heat and sore feet, it's always nice to see a friendly face.

Dyan Lancaster has been one of those faces for 25 years. She works for Guest Services in the fair's information booths, dispensing maps and advice.

Lancaster understands her role as a counselor to the harassed and helpless who wash up at her booth, often in a puddle of sweat.

"It's always hot, they fought traffic to get here, parking cost more than they thought, they parked way out in Timbuktu, the kids are cranky and here they are," Lancaster says cheerfully.

If fairgoers are arriving, she and her cohorts – there are three such booths, with two or more employees at each – stand ready with maps of the sprawling fairgrounds and schedules of the day's events.

If people are leaving and have final questions, Lancaster offers words of advice, always with a friendly, energetic style.

"Get 'em happy before they hit the road to go home. That's our main job," Lancaster says. "We try to have everybody leave with a smile."

This year she's staffing the booth by the White Avenue entrance near Plaza de las Americas. A man walks up as the two of us talk. He's pushing a toddler in a stroller and asks for recommendations.

"How old is the child?" Lancaster asks. Eighteen months, the man responds, plus there's a 2-year-old sibling nearby.

"Try Building 10. There's things in there they might enjoy," Lancaster advises, turning to point to the America's Kids building behind her.

Grabbing a schedule, she circles in pen the times of the Peking acrobatic performances – "but get there a little early," she says, "so you get a good seat."

I learned about Lancaster from one of her children, Kathleen MacGregor, who told me her mom is a walking history book of the fair and that her "dynamic smile" is a tonic for even the grouchiest fairgoer.

"No matter what changes or cutbacks have been made," MacGregor says, "every year she is always determined to make it a great experience for each customer as they come to her information booth."

Speaking of cutbacks, fair poobahs dropped tram service this year on the grounds, putting the trams in the parking lots instead. They claimed the trams could no longer maneuver among the crowds on foot.

I suspected this decision would not go over well with seniors and apparently that's true: Lack of trams is the No. 1 complaint this year. (No. 2 is the demise of the P-Nuttles stands.)

"The trams are missed. They are very much missed," Lancaster admits.

Besides handing out complaint forms and listening to problems, employees in the information booths answer strange questions.

Fairgoers will show Lancaster a piece of jewelry bought at the fair last year and ask where the vendor is this year. She offers her best guess.

A woman once reported that she'd lost her cell phone. Lancaster, offering use of the booth's phone, suggested calling the cell number.

"How can I answer it when I don't know where it is?" the woman asked, confused.

Lancaster explained that someone else might hear the ring and pick it up.

"But I won't be able to hear it," the woman said.

Nevertheless, the woman dialed her number, someone answered and she arranged to get the phone back. She was a blonde, Lancaster notes.

People also forget where they parked. Not where in a particular parking lot, but which parking lot.

"What was the first thing you saw when you came in?" Lancaster will ask.

A common response: "People."

"Did you come in by the rides or through the tunnel?" Lancaster will ask, trying to jog their memory.

Tickets now indicate which entrance was used, which is a big help, Lancaster says.

She got involved with Guest Services through her husband, Jack, a retired firefighter who worked a booth for fun. But the Montclair woman's history with the fair goes back much further.

Her parents, Bob and Frances McDonald, sold food at the fair for decades beginning in the late 1930s.

At one point the family had four food stands. They were the first to bring Mexican food and imported beer to the fair, Lancaster says.

"My dad started off with sodas and added popcorn. All of us had family scars from making popcorn," Lancaster says with a chuckle.

The eight McDonald children pitched in. Dyan switched to Guest Services after some 35 years at the food stands, "tired of popcorn burns," she cracks.

Her sister, Tammy Lawler, joined Guest Services in the mid-1990s and staffs the booth near the Clock Tower. Yep, two sisters, both working at the fair's information booths.

Is that too much information?

"She loves it," Lawler says of her sister. "It's part of her life. She takes it very seriously. She's great with the older people. She's very proud of her job."

Cindy Castaneda, who directs Guest Services, says the sisters are important to the operation, which employs 38, and to her personally.

"They know everything about the fair. This is my fifth fair.

They're my go-to people," Castaneda says.

Lancaster isn't the longest-serving Guest Services employee – that would be Terri Carver at 32 years – but then there's her previous fair experience.

"It's 60 years with the fair. It's 25 years with Guest Services and 35 years before that with my folks," Lancaster says.

MacGregor, her daughter, told me: "Her goal was to work 60 years so I have a feeling she may call this one her last."

Lancaster, who's 75, says the first fair she worked was 1948.

"The same year as Thummer the pig!" she exclaims. Thummer is the fair's mascot, whose classic pose is standing with arm cocked, as if thumbing a ride.

("At that time, it was common to hitchhike to the fair because of gas rationing," Lancaster explains. "That was one of the ideas, hitching a ride to the fair.")

Is this her last fair? Maybe.

"I always said when I got to 60 years, I could retire because I would have accomplished something in my life," Lancaster says with a laugh.

But if her first year was 1948, then her 60th would have been 2007. This would be her 62nd fair.

Well, maybe the math doesn't pencil out precisely. Retirements at the fair don't always go as planned, anyway. September rolls around and employees who swore they were done can't resist returning.

Lancaster isn't ruling it out either.

Just to be safe, though, better say hello to Lancaster by the fair's end, October 4. She'll give you that dynamic smile and you'll both feel better.

THIS BATMOBILE HAS NO POW! NOT EVEN A BAM!

THE Batmobile is parked in Pomona.

Specifically, it's parked in the National Hot Rod Association Museum at Fairplex, but only through Friday. This isn't the Hummer-like Batmobile from the recent movies but the Adam West Batmobile from the 1960s TV series.

"We've had kids who say it doesn't look like the Batmobile," museum spokeswoman Monique Valadez says. "Their parents explain about the TV show and share their memories of watching it."

Must be (yawn) fascinating for the kids.

Well, this may be their father's Batmobile, but it's also mine. So when Valadez invited me to view the vehicle and even sit inside – a privilege not afforded the general public – I escaped from the death-trap that is the *Daily Bulletin* and hopped in my Corolla.

Engines to power, turbines to speed ... OK, let's move out.

Batman aired from 1964 to 1966 on ABC and presented a silly, pop-art version of the Caped Crusader. For murky reasons, either control of the rights or the out-of-fashion version of Batman as high camp, the series isn't on DVD.

But during my childhood in Illinois, the show was must-viewing for me in syndication, and apparently I even watched the tail-end of the original broadcasts.

Because when I was 2 or 3, my babysitter and I used to play Batman and Robin. Mrs. Boehm, whose own children were grown, would re-enact superheroic moments with me. For instance, the two of us would stand side by side against a living room wall and pretend to climb our Batropes hand over hand.

Holy nostalgia, Batman!

These days the Batmobile tours the country for people to ogle. Original designer George Barris built a few replicas, but the one in Pomona is said to be the original.

Parked in the museum, which is a neat place but a poor substitute for the Batcave, the Batmobile is roped off, like a precious artifact, which I suppose it is.

"It's been a big hit during the fair," Valadez says. "We've had people come specifically to see the Batmobile. We've had all ages, across the board, wanting to pose next to it."

The museum is open the same hours as the L.A. County Fair and can be found just south of the Millard Sheets Gallery. Admission with your fair pass is $1.

The Batmobile is leaving sometime Friday for a car show, but it's scheduled to return October 7 for one night only, the NHRA Twilight Cruise, from 4 to 8 p.m. That event is free.

I was there Monday, when the museum, like the fair, is closed – thus sparing the feelings of children who couldn't climb inside the Batmobile like the dorky grown-up.

This Batmobile looks like you'd expect, sleek and stylish, unlike the armored tank from the movies. Its exterior is a shiny black with fluorescent orange highlights, all in perfect condition.

I notice a car duster behind the front seat. Property of Alfred the butler?

Museum facilities manager Wayne Phillips, not to be confused with stately Wayne Manor, arrives to power up the car for me.

A radar-like antenna rises from the center of the hood, lights on the dash come on. But the battery is low and the engine won't turn over, nor will the siren-like red light up top shine.

"Is it essential for what you're doing that everything work?" Phillips asks.

Well, it's not like I'm chasing the Riddler here. All I really want to do is sit inside.

Phillips flips a switch inside the door to open it. Better than my jumping in like Adam West.

Inside the exposed cockpit, the car looks old, in a way – the Batmobile is a modified 1955 Lincoln concept car – and yet it also looks more like the Batmobile than expected.

There's the giant compass on the dash and plenty of dials and switches to control the After Burner, the Bat Chute, the Bat Phone and other gimmicks – even if they don't really work.

You can imagine you're really Batman. If only Mrs. Boehm were in Robin's seat!

Speaking of the Bat Phone, Valadez points it out on the floor and suggests I pick it up. The bat-shaped red receiver is attached to the base by Velcro.

I pretend to take a call while Valadez kindly commemorates the moment by taking a photo.

I imagine that back in Gotham City, Commissioner Gordon, who has lifted the glass bell off the Bat Phone in his office to place that dreaded call, is filling me in on the latest caper while Chief O'Hara is in the background, looking grim.

(Which he should, since he's such a failure as a police chief that he has to let a man in a cape and skintight suit catch crooks for him.)

"I'll be there soon, Commissioner," I might say. "Just as soon as Wayne Phillips recharges the Batmobile's battery."

Back in the newsroom, I get some mileage out of my Batmobile story. Joe Blackstock, one of our editors, is duly impressed.

"You might as well chuck it," he says of my career. "I don't think there's anything else you can aspire to."

Holy pinnacle, Batman!

No hair's-breadth escape from jokes

THE photo of yours truly behind the wheel of the Batmobile in Wednesday's newspaper prompted two Batmaniacs to kid me that rather than the Caped Crusader, my bare dome made me look a lot more like the TV villains Mr. Freeze (says Derek Deason) or Egghead (says Steve S. from Chino). After that "Pow!" and "Bam!", my ego went "Splat!"

* * *

At the L.A. County Fair the other night, I parked near a KIIS-FM van with images of Chris Brown and Rihanna paired on the side – seven months after his post-Grammy arrest for beating her – and, both amused and horrified, snapped a photo, then put it on my blog.

Not only did "LA Observed," a well-read blog, pick up on the item, but Fox 11 News aired a segment about my photo on Thursday, with full credit.

See what you're missing by not reading my blog?

(Although it's puzzling why it took a guy in Pomona to notice that this van is still driving around.)

MISTY CHOCOLATE-COVERED MEMORIES OF FAIR

S IGHTS, sounds and smells from the L.A. County Fair, which ends today (with $1 admission before 1 p.m.):

- Most literal-minded name for a food stand: Everything is Smothered in Chocolate.
- For my frozen cheesecake dipped in chocolate, I paid with exact change, worried that otherwise I might get back chocolate-covered currency.
- Near the lagoon on a Friday night, a video screen had a live feed from the Donna Summer concert occurring on the racetrack. A small, mellow crowd sat on the short stone walls, eating barbecue and enjoying the show. Now *that's* an "End of Summer" concert series – one with Donna Summer herself.
- The P-Nuttles stands are gone this year. I never went there, nor am I clear on what they sold. Did I miss anything?
- At the Garden Railroad, the outdoor model train layout that remains one of the fair's treasures, a water problem damaged the drive-in theater scene. Its miniature parking lot is empty of miniature cars. In acknowledgment, the theater screen has the message "It's intermission time!"
- Also at the Garden Railroad, a Mexican village scene once again has a Zorro figure, sword brandished, on a flat roof. The figure had been missing and the railroad crew assumed it was stolen, volunteer Carlton Dudley told me.
Then, while replanting the landscape, someone found the figure, which had simply fallen into the shrubbery. It's been glued back into place.
Viva Zorro!

- At the fair, no vegetable is safe. Sign at a barbecue stand: "Chocolate Dipped Corn."
  What worries me is that some fairgoers probably put mayo, butter and salt on their chocolate-dipped corn.
- Theme for the America's Kids building: "Under the Sea." One area is called Shark Shack, which when I was 10 would have been my favorite part of the fair.
  The docent stands inside a shark cage. Shark jaws are on view along with a list of shark facts and myths. A display shows "Tiger Shark Stomach Contents," illustrated by such objects as a pair of sneakers, a sack of Yukon Gold potatoes and a tire.
- Meanwhile, the children's competition features multi-colored, multi-tentacled octopi made of various materials. Also on display are binders of student-penned stories with provocative titles.
  Among them, all from Ontario children: "The Story of My Dogs," "The Wizard of El Camino Elementary" and "The Secret Spy."
  Not just a spy, mind you, but a secret spy. Ooooohh!
- At the Pink's Hot Dogs stand, they're celebrating 70 years since the Hollywood landmark's 1939 founding. I was happy to help them celebrate by buying one of their delicious chili dogs.
- Among the products for sale in the Shopping Plaza: the Poodle Glove, the Shopping Jeep and a video console billed as "76,000 Games in One."
- Looking at the animals in Fairview Farms is always a highlight. Chickens, cows, goats, sheep, even llamas, all there for the viewing. The pigs seemed especially content, unaware that elsewhere on the fairgrounds, stands were selling chocolate-drenched bacon (shudder).
- Disturbing sign outside Building 4: "Santa is Visiting the Fair." Let's hope he's there for vacation, not work.
- In the Culinary Styles area, there are creative homemade cakes in the shape of a pirate chest and a woman's high-heeled shoe.
- One of the tablescaping categories, Motion Picture Perfect, caused a controversy. A table set for a romantic dinner with such elements as a small piano, pair of shoes, airplane, cell phone and fake money prompted this comment on the judging sheet: "Use of

theme is unclear and incohesive ... *Casablanca*?"

Someone wrote in pen: "Hello! *Pretty Woman*," proceeding to explain how each element figured into the movie's plot. Piano: "They made love on it." The plane and the red dress was for their trip to San Francisco, the shoes because she made him take his off and walk barefoot in the park, etc., etc.

As for the cash, that is for "paying for her services."

At least during my visit, the judging sheet garnered a lot of attention, and chuckles, from passersby.

- In the Millard Sheets gallery, the modest theme is "The Making of Art: The First 30,000 Years." Now that's value for the money!
- Baffling food stand sign: "Meat Lover's Ice Cream." What are the sprinkles made out of, pepperoni?
- In the annual Spam cooking contest, the children's winner was a Chinese noodle dish. According to the fair's PR department, when young chef Connor Stitz of Covina was quizzed on where one might find the crispy noodles he used as his topping, he replied: "Aisle 9."
- No matter how much I roam around the fair, I can't get everywhere or see everything. For instance, somehow I missed the "Jurassic Planet" exhibit, said to present "a dramatic prehistoric world of over 20 dynamic animated dinosaurs."

Perhaps the exhibit answers that age-old question of why the dinosaurs died off.

My guess: They smothered in chocolate.

BIG CROWDS, BUT NO BOOM

THERE was less boom and fewer bright lights at the L.A. County Fair this year: The nightly fireworks show at closing time was doused.

Reader Randall Volm brought the absence to my attention, telling me he and a friend had been comparing the fair with previous runs while driving home from Disneyland (the L.A. County Fair of the south).

"The one thing that stood out in the conversation was the nightly fireworks show, or lack thereof," Volm said. "Was the decision due to cost? Or nearby residential noise complaints?"

Cost, says fair spokeswoman Michelle DeMott, telling me the demise of the fireworks was "an economic decision we had to make."

Early-to-bed types in Pomona and La Verne probably didn't mind a bit.

2009's Never Ending Fair, as I like to think of it, started September 5 and ended October 4, carrying through five weekends, which may be a record.

Attendance was 1,372,383. (It would've been 1,372,380 without my three visits. Every little bit helps.)

The early opening on Labor Day weekend was a smash hit, drawing 265,000 stay-at-home types. To lure crowds in a tough economy, the fair offered plenty of $1 admission deals and a $25 pass good for the entire run.

Tentative dates for the 2010 fair repeat the five-weekend concept and pre-Labor Day opening.

I'm pleased to know that unlike the nightly fireworks, the fair didn't fizzle.

LET'S GIVE A HAND TO
P-NUTTLES

THE perennial P-Nuttles stands at the L.A. County Fair were (gasp) absent this year, which was noted here along with an admission that I'd never had a P-Nuttle and wasn't clear on what they were.

"What a shame!!" shocked reader Lorae Vanden Berge says. "You have truly missed out on one of the highlights of the fair."

She enlightens me that P-Nuttles are toffee nuts and that the experience of stopping at the stand was even better than the nuts themselves.

The reason: free samples.

"Outside the stand were women dressed in P-Nuttle outfits holding little white plastic spoons and a bag of P-Nuttles. They would hand out samples by taking their spoons and placing two or three – and only two or three – P-Nuttles in the palm of your hand," Vanden Berge says.

"They tasted so good served that way, and the sample was just enough to whet your appetite so you would buy the overpriced bag of P-Nuttles!"

Now that's marketing. Vanden Berge says she used to always visit a P-Nuttles stand at fairtime until she "wised up" and discovered that $4.99 will get you two cans of toffee nuts at Stater Bros.

"They taste the same," Vanden Berge adds. "At least they do when we eat them two at a time off a white plastic spoon."

FAIR'S FOOD COURT SWALLOWED UP BY BULLDOZERS

THE sun has set on the Sunset Cabana, the food court of the L.A. County Fair.

The open-air food court, a fixture since the 1930s, has been demolished. The move is giving preservationists a stomach ache.

"I'm so mad at them," sighed Charles Phoenix, who has led tours of vintage architecture at the fair but laments the increase in demolition in recent years.

"To me," Phoenix said, "they need to bulldoze the people who make these decisions." Ouch.

The food court lay north of the Clock Tower and southwest of the Grandstand. Forming a semi-circle, the food court featured a half-dozen eateries, their cuisine spelled out in neon script.

An art deco tower rose from the courtyard, where tree-shaded tables offered an oasis for a quick meal or a short break.

Original food stalls included Bonnie's Southern Fried Chicken, Hap's Cafe, Hamburger King and Brock's Swiss Steak. A vintage photo of the court also shows signs for Baked Ham and Creamed Chicken.

Did those come deep-fried?

The food court, originally the Food Circle, was erected in 1939. It became Super Diner in a 1986 remodeling that added stainless steel accents and Sunset Cabana in a 2003 retooling that gave it a Jimmy Buffett feel.

Burgers, Hawaiian barbecue, Mexican food, fish and chips, Chinese food and funnel cakes were among the foods sold in recent fairs.

To be honest, I never ate there because the stands felt second-rate. But on occasion I did enjoy the free entertainment – a cappella acts performing pop oldies – and the shade, a welcome thing in a sea of hot asphalt.

Phoenix is among those upset that the fair's quaint permanent attractions such as the Pie A La Mode, Ernie's BBQ and Toad in the Hole stands and the Clock Tower have been razed and replaced by temporary structures.

"Just the presence of the food court helped give that historic essence to the fair, which to me is the most important reason to go," Phoenix said. "All the new features are kind of the same."

The food court was demolished in December. Sorry, but nobody told me until last week, and this isn't the sort of thing the fair trumpets in press releases ("Look what we're destroying now!").

Fair officials say the structure had outlived its useful life. The food court fell victim to age and changing priorities.

"It had no historical value as far as being a landmark," spokeswoman Sharon Autry told me. "And the space can be better utilized year-round instead of just during the 18 days of the fair."

There's talk of moving the Fun Zone carnival rides south to the territory between the Grandstand and the Flower and Garden Pavilion, including the former food court area. The idea would be to shrink the sprawling fair's footprint and make it easier for fairgoers to navigate.

Autry wouldn't comment in detail on that rumor, saying "we're exploring layouts for the fair" and that nothing is ready to announce.

She added, however, that the space in question was "where the carnival was located during the 1930s" – speaking of history.

* * *

More fair: Excavation for the fair's trade and conference center recently unearthed two reminders of the 1960s: a bomb shelter and a swimming pool. Both were remnants of a model home showcased at the 1961 fair.

"It was during the bomb shelter frenzy of the '60s," Autry told me.

At the site, fair employees and the construction crew marveled at the pool's elaborate diving platform and, especially, the bomb shelter.

One person remembered seeing the bomb shelter as a child but didn't understand what it was.

"He had thought it was a little fort you could put in your backyard," Autry said. "I guess that's how a little kid would look at it."

LESS SPRAWL AT FAIR BUT SAME FUN

THE L.A. County Fair returns Saturday, and it's smaller than ever!

No kidding. The fair will relocate its Fun Zone carnival rides and pull its northern boundary back to the Grandstand and Flower and Garden Pavilion.

The result will be a fair more than 10 percent smaller than usual.

"The fair is 89 percent of what it was. It's an 11 percent difference," fair spokeswoman Sharon Autry told me.

Shrinkage? What would George Costanza say?

Speaking of shrinkage, anecdotal evidence was that crowds seemed sparser last year. Fair officials confirmed that.

While 2009 attendance was up slightly from 2008, to nearly 1.4 million, average daily attendance was down because the fair lasted 23 days rather than 18.

"It may seem crowded on Saturday when it's shoulder to shoulder and you're trying to shuffle down Broadway," said Michelle DeMott, the fair's marketing manager, referring to one of the fair's bigger streets. "But the outlying areas aren't getting the traffic flow."

As a fairgoer, I have to agree that the event sprawled to the extent that it was hard to get around. By the time my slog around the grounds brought me to the Fun Zone, I usually turned around.

"The walk from Blue Gate (across White Avenue) through the tunnel to the carnival was about a mile," DeMott said.

This year, the fair is withdrawing from 12 acres, bringing the event's size to 110 acres. (The unused space will be used for parking.)

In the biggest change, the Fun Zone will be placed between the Grandstand and the Flower and Garden Pavilion, both of which will roughly constitute the northern border of the fairgrounds.

The space between the two landmarks was formerly taken up by tents of vendors selling such wares as big-screen TVs and hot tubs.

Those vendors have been relocated to the shopping areas, grouping all the commercial space at the fair's south near Red Gate. In a boon of sorts, this allows one-stop shopping for Sham-Wows, backscratchers and billiard tables.

Said DeMott: "We felt we could compress some of the things and get rid of the redundancies."

In other words, look for less competition among vendors hawking jewelry polish and miracle cookware.

Making the carnival's move simpler was the demolition of the semi-circular Food Court building from the 1930s, a loss for architecture and shade but a gain for tastebuds (the vendors were awfully generic).

The new layout may be a blast from the past for older fairgoers.

"It's more reflective of how the fair was in the '50s," said Leslie Galerne-Smith, a fair spokeswoman.

The compact fair will be "more navigable" for fairgoers, she added.

The trams, exiled to the parking lots for the 2009 fair, will be back, although they won't offer the guided tours of years past. Their absence was the top complaint last year.

They will shuttle fairgoers between Yellow Gate, near the Fun Zone, and the shopping areas.

"They'll go through service roads, not the heart of the fair. That was our problem," DeMott said, referring to conflicts between trams and pedestrians.

We've already printed a Page One story about the fair's big attractions. But let me hit a few highlights:

"Mojo's Jungle," featuring capuchin monkeys, kangaroos and snakes; "LA in Ice," in which Los Angeles landmarks will be carved in ice; a celebration of Mexico's bicentennial in the Flower and Garden Pavilion; a traveling circus and a double-decker carousel;

and another outing for "Jurassic Planet" and its 20 animatronic dinosaurs.

Most startling may be "Our Body: The Universe Within," in which plastinated cadavers – essentially, skinned and preserved human bodies and organs – will be on display under the Grandstand (for a $7 extra charge).

A similar exhibit has drawn throngs, and mild controversy, to L.A.'s Exposition Park and other museums across the country.

Fair officials say this is its first-ever exhibit at a fair.

Making its last-ever appearance is the Giant Slide, which debuted at the fair in the 1960s.

"This is its final year. We're encouraging people to ride it one last time," Galerne-Smith said.

There should be plenty of chances to do so with the fair again open 23 days. For Labor Day weekend, the fair is open Saturday through Monday. From that point, it will operate Wednesday through Sunday through October 3.

Season passes were introduced last year at $24.95 and are back. Passes pay off if you're planning to visit at least twice and also include parking upgrades.

"We sold more than 30,000," DeMott said about 2009. "Our goal was 10,000. We're hoping to sell 50,000."

Regular admission is $17 for adults and $12 for children 6 to 12, but the fair is offering other deals to lower the cost, such as discount tickets sold through Ralphs and McDonald's, $5 admission after 5 p.m. on weekdays or free admission on Fridays with the donation of five cans of food.

Metrolink will still deliver fairgoers who want to avoid the $10 parking fee, but only on Saturday and Sunday due to lower demand the other days.

Concert highlights include Hall & Oates on October 1, Darius Rucker on September 12 and Bad Company on October 2.

As for food, the fair promises to mix it up with a selection of food trucks, following a trend in L.A. Not to mention the usual high adventures in cholesterol.

"We will have bacon-wrapped Oreos dipped in chocolate," Galerne-Smith said.

I can't wrap my head around that.

To sum up, the 2010 L.A. County Fair may be smaller than usual, but the slate of fun continues to be expansive.

DANCE LED TO ROMANCE

TODAY is Pomona Day at the L.A. County Fair, when two noted citizens will be honored. Surely you already know about Joe Romero, the former police chief, so let me tell you about Beth Brooks, the other honoree.

President of Fairplex Friends, a support organization, Brooks has been visiting the fair since childhood. And without the fair she wouldn't be here – that's where her parents met.

It was a Valentine's Day dance in 1942, held at the art gallery. Marcia Fredendall was there with a group of girls from Pilgrim Congregational Church.

Clyde Warren was there too. He was a soldier stationed at the fairgrounds, which during World War II was taken over by the U.S. Army.

Fredendall was dancing with a soldier when Warren cut in. The North Carolina man made quite an impression on the Pomona woman, and vice versa, despite the, um, language barrier.

"The next day, Marcia told her mother that if someone called who could not pronounce her name, that was Clyde," Brooks told me.

There's one reminder of her father at the fair. The building in which he was stationed during wartime is now the NHRA Motorsports Museum, behind the art gallery.

"There is a closet to the right of the front door and since he was a captain in the army, he got to use that closet," Brooks said. "I pay my respects to the closet each year."

Clyde's closet, she calls it. Cool.

Fair's art gallery features fresh Sheets

Tony Sheets says his goal is "to bring art to the people." Not coincidentally, that was his dad's goal too.

Sheets runs the L.A. County Fair's art exhibition, the one his father, Millard Sheets, spearheaded for a quarter-century.

The elder Sheets, a famed watercolorist and muralist who was born in Pomona, ran the Fine Arts Exhibition from 1931 to 1956. In testament to his influence, the Fine Arts Building was named for him in 1994.

Fifty years after Sheets left the fair, a second-generation Sheets has entered.

Tony, 68, is exhibit director of the Millard Sheets Center for the Arts, dreaming up and carrying out ambitious themed displays.

"In my office I have a photo of this place, empty, 12,000 square feet," Sheets told me. "That's my challenge. Fill it up."

He led me on a tour Wednesday through the five-room gallery to show off "From the Industrial Age to the Computer Age," an exhibit that explores the connection between art and technology from 1700 to 2000.

Last year's exhibit was titled "The Making of Art: The First 30,000 Years."

Whew! Sheets doesn't kid around.

Actually, Sheets does kid around – his tastes run to the whimsical. The first piece visitors see is a kinetic sculpture featuring motor-driven metal birds on an aluminum tree branch. The birds slowly flutter to life, one at a time.

Visitors will also see an engine from a linotype machine, a neon sign, weavers' looms, a steam-run popcorn machine and a display on great 20th century photographers.

Storytellers roam the galleries, slipping into character to add insight to the pieces.

Artists are at work throughout, at multiple stations, weaving threads, blowing glass or crafting metal.

"People love to see artists at work. It makes them see they can do it," Sheets said.

The fair, which opened September 4 and continues through October 3, attracts nearly 1.4 million visitors a year – 300,000 of whom visit the Sheets Center.

"It's everyone from museum-goers to kids who have a hard time keeping their hands off everything," Sheets said of the audience. "And everyone in between."

Millard Sheets isn't absent from his namesake center. A display at the entry includes work he did for the 1939 Golden Gate World Expo. A nearby poster is based on a cover he did for *Fortune* magazine in the 1940s.

Five panels of a mural Sheets painted on walnut for Pasadena Home Savings, about the history of the Tournament of Roses, are displayed within the gallery.

Its presence highlights Tony Sheets' other late-in-life role: protector of his father's legacy.

Much of Millard Sheets' work was done as commissions for banks and public buildings. He designed some 40 Home Savings Bank branches, including murals, mosaics and stained-glass windows, many depicting the history of the city they're in.

But as banks fail and change hands, and as mid-century buildings age, his works have increasingly been obscured by plexiglass at banks or endangered.

In 2008, a Sheets mural in a San Francisco bank was painted over. Chase Bank, the culprit, has since become more sensitive to its new holdings.

The bank helped Tony save the Pasadena mural, which is likely to be incorporated into a renovated Pasadena Convention Center.

In San Jose, a mural in a 1970s airport terminal was believed to be doomed because the terminal was set to be demolished and the mural – a pastoral scene of Indians, Spanish settlers and American pioneers – was thought to be permanently attached to a 28-ton wall.

As late as June, Tony Sheets was ready to give up on it too – until taking a closer look. He figured out how to roll the mural off the wall intact. The 24-by-35-foot mural is now safely in storage.

"They're going to put it up in the new terminal. I think that's great," Sheets said.

He's practical about these things. Some of his father's art can't be saved. While ready to invoke the California Art Preservation Act as pressure, he told me he only wants to sue as a last resort – because a lawsuit might discourage anyone from commissioning murals like his father's again.

Westways magazine has a six-page feature in its September issue about Sheets' murals at Home Savings Bank branches, including Pomona's.

Tony is actively cataloging Millard's work at *www.millardsheetsart.com* and tracking renovation plans nationwide. He's been doing so since the 1980s, but his activities have stepped up in recent years.

"The problem is, saving his art doesn't pay," Sheets quipped.

Sheets, who was born in 1942, grew up in the family's Padua Hills home and attended Webb School, Claremont High and Cal Poly Pomona, although he had trouble settling down, which he blames on undiagnosed attention deficit disorder.

He studied under such Claremont artists as Albert Stewart, Jean Ames, Phil Dike and Paul Soldner. He worked as an "imagineer" for Disney.

"I've been making a living as an artist since 1972," Sheets said.

He and his father turned around an awkward relationship.

"When I was a teen it was tough. He was gone a lot and I was rebelling a lot. Once I got out of Cal Poly and had a direction, he was extremely supportive," Sheets said. "When I went to work for Disney, he thought that I was finally growing up."

In repose, Sheets has the stolid features of his father – at least when viewed from the right. His left ear on Wednesday sported a small earring that on closer inspection turned out to be Mickey Mouse ears.

Father and son worked together closely in later years. And Sheets spent his childhood at the fair helping his dad set up well-regarded shows that might include loaned pieces from the Metropolitan Museum of Art in New York.

Tony joined the board overseeing the gallery in 2000 when his brother, David, died.

"He made me promise I would stay involved," Sheets said.

A disastrous 2006 show of environmental art didn't connect with the public. Sheets said he persuaded fair officials to let him curate a show for the centennial of his father's birth rather than shutter the gallery.

After that 2007 show, Sheets had an idea for a horse-themed exhibit for 2008, reflecting another interest of his father's.

"I don't try to fill his shoes. I try to fill his spirit," Sheets said.

His wife, Flower, and daughter, Summer – "what can I say, we're hippies," Sheets joked – and longtime friends such as Nelson Scherer are part of a team of more than 30 people who make the exhibits happen.

"He and Flower are absolutely amazing," said John Svenson, an Upland sculptor who has done work at the fair since the 1950s.

"I think he's a spinoff of his dad," Svenson said, saying father and son share art-world connections and a sensitivity to public tastes.

The Sheetses live in southern Oregon and are staying in an RV near Tony's childhood home in Padua Hills.

He doesn't know how long he'll continue at the fair, but he's already planning the 2011 show, about collectors and collecting.

"In this economy, it's nice to have a steady paying job," Sheets admitted. "Doing these exhibits each year isn't what I expected to be doing at this point in my life. But I love it. It's a real challenge."

FAIR RIDE SLIDING TOWARD THE SCRAP HEAP

A s Jan and Dean once sang, "Gotta take that one last ride."

And so on Wednesday, I climbed the metal stairway, burlap mat in hand, to pay my respects to the Giant Slide.

The L.A. County Fair attraction, erected in the 1960s, will be torn down after the fair ends October 3.

"We're encouraging people to ride it one last time," fair spokeswoman Leslie Galerne-Smith said recently.

The Giant Slide is a daunting thing. Even the operators don't know its dimensions for sure, but it's believed to be 50 feet high, 20 feet across and 120 feet long.

Getting to the top means hoofing it up 95 steps, a mild workout in itself. Each step drives home the feeling that this is one Giant Slide.

So does the view from the platform at the top.

"Once you get up there, it's a lot higher than it seems," ride manager Larry Coleman said before I started my ascent.

The employee at the top spread out the mat for me. A helpful diagram shows how to sit: leaning slightly forward, palms on the mat. (Head-first slides are banned.)

The Giant Slide has no runners to keep you hemmed into a lane. What you see spreading out below you is a Giant Expanse. A practiced Giant Slider might be able to slalom the whole course.

I am not a practiced Giant Slider. I rode it once before, in 1999. Nerves almost kept me from taking the plunge once I gazed down the Matterhorn-like distance to the ground far below.

But that ride went fine. Knowing that, this time there wasn't much trepidation. I sat on the mat and inched myself forward. And forward. And forward some more.

At about the point when you wonder if you're ever going to move, you move.

I took off like a rocket. I even fell backward a little, then remembered I was supposed to be leaning forward – which isn't easy to do when you're plunging downhill – and righted myself.

The descent takes you over four wave-like humps. In the final yards, I raised my arms. By that point in the ride, the diagram doesn't apply. Right?

Other riders Wednesday seemed to have just as much fun on the $3 journey.

"It was a thrill," exclaimed Ryan Mangerina, 13, who had been dubious on his way up.

The Giant Slide appears to have debuted in 1967, according to a *Progress-Bulletin* photo found at the Pomona Library. The fair says the slide came in 1965.

Slide owner Gary Barham doesn't know. His dad, Dave Barham, built the slide. The elder Barham founded the Hot Dog on a Stick chain.

The Missouri native had moved west during the Depression and worked for Lockheed before deciding a life at the Muscle Beach boardwalk selling hot dogs and lemonade in the sun was more appealing.

A fellow vendor named Peanut Bill told Barham he could make as much at the L.A. County Fair in 10 days as he could in a whole year in Santa Monica, Gary said.

Hot Dog on a Stick's first fair was in 1948. Barham, an idea man, had trailers custom-built with big windows to show off both the food preparation – he called it "exhibition cooking" – and the uniformed young women.

"He invented 'sex sells,' a little bit," Gary said.

The Giant Slide was another way to draw attention to the stand. Barham saw a similar slide in San Bernardino and decided he should have one too, only bigger.

His brother, Jack, engineered it and a friend, Fred Pittroff, set up the scaffolding. (Pittroff went on to oversee more than 40 other Giant Slides across the country and in Australia.)

Gary Barham remembered a hitch the first year: The humps sped up riders so much, "they were probably zipping through the fence" at the bottom. He said the humps were fixed overnight.

Other than replacing the wooden steps with metal ones the ride has stayed basically the same, Barham said. Restrictions on riders, however, have risen alongside insurance costs.

In the evenings, after a few beers, riders used to ski down, standing up. That's now a no-no.

"Get a good ride, give them a thrill – but you can't leave the ground," Barham said.

People of all ages ride the Giant Slide. Coleman, the manager, said grandparents who rode as children now bring their grandchildren.

The most devoted rider is Doug Davidson. Now 53, the Los Angeles man, who was born blind, has been riding since the late 1960s. He's missed only a few fairs due to college or illness.

Each visit he rides multiple times. His personal record is 95 rides: "95 times, 95 steps," he told me. It took four hours – plus 95 hikes up all those stairs, to the amazement of ride operators.

Davidson and other special-needs people ride for free. Employees have felt a connection to Davidson after so many visits.

"The Giant Slide has contributed a lot to his life," said his mother, Margaret. "It's a challenge that he could take on. I guess freedom is the one thing that slide gives him."

Davidson and his parents visited September 9 and learned the slide would be dismantled. Barham's daughter saw him and, knowing this would be his last visit, burst into tears.

Erick Gomez of Victorville didn't cry, but he was startled when I told him Wednesday the slide would be taken down.

"No way! That's stupid," Gomez said as his two children rode. He had enticed them here by describing the slide as "the biggest thing I've ever seen."

Fair officials have removed many permanent structures, including food stands, in the past decade to make the fairgrounds more flexible the rest of the year.

The Giant Slide is another permanent structure. The fair wants slides, but it wants ones that can be taken down and rebuilt each year, Galerne-Smith said.

The Fun Zone carnival operator has a Euro Slide not far from the Giant Slide and it appears almost as tall. It's probably safer, since riders have lanes in which to stay and they descend in sleeve-like mats that enclose their feet.

Still, if the Giant Slide means anything to you, better visit soon.

In a little more than two weeks, it will slide into oblivion.

Wheeeee!

They've logged six decades at county fair and are still going strong

NOT every beloved feature at the L.A. County Fair has lasted, whether it's the Toad in the Hole stand or the Clock Tower, both gone, or the Giant Slide, doomed after this year.

And yet outside the Millard Sheets Center for the Arts, a redwood sculpture of Pomona's founder has gazed at fairgoers for almost 60 years.

And inside the center, the figure's sculptor, John Svenson, is gazing at fairgoers too.

Svenson, 87, is displaying examples of his work, hawking his biography (written by his son) and holding forth most days of the fair, which ends Sunday.

The white-haired San Antonio Heights resident now uses a walker and was recently fitted for a hearing aid, but his sly sense of humor remains intact.

Of the fair audience, Svenson says: "This is a cross-section of humanity – which is enough to scare you half to death sometimes."

How did the Ranchero figure come to be? With Svenson ensconced only yards from his creation, I decided to ask.

In 1952, the fair got a portion of a 2,000-year-old Coastal redwood and contracted with Svenson to carve it into something Mexican-related.

He had already been working with Albert Stewart on "Bull Wall," a brick relief sculpture that likewise still stands on the Sheets patio.

The redwood deal was masterminded by Tevis Paine, the fair's publicity manager, who milked even the transport of the log for free ink.

"At that point you could haul 20-foot logs legally. Tevis Paine, being the publicity agent, cut it to 22 feet," Svenson says.

According to Svenson, police in every town stopped the truck and wrote a citation, and every newspaper along the route had a photo of the truck's oversized load, each noting that it was bound for the L.A. County Fair in Pomona.

Now that's genius. The first idea of what to do with the log, however, was a dud.

Two Mexican-American consultants from L.A.'s Olvera Street advised the fair to produce a condescending, stereotypical image.

"They wanted a giant saguaro cactus and a Mexican guy with a big hat against it sound asleep," Svenson says. "I said, 'Are you out of your mind?'"

Over objections, he says, he pursued his own concept. It was based on lore about Ygnacio Palomares, who with business partner Ricardo Vejar got a land grant from Mexico in 1837 for 22,000 acres of present-day Pomona, La Verne, Claremont, Covina and environs.

From atop Ganesha Hill, adjacent to today's fairgrounds, Palomares' land grant "extended as far as the eye could see," Svenson says.

And so he sculpted a towering figure of Palomares, dubbed "Ranchero" after the *Californio* ranch owners of the era. The figure wears a cape, carries an ax for tree-clearing and gazes down at his holdings – or in this case at people eating food on a stick.

It was the largest figure the young Svenson had ever attempted. He first created a one-fourth-size version, which he's showing off at this year's fair. Then, using that model as a guide, he climbed scaffolding to carve the figure's face and shoulders, working his way down the 22-foot log.

He spent a couple of days a week for a year, from September 1952 to September 1953, sculpting the figure.

Fairgoers observed him at work. One woman, evidently not believing the strapping, wavy-haired Svenson could be a sculptor, asked him when the artist would return. He told her to keep an eye out for a weaselly guy with a mustache and beret.

Others asked if the redwood sculpture would continue to grow.

"Yep, they'll probably have to prune it once a year," Svenson liked to reply.

Svenson's resume is too long to include here, and besides, you should buy his book, *Exploring Form*. But as far as the fair is concerned, he worked from 1961 to 1987 as its part-time design consultant, choosing colors, overseeing architecture and creating features such as fountains, the monorail and Heritage Farm.

"Ranchero" stood for several decades in the Court of the Redwoods and was moved to the front of the Sheets Center in 2001. Svenson says there's talk of moving it to an indoors setting.

"The whole top has rotted off, water has gotten inside it and termites have been eating it. I think it's shrinking. The head is narrower than it was then," Svenson says.

But that, he adds, may have improved its proportions.

"Looking up at it," Svenson says, "I'm more satisfied with it now than I was then."

FAIR'S CADAVER DISPLAY COULD BE ECCH-RATED

CALLED "Our Body, the Universe Within," the L.A. County Fair exhibit may show a little more of the universe within than squeamish fairgoers would wish.

Cadavers donated to science have been preserved through the miracle of plastic and placed on view for educational display, innards exposed.

The results are eye-opening, and possibly stomach-churning. It could be titled "Our Body, the Yuckiness Within."

I saw the exhibit one afternoon last week. But first things first: I had lunch. It was less likely, I reasoned, that the exhibit would make me lose my lunch than that it would make me lose my appetite.

"Our Body" is under the Grandstand. Signs warn against photography, cell phone use and food or beverages. I imagine organ meats and beef ribs are double-banned.

Inside, dim lighting, velvet ropes and spotlights are employed. The atmosphere, unlike almost anywhere else at the fair, is hushed.

(It's not quite a museum environment. Late in the exhibit, I could hear a horse race being announced.)

The first figure is labeled "skeleton with joints and partially cut muscle and tendons." He's posed atop a bicycle, as if racing away from the examination table in mid-dissection.

Another figure, in the running position, must be fleeing on foot from the same fate. All his muscles are attached but flayed away from the bone.

"What happened to him?" a woman near me asked. "It looks like he exploded."

Some of the figures are reduced nearly to skeletons. Most look mummified, with unrecognizable features.

Each has pieces missing – the bones on that one, internal organs on another – to allow us to see how they, and we, are put together. Diagrams explain what we're seeing.

One standing figure is pretty much intact, except without skin. All you see are muscles, tendons and nerves. He seemed to have been very fit. At any rate, he has great abs.

Evidently no obese people are on display. Other than among the paying guests. Another male cadaver is holding a baseball glove and appears to be making a catch.

A smaller number of female cadavers are on display and are likewise posed in the altogether. Less energetic in their post-life than the males, the females tend to be at rest or standing. At least they aren't posed knitting or baking.

As for the males, one can't help noticing that sex organs are delicate, but durable, even in death. Emotion welled within me. I think it was pride.

Individual organs are also on display inside clear cases: a vertebrae, a pelvis, knee joints and parts of the brain, for instance.

The brain, by the way, looks undersized. Are all brains so small? Perhaps it formerly belonged to one of our local elected officials.

A spinal cord and nerves look like a long, many-legged insect. Anyone with lower-back trouble might feel a pang of sympathy eyeing the section labeled "lumbar nerves."

Like something from the butcher case, a tongue and pharynx, sliced in half down the middle, lie there, inert but enormous.

I almost clutched my throat. I was reminded of the *Peanuts* strip in which Linus told Lucy in horror that he had suddenly become aware of his tongue.

After the tongue, my journey through "Our Body" brought me to the stomach, liver and gall bladder. I seemed to be traveling southward, a fear confirmed by my, um, movement to the small intestine and rectum.

The nether regions rest in a case, each helpfully labeled for our detached inspection.

Did you know the rectum has a part known as the anal sinus? Next time someone passes gas, politely say "gesundheit."

One of the most remarkable sights, in an exhibit full of them, was a skeleton, seated, legs crossed, with its blood vessels still in place – a few draped across the skull, many more slithering over the rest of the bones. The appearance was of a skeleton being slowly overrun by gossamer tendrils of red moss, and oddly beautiful.

That was my feeling about the entire exhibit. If you can get past the ick factor, its effect is to make you appreciate just how fragile we are.

So much stuff is shoehorned inside us – if we are luggage, God is the master packer – that it's a wonder most of us function at all.

I found myself not only aware of my tongue but of the joints, muscles and other mechanisms enabling me to walk through the exhibit. The effect, thankfully, wears off, or we'd be too self-conscious to do anything. But the impression lingers.

The audience included a lot of medical students, based on technical discussions I could hear, but also included lots of ordinary adults, a disconcerting number of whom brought in young children.

Few fairgoers seem to have demanded their money back. Some 60,000 have seen the exhibit and response has been positive, fair spokeswoman Sharon Autry said. The fair ends Sunday.

Getting inside "Our Body" is $7, or $5 if paid online, on top of your fair admission. That fee, and the visuals outside the hall, were designed to keep people from simply wandering in without knowing what they were getting themselves in for, fair officials said.

Several competitors mount exhibits of so-called "plastinated cadavers." You may have seen them at the Natural History Museum in L.A., where the inaugural 2004 exhibit caused a sensation.

While such exhibits have been shown in museums around the world, this is said to be the first at a county fair. Another first for Pomona.

"Our Body" ends with restrooms (I did not hear the sound of

retching) followed by a case about 18 feet long containing a human body in 0.5-inch horizontal slices, each spaced apart an inch and standing on edge, like cuts of meat.

It does not increase your desire for a steak.

On the way out, you pass professionals from hospitals and medical schools, ready to answer questions, or perhaps fan you if you're feeling faint.

Mad magazine used to bill itself, deprecatingly, as "the Number One *ecch* magazine," based on its supposed nauseating qualities.

"Our Body, the Universe Within" ought to proudly adopt a related slogan: "the L.A. County Fair's Number One *ecch*-xhibit."

P-NUTTLES AT THE FAIR

THERE'S no official P-Nuttles stand at the L.A. County Fair anymore, although at least one stand does sell the nuts among other products. The stand across from the Clock Tower, the one people remember, didn't return for the 2009 and 2010 fairs. Some fairgoers fondly recall how employees standing in front of the stand would put a scoop of the toffee-coated peanuts in your hand.

Jean Nist worked at the stand for years going back to the 1970s. Her son Jon Nist and daughter-in-law Ruthie Baudoin sent me two snapshots and a tip.

P-Nuttles, introduced to the world in 1946, are still made by Adams & Brooks and can be found in stores. As well as at the fair, if you know where to look.

"There are two sisters (Kim and Corey) who still give out these samples at one of the fruit smoothie stands which offer P-Nuttles," Baudoin writes. "The sisters worked with Ms. Jean and Jon back in the day. Long live P-Nuttles and the old stand!"

Sight bites from the 2010 Fair

DIDN'T make it to the L.A. County Fair, which ends tonight? Here's what you missed:

- A re-thinking of the fair layout put the Fun Zone closer to the heart of the fairgrounds. It works.
  Who would have thought that replacing vendors with carnival rides would actually class up the place?
- Evidently there are capuchin monkeys and other critters up on Picnic Hill, refashioned this year as Mojo's Jungle. The only time I thought to look for them was one evening, when the show was long over. So that's what I missed.
- AWOL this year: the Ten Pound Buns stand. Reader Mary Lapeyrade cared, saying she'd been going there since childhood: "They are really more like a cheesebread or pizza-bread type thing than a bun. It's a slice of really good bread with cheese and garlic, or you could add tomatoes, pepperoni, jalapenos."
  I always assumed the stand sold enormous cinnamon rolls. Guess I missed out.
- Also missing: a French Dip stand near the Grandstand, whose sign (if memory serves) always said it had been in business since 1948, and all pay phones, removed by Verizon due to a reported lack of use.
  Tell that to kids who were supposed to phone their parents.
- More significantly, even the recent Erector-set version of the Clock Tower was gone this year. (Although it was still on fair maps.) Don't say to anyone, "Meet me at the Clock Tower." You might all end up in the Twilight Zone.
- A tent of Toyota vehicles fills the old Clock Tower space. I guess someone could meet you there. But watch out for sudden acceleration!

- In the Tapestry of Tradition home arts area, you can see a pencil portrait of Ozzy Osbourne and a pencil drawing saluting the four branches of the military, both just a few feet apart.
- Elsewhere, decorated dining tables have such themes as the Galapagos Islands, *The Nightmare Before Christmas*, Frida Kahlo and *Twilight*.
Contest judges continue to pay close attention. For a 1950s-themed table with a clever "Mom's Diner" sign and counter-style stools in place of chairs, they note: "Stools are creative, but not the correct height for the table."
- In the cake competition, imaginative cakes resemble a farm with a tractor, a box of tissues, Ms. Pac-Man, a bathtub, a bowl of spaghetti and Van Gogh's "Starry Night." The baker explains regarding the latter cake: "Like the real painting, it is best viewed from a few feet away."
- It was hard to know how to dress this year. Opening weekend was near 100. Days later, the high was in the 60s and, clad in long sleeves at 2 p.m., I watched in amazement as a passerby donned a sweater.
Just when it seemed the fair could clean up with hot chocolate and clam chowder, the mercury spiked again.
- I saw cookware advertised with the slogan "waterless, greaseless cooking." Fair vendors ought to invest in some.
- Best food items I ate this year: coconut lime shrimp from The Shrimp Guys and a filet mignon taco from The Street Kitchen (where the tacos are an affordable $3 to $4). Worst item: a dried-out chicken kabob from Chicken Charlie's that had been sitting under a heat lamp for a while.
- I'm not one for what I call stunt food, but several of us shared a deep-fried Klondike bar and were unimpressed. All we tasted was batter. It was a waste of a perfectly good Klondike bar.
- The salute to Mexico's bicentennial in the Flower and Garden Pavilion is colorful and cool.
- A sardonic T-shirt seen at an American Indian-themed stand shows an Old West photo of Indians above the following motto: "Homeland Security. Fighting Terrorism Since 1492."

- "Jurassic Planet," which features 20 animatronic dinosaurs who move their jaws, spit water and wave their puny arms, is free and worth seeing. If I were 10 years old, I would spend all day there; as an adult, I lingered longer than expected.
- "L.A. on Ice" is said to feature city landmarks carved in ice within a giant walk-in freezer and costs $1 to enter. I paid my buck and walked in.

  Inside you mostly find objects encased in a block of ice, like a Dodgers logo, and only a few objects, like a dragon and the Hollywood sign, carved in ice. Lame.

  But on a blazing hot day, I did emerge feeling crisp and refreshed, which was worth the dollar. A sno cone is five bucks.
- The fair is 11 percent smaller this year after pulling in its northern border, but at 110 acres it remains enormous and impossible to fully explore, even on multiple visits.

  Still, officials insisted the event wasn't so much smaller as it was more compact.

  It was a familiar argument. That's what we say these days about the newspaper.
- In the Farmhouse Kitchen area of the McDonald's Garden, coloring pages of a cow are posted. Each has a few words about what the child learned from a presentation.

  "I learned that the cow has four stomaches," one wrote.

  "Today we learned that cows have six tummys," another wrote.

  Let's split the difference and say five.

  Another child, who has a future in padding school essays, or perhaps in padding newspaper columns, wrote: "I enjoyed the cow Shena. Shena is a very good cow named Shena."

IT WASN'T ALWAYS FAIR WEATHER

A T the L.A. County Fair this year, attendance held steady despite an unwelcome thrill ride: roller-coaster weather.

The fair saw record highs and record lows, with temperatures swinging 40 degrees in a span of days, during the event's four-week run ending October 3. The final days also brought light rain, twice.

Still, attendance was 1,374,673, a modest bump of 2,290 from 2009 figures.

The big surprise was the evening crowds. The fair's $5 after 5 p.m. promotion on weekdays drew 50,000.

"We've become a great evening destination. We were seeing people entering the fair at 8, 9 o'clock at night," said Michelle DeMott, a fair spokeswoman. "Even at 12, 12:30 at night, we saw families on the grounds."

Jim Henwood told me that in his 15 years as the fair's CEO, he'd never seen so many people entering the fair at night. Safety, he said, seemed to have evaporated as a concern.

Indeed, safety barely came up in exit surveys.

Neither did the Giant Slide, which will soon be torn down after more than four decades. Most riders seemed content to bid the 50-foot-high fair staple farewell.

While "there are a lot of people who are attached to the Giant Slide," DeMott said, "there wasn't as much concern as we might have thought."

After an estimated 4 million rides in four decades, fans must have decided to let it slide.

The new layout of the grounds proved popular with fairgoers and vendors, DeMott said. The carnival was moved closer to the center and most retail vendors were clustered together. The layout will probably be repeated next year.

Concert revenue was up, with pop singer Selena Gomez the biggest draw.

2010's blockbuster was "Our Body: The Universe Within," an exhibit of preserved human bodies and organs to illustrate their wonders. Despite needing to pay up to $7 for admission, some 75,000 people saw the exhibit.

"It was the first time it was ever shown outside a museum setting," DeMott noted. "I think the owners were very pleased. We certainly were."

Typically the top reason fairgoers give for visiting is either eating or shopping, followed by the carnival or the animals, DeMott said. But on some days, "Our Body" ranked third in exit surveys, higher than the carnival or the animals, on why people visited.

The number of first-time fairgoers was up 5 percent this year, much of that due to the "Our Body" exhibit, DeMott said.

That's got to have fair officials wondering what they can do in 2011 to equal it.

Here's my idea: Bring back the preserved corpses – and send them down the Giant Slide.

THIS YEAR'S FAIR WILL FEEL FAIRLY FAMILIAR

THE arrival of the L.A. County Fair is always like greeting an old friend – and this year you'll have more than usual to reminisce about.

Because if you liked the 2010 L.A. County Fair, with its smaller layout, animatronic dinosaurs, food trucks, capuchin monkeys and (*blecchh*) preserved cadavers, the 2011 fair will look awfully familiar.

All those elements, and more, are back at this year's fair. Admission ($17 maximum) and parking fees ($10) haven't budged, either.

The fair opens Saturday, the first day of Labor Day weekend. But it may feel more like the movie *Groundhog Day*.

(There are worse things than reliving the L.A. County Fair over and over, though. For one thing, all the day's calories would disappear overnight.)

"We tried not to switch things up too much. Last year we changed the layout. This year we're lying low," quipped spokeswoman Leslie Galerne-Smith.

In other words, the big change at the 2011 fair is that there aren't many changes. Other than the Giant Slide, which slid into the sunset last year after a 44-year run, no fair favorites have been demolished.

As for the new layout, it put the carnival rides in the thick of the fair, between the Grandstand and the Flower and Garden Pavilion. Displaced retail vendors moved east to the shopping area and the former carnival area was converted to a parking lot.

Fairgoers said in exit surveys that they liked the new layout, which made the fair more compact.

Aside from the tried-and-true, the fair does have new elements, of course – some of them fried-and-true.

Deep-fried watermelon on a stick, deep-fried Kool-Aid and maple bacon doughnuts are on the menu, as is wood-fired (note the rearrangement of letters) pizza.

Food trucks will be back, and on September 11, they'll be back in force. Some 35 trucks will be grouped on the infield of the horse racing track for one-stop snacking. No separate admission required.

The fair will be open 23 days, just like last year, open all of Labor Day weekend and thereafter closed each Monday and Tuesday, ending October 2. Admission this weekend is $1 before 1 p.m.

The $5 after 5 p.m. deal also returns this year on weeknights. For hard-core fairgoers, season passes are $30 at the fair ($5 more than in 2010), or $25 at Walgreens, and are a good deal if you intend to visit three times or more.

If you visit even once, you're almost certain to see animals. More animals than ever will be part of the fair, and not just in the form of giant turkey legs (and those who devour them).

Kangaroos and wallabies will join a capuchin monkey in "Mojo's Jungle," as will an attraction called Insect Encounter. (I use the word "attraction" advisedly.)

A shark tank will add bite to Building 5, and various critters will cavort in the Flower and Garden Pavilion. The former Pirate's Cove area this year will combine pirates, parrots and – why not? – stunt dogs. New name: Pets Ahoy!

I haven't seen it, but this is my new favorite part of the fair based on the premise alone.

"Our customer service research shows people want more animals, so we've taken that to heart and have tried to incorporate animals into more exhibits," Galerne-Smith explained.

Of course, the best place to see animals is Fairview Farms, which will have the usual sheep shearing, live births, goat milking and petting zoo. Or the racetrack, which will have 13 days of horse racing.

An alley will again host Esmeralda's Traveling Circus, with trapeze acts, animal freaks, a flea circus and elephant rides. The latter has come under fire from People for the Ethical Treatment of Animals.

The band Styx, which is performing September 25, sent a letter of protest about the rides. (Styx's letter did not begin: "Laaaadyyy ...")

While we're on the subject of culture at the fair, the Millard Sheets Center for the Arts this year spotlights people's collections, from marbles and lunch boxes to buttons and license plates.

Titled "Eclections," a pun on the eclectic nature of the collections, the exhibit looks like a lot of fun, based on a preview I saw Monday. I didn't see any animals, though, and thankfully, the hobbies on display did not include taxidermy.

Fairgoers will, however, be able to see plastinated cadavers at the fair. This is a sequel to last year's "Our Body, the Universe Within" exhibit, in which medical specimens were displayed in educational and only somewhat nauseating ways.

(The euphonious phrase "plastinated cadavers," by the way, might make a good workplace-safe curse. "Plastinated cadavers! Why doesn't anyone throw out the coffee filters around here?")

Also back this year is "Jurassic Planet," a building full of animatronic dinosaurs.

Some shake their head from side to side, perhaps in commentary on fairgoers' attire, or open and close their mouth. A new dinosaur this year spits water.

"That might be a popular area on hot days," Galerne-Smith mused.

Will the fair have hot days this year? No doubt. But will it also have cool days? Possibly. Last year the fair had temperature swings wilder than any ride, with record highs and record lows.

"I took to calling the weather one of the attractions," Sharon Autry, another spokeswoman, remarked. "We had thunderstorms a couple of days. We have a great photo of a rainbow over the Pirate's Cove."

The fair is repeating a lot of things this year, but they probably won't repeat that.

FAIR SHOWS THERE'S AN ART TO COLLECTING

THE L.A. County Fair is known for new foodstuffs and new thrills – but new words?

They've coined one at the Millard Sheets Center for the Arts: eclections. "Eclections: The Art of Collections" is the title of the exhibit this year, which spotlights collectors and their collections.

Comic books, marbles, toy robots, lunch boxes and salt shakers are among the items on display. Also, buttons, toy trucks, etched glass, hand fans – and more.

"If you look at the whole of it, it's very eclectic," Tony Sheets, the center's director and the son of its founder, told me. "That's where 'Eclections' came from: eclectic collections."

Got it. Now tell it to Webster's.

"Eclections" is a collection of collections, a meta-concept that makes me think of Kramer's coffee table book about coffee tables on *Seinfeld*.

The Sheets Center is the museum-like building by Gate 1. Inside the entrance, license plates for each state are affixed to a giant map. Nearby are tether cars, a hobby with which I was unfamiliar.

The small race cars have model airplane motors. The cars can be attached by a tether to a rotor within a circular racetrack. The rotor whips the cars around as if they're driving.

Further along is a display of elaborate iron banks. One is fashioned like Jonah and the Whale. Alas, it's behind clear plastic, so you can't drop in a coin to watch Jonah get swallowed.

"This is a four-generation collection of shells," Sheets remarked concerning a case of seashells resting in sand. His parents, Millard and Mary Sheets, started the collection, which has been continued by Tony and his wife Flower's grandchildren.

The exhibit has no Beanie Babies, but there are Hummel figurines and Painted Ponies.

Salt and pepper shakers often come paired. Among the ones on display are a Dutch boy and girl kissing, a couple on a beach and two astronauts in a Moon Rover. LBJ and Lady Bird and JFK and Jackie represent dual pairs.

(Want a dash of pepper? Jackie's description of Indira Gandhi as "a prune" might qualify.)

Some might gravitate toward the weaving and spinning wheels from several continents. Me, I was entranced by the comic books, including *Iron Man* No. 1, and the chalk figures of comic strip characters the Shmoo, Spark Plug and Popeye.

An assortment of ray guns and tin robots, some from the 1930s, remain idealized artifacts of a future that hasn't happened yet.

A giant display case that cleverly resembles a lunch box holds dozens of lunch boxes, including ones for the Beatles, Disneyland and *The Six Million Dollar Man*.

Two friends and I admired the lunch boxes one night last week. I pointed out one for *Gentle Ben*, my favorite TV show when I was a tot.

"Was it a good show?" Neil asked.

I explained that it was about a small boy, not much older than me, who was friends with a bear. How could it not be a good show?

We chuckled at a Vietnam-era G.I. Joe lunch box showing Joe running through a rice paddy with two explosions occurring near him, but not too near him.

Wes jabbed a finger at the lunch box and hit the almost-invisible plastic barrier. Good thing it wasn't electrified.

By the way, I don't know who carries the giant lunch box with all the lunch boxes inside. Maybe the giant Ranchero statue out front?

The back portion of the Sheets Center is devoted to the gift shop – one treat this year is original citrus-crate labels – and an area for children's crafts.

Mary Flynn, the center's supervisor, said they've come up with 20-minute projects for kids who drop in or come by on school tours. She showed me a mobile of abstract butterflies, each one made from paper triangles. (Making one of these might take me two sessions.)

Outside on the patio are vintage neon signs, as well as neon artists repairing broken signs.

Among them: Pie A La Mode, once a popular fair stand. Another familiar one is from Midway Building Materials, a longtime Montclair business. The animated sign depicts a man building a brick wall.

The signs are the property of the Museum of Neon Art, formerly of downtown Los Angeles. The museum is closed during its anticipated move to Glendale.

"During their move, they're here," Sheets said.

A bright idea.

But back to "Eclections," where the human story is that of the collectors who amassed these collections.

Jim Cogan, a storyteller, interviewed the collectors and boiled down their stories to video and audio clips or display cards.

What trait was common to all the collectors?

"Incredible passion for what they collect," Cogan told me.

(As a collector myself, I'm relieved he didn't say "mental illness.")

Many collections began in childhood. Each item might have a story behind it. The collectors were all too happy to show off their items, natter on about them and loan them to the (heavily insured) Sheets Center.

"'Eelectic' is a good word," Cogan mused. "'Eccentric' might be too."

Should we combine those words into "eclentric"?

Nah. Let's leave well enough alone.

L.A. COUNTY FAIR: LIGHTS, CONES, ACTION!

SIGHTS, sounds, tastes, smells and tactile sensations from the 84th edition of the L.A. County Fair, which ends Sunday:

- In an ironic touch, "Our Body: Live Healthy," an exhibition of preserved cadavers and organ specimens that focuses on what unhealthy living can do to you, is catty-corner from Chicken Charlie's, the stunt-food stand that deep-fries everything, including beverages. Wonder if anyone goes directly from one place to the other?

- They had horse racing under the lights this year for the first time in 30 years. According to a friend who's a racing aficionado, this meant that off-track betting facilities across the country would have ended the night with nothing on the tote board but Pomona, the only racing at that hour in America. Neat, eh?

- There were more live animals at the fair than usual: Not just the usual goats and pigs, but also sharks, elephants and a bear. Oh my.

- In the non-live category, a mechanical bull enticed riders to a ring near the Bubba's Big Bad BBQ stand. One evening, a group of us eating barbecue watched a series of riders, from children to adults. Then a comely young woman climbed onto the bull. Men were drawn to the ring like moths to a flame. Let's just say the ride suddenly became PG-13.

- Another night, a group of us stood in line at the expansive Juicy's BBQ stand, where the public address recording, by a man with a Texas accent, memorably begins: "Is yore belly button gnawin' at yore backbone? Come tah Juicy's." The recording continues with a list of recommended items, ending with three beverage choices: "Lemuhnade, lemuhnade an' more lemuhnade." By the time we got to the front of the line, we were able to recite the spiel along with the recording.

- The Giant Slide went out with great fanfare last year, with everyone encouraged to take one last ride. While there's no Giant Slide this year, two slides that are slightly smaller, and safer, by the looks of them, are up. My nickname for them: Medium Slides.
- The only thing of importance to me that isn't back this year is the Gingerbread House, a charming stand that resembled a pink-and-white gingerbread house. It sold gingerbread, apple crisp and strawberry shortcake and had been there for years. Hey, fair, last year we might have bought one last item – and come back for a few more last items – if we'd known!
- The Live Shark Encounter features sharks in a long tank. Four times a day, people gather for a show in which a man enters the tank and cavorts with the sharks. He holds one horizontally and plays air guitar on its belly. He "dances" with another and moves the flipper of another to make the shark wave to the crowd. One can only assume the sharks were fed immediately before the show, or that they're vegetarians.
- Priorities Dept.: Some 300 people – 100 seated, 200 standing – caught the same Live Shark Encounter show as I did last Sunday. This is roughly 285 more people than attend an Ontario City Council meeting.
- At Dr. Bob's, reputed by experts to be among the best ice cream in L.A. County (and I wouldn't disagree), we got kid cones, a size which is plenty big. One of our group unwarily got the next size up, the small cone. It's roughly the size of one of the fair's giant turkey legs.
- Signs seen in booths in The Shopping Place: "Bling Jewelry $5.99," "Got emu oil?" and "End wallet butt! World's thinnest wallet." (Anything that slims some of the butts seen at the fair would be welcome.)
- A vendor in The Shopping Place sells one kitchen product named Smart Chop and a second named Quick Chop. How does one decide which is better?
- Bags of swag were handed out one evening by a satellite dish representative. One of us, after scrutinizing the items, remarked:

"It's all brands that will soon die: a Dish Network for Latinos bag, a Blockbuster keychain and an Oprah Network chapstick."

- At Pink's, the famous L.A. chili dog purveyor that always has a stand at the fair, they give you a card with a celebrity name to call your order by. When "Matt Damon" was called, I raised my hand.
- Another Pink's customer was "Bill Cosby." A man near me was "Ellen DeGeneres." Understandably, he asked if he could be "Manny Pacquiao" instead.
- "Sir! Are you a homeowner?" a shutter salesman asked as I passed by his booth. "Nope," I said. "Me neither," the salesman admitted.
- We watched a demonstration of the Sham Wow, which took place before an enormous "As Seen on TV" banner. The pitchman splashed water onto a counter and dragged the cloth across, soaking it all up. An off-brand soda was poured onto a swatch of carpet and the Sham Wow soaked that up too. The Sham Wow is said to have the ability to pick up "21 times its weight" in liquid.
- Meanwhile, another booth in the same building touts a cooling cloth named Mr. Cooley Towel. This product, according to a sign, "is made with a hyper-evaporating material." Huh! Hyper-evaporating towels, hyper-absorbent Sham-Wows – everything at the L.A. County Fair is extreme. Except for the slides, which are medium.
- As we strolled down the midway, one of our number took a deep breath and said with satisfaction: "I can almost taste the fat in the air."

Only three days left. I may have to go again.

AN EARLY START TO 24 DAYS OF FUN AT FAIR

IT'S not only Halloween and Christmas that seem to come earlier every year. It's also the L.A. County Fair, which opens today – which if you haven't noticed is still August.

The fair, whose inaugural edition in 1922 began October 17, has opened for Labor Day weekend since 2010 as a way of appealing to people in a lousy economy who are staying home that weekend.

I asked when the fair had last opened in August.

"Never," spokeswoman Sharon Autry said. "This is the earliest we've ever opened. Last year was the earliest, September 3."

Labor Day comes early this year, on September 3, and rather than open Saturday as the fair has been doing, it's opening Friday, albeit late, at 3 p.m. Hence, an August start.

"We've added a day. We're open 24 days, not 23," Autry explained. The fair ends September 30 rather than in October.

I consulted my friend Paula on the switch. "The fair should start in September," she declared. "The fair is starting early, school has already started. What is the world coming to?"

What indeed?

"Pretty soon," Paula added, "the fair will be starting in April."

Ah, springtime at the fair.

Well, we'll cross that bridge when we inch up to it, a day or two per year. In the meantime, I took a tour of the grounds earlier this week for a preview of coming attractions.

Remember the Giant Slide, which was torn down in 2010? The fair has built a replacement into the side of Picnic Hill. They've dubbed it Timber Mountain Slide.

The dimensions are comparable: More than 90 steps to the top, a half-dozen humps, 130 feet long. And just like the old slide, you'll ride down on a burlap sack.

The slide won't be the only way to see the fair from a high perch. A zipline is new this year. You'll climb into the harness and, from a height of 60 feet, traverse 800 feet of the fairgrounds.

Add to that the aerial tram, the giant Ferris wheel and the bungee jump, and a dedicated altitude junkie will only have to return to earth to buy more ride tickets and to throw up.

Speaking of above-ground modes of transportation, an exhibit of photos and memorabilia about the fair's old monorail system will be part of the Millard Sheets Center for the Arts.

The Sheets Center is paying tribute to the fair's 90th anniversary with California history – citrus crate labels and advertising art touting the Golden State's charms – and fair history. You'll find looks at its architecture, performing artists and past art exhibits, plus contemporary images of the fair too.

For more of the finer things in life, you'll want to see the Flower and Garden Pavilion. One of the loveliest spots at the fair, and reliably air conditioned, the pavilion this year has a London theme.

Two Union Jacks fly outside the entrance near a replica of Big Ben and the Tower Bridge. Inside, Mary Poppins umbrellas are attached to the ceiling and a portrait of Queen Elizabeth has been fashioned out of seeds.

Oh, and they have flowers, too.

"Rock of Ages," an exhibit on the history of rock and roll, will occupy the space under the Grandstand starting September 6. Fairgoers will have the chance to try out instruments and sing. I forgot to ask if they get a soundproofed room so the rest of us don't have to hear.

Ray Cammack Shows is back with its carnival rides, which again will be located in a more central location rather than in the fair's hinterlands.

Esmeralda's Traveling Circus is back too, with its trapeze acts, flea circus and animal freaks. (The elephant rides, as promised, won't be back.)

Animals, of course, remain an important part of the fair, with Fairview Farms and its sheep shearing, goat milking, petting zoo and live births – as you watch!

The track will have horse racing from September 7 to 23, with wiener dog racing on the same track September 8 after the horses are done. You won't be able to rely on the Daily Racing Form for that.

Grandstand concert acts this year include Boyz II Men, the Charlie Daniels Band, Grand Funk Railroad, the B-52s and Earth, Wind and Fire, all free with fair admission.

"Genius" is an exhibit focusing on 50 inventors, from Ben Franklin to Steve Jobs, with such products on display as 19th century fire-fighting rigs, Edison recording equipment and a Zamboni.

Over in the shopping areas, hot products are expected to be barrels for home vintners to age their own wine; two-flavor lip balms known as Kisstix for couples; and the Miracle Whisk. I don't know what the Miracle Whisk does, but it must be extraordinary.

Extreme foods this year include a two-pound beef rib on a 17-inch bone and, at the Chicken Charlie's stand, a deep-fried Dodger dog and deep-fried cereal: Cinnamon Toast Crunch or Trix.

Trix is for kids. It's also for frying.

Also, a contest on Facebook to nominate a Pomona fair-only food-stuff for Chicken Charlie's was won by deep-fried cookie dough.

Meanwhile, the Garden Railroad ("since 1924") continues as usual, its model trains chugging along an elaborate outdoor layout. New this year: a Renaissance Faire section, featuring a miniature castle with a dragon and fighting knights, and a Death Valley corner, in which laborers dig up borax and a 20-mule team hauls it away.

A few feet away, a Lego train travels a smaller track on a tabletop around a Hollywood scene that includes – why not? – a zombie. This was designed by 12-year-old Shaun Gross of Chino.

Fair parking and admission are unchanged from last year: $12 to $15 for parking, $12 to $17 for admission. Frequent fairgoers can splurge on a $25 season pass from Walgreens and a $60 parking pass.

This weekend you can get in for $1 the first three hours, and there are various promotions on the fair's website, *lacountyfair.com*.

As usual, other than Labor Day, the fair will be closed each Monday and Tuesday.

The fair began in 1922, and officials are touting this as the 90th anniversary.

A woman named Happi Moore, a Pomona native, saw the first fair as a 4-year-old and, if you can believe it, hasn't missed one since.

"She has attended every single L.A. County Fair. Every one," Autry said. "She comes back every year and goes to MacPherson's for ice cream, Hot Dog on a Stick and Mackinac Fudge. She just loves the fair."

Moore rode in the 75th anniversary parade in 1997 and will ride in today's 5 p.m. parade too – assuming she remembers the fair starts in August and shows up.

THE SIGHTS, SOUNDS AND SMELLS FROM THE L.A. COUNTY FAIR

OBSERVATIONS from this year's L.A. County Fair, which ends its 24-day run on Sunday:

* * *

Sign seen at Bubba's Burgers and Fries: "Home of the 2 Pound Belly Buster." A friend, jaded by the fair's excess, yawned and remarked: "Only two pounds?"

Several of my friends shared a single turkey leg the size and shape of a bowling pin. Nearby, I spotted a boy with a foot-long corn dog on a two-foot stick, the whole thing resembling a battered, deep-fried baseball bat.

The L.A. County Fair, needless to say, is no place for Michelle Obama or Michael Bloomberg.

* * *

Filling one exhibit hall is "Genius," which is devoted to American inventors.

It includes two rows of giant mock iPhones, the screens listing some 300 patents assigned to Steve Jobs. Spies from Samsung are no doubt lurking about.

The exhibit pays tribute to 50 inventors, among them the well-known Henry Ford, Ben Franklin and the Wright Brothers and some you may not know, such as Linus Yale, of lock renown, and Thomas Jennings, an African-American who invented dry cleaning. (Jennings did not invent excuses for why your buttons were broken.)

Among the lesser-heralded inventions celebrated in the exhibit: the Zamboni, the Super Soaker, liquid paper and disposable diapers.

A space devoted to Thomas Edison includes a re-creation of a 1905-era recording studio, when giant horns were used as microphones to record sound onto wax cylinders. Neat. But was this really what a 1905 recording studio was like, man? I expected to see bottles of nerve tonic and bags of snuff.

Pertinent Edison quote on display: "Genius is 1 percent inspiration, 99 percent perspiration." With eight 100-degree days in September, fairgoers know what he means. Thankfully, among its other marvels, the exhibit hall demonstrates the wonders of air conditioning.

* * *

If you love the fair, you should spend time in the Millard Sheets Center for the Arts, where the exhibit this time is less about art and more about the fair's 90-year history.

A few facts gleaned from "Art & Fair: A 90 Year Celebration": the model train layout, still chugging along, began in 1939; the fairgrounds was used during World War II as an internment camp, POW camp and ordnance depot; Louis Armstrong and Dave Brubeck performed in 1956; and a couple got married at the fair in the 1970s.

In 1950, the fair exhibited art by Picasso, Monet, Cezanne, Van Gogh and Toulouse-Lautrec. They were already famous, so, no, they didn't win blue ribbons.

Headline from a Sheets display: "1951 Fair to Exhibit Statue Made 33 Centuries Ago." Oh? The 2-ton statue, on loan from the Metropolitan Museum of Art in New York, was a representation of Sekhmet, an Egyptian goddess, and was made in 1340 B.C. during the reign of Amenhotep III.

I hope Sekhmet enjoyed Pomona.

* * *

Some of the best food stands at this year's fair: Harold and Belle's, Street Kitchen, Chuckwagon BBQ, Pink's Hot Dogs, Eddie's Italian and Dr. Bob's Ice Cream.

The Hollywood-based Pink's hands out a laminated card with a celebrity name rather than an order number. "We're going to call you Ashley Tisdale," an employee told me Wednesday, referring to the *High School Musical* actress. Then she called out an order: "Amy Adams! Amy Adams!"

Stunt food is not my thing. I tried deep-fried cookie dough, one of the new items this year, and it rendered sweet, dense cookie dough into something as insubstantial as cotton candy. Ehh. Might be your thing, but I gave away the second piece.

Not to say fair food is pricey, but at one stand, a sandwich, fries and soda combo for $12 was touted as a "value meal." (Technically true: Ordered individually, they would cost $15.75.)

* * *

Vendor signs seen in the Shopping Place: "Dinner in 12 Minutes!" (for cookware), "Touch of Purple Jewelry Cleaner" and, a tough sell, "Children's Dental Fun Zone."

Also: "Original Ultimate Hose Nozzle" – evidently other ultimate hose nozzles have crowded onto the scene – which promises enticingly that it's "the only nozzle you'll ever need."

Among the strangest sights I saw at the fair was a teeth-whitening booth in the Shopping Place. A woman in sunglasses reclined in a dentist-type chair, her teeth bared in a grimace smile, with a lamp aimed directly at her teeth shining a mysterious blue light.

Best to continue walking.

* * *

The America's Kids hall this year has a books theme and is titled "Living Library of Fun." I prefer the Pomona Public Library, but I have to admit the fair's "library" has better hours.

In a superhero-themed area of the building, people can don a cape and pose nobly for photos against a blue-sky backdrop. You can also spin two wheels – one with an adjective, one with a noun – to find your superhero name. Mine was Colossal Gladiator. Fun, but I still like my other recent nickname, Unicorn.

During the hall's Wizard Show on Wednesday, done on a stage with a castle-like backdrop, an actor portraying a wizard brought up a young girl named Natalia, who started to give her age as 6 before quickly saying 7.

"You must have just turned 7," the wizard said. The girl nodded proudly.

"I do the same thing. I'm 129," the wizard continued, quickly correcting himself: "130."

Child science projects on view in the hall have such titles as "Levers," "Germs," "The Effect of Pillows on Sleep" and "How Does Temperature Affect the Tuning of a Guitar."

My favorite science project, for obvious reasons, was titled "Column Shapes," which attempted to answer the question "Which shape of column is the strongest?" For professional reasons, I paid close attention to the answer, which is "cylinder." (I hope this inside tip won't be stolen by my colleague Diana Sholley.)

Sarah Sandoval of San Dimas, who got second place for the above display and hopes to become an architect, writes: "I was also surprised to find out that the shorter columns were able to support more weight than the taller columns."

Taking Sarah's advice, I'll end here.

County Fair: Owls, bacon, mermaids, oh my!

BARN owls, zebras and monkeys are headed to Pomona. No need to cower inside your homes, though: They're not running wild in the streets, they're arriving in an orderly fashion as part of the Los Angeles County Fair.

The fair starts Friday at 3 p.m. and brings the usual (scary rides, turkey legs the size and shape of bowling pins, farm animals, mystery products) and the unusual (bacon cotton candy, mermaids).

Mojo's African Jungle, an attraction on Picnic Hill, is back with two zebras, named Barcode and Stripes, and a capuchin monkey, among other critters. The newcomers include two camels – a Facebook contest offers a chance to name them – and a baby zebra, a spider monkey, actual spiders, a two-toed sloth and an anteater.

Wouldn't it be charming if the fair sold handfuls of ants for children to feed to the anteater? OK, never mind.

Over in Fairview Farms, where typical farm-type animals can be seen, Max's Country Farm Show will focus on "our country neighbors," such as a fox, opossum, tortoises, king snakes anda barn owl.

"When we get new animals, our guests get so excited," said Renee Hernandez, a fair spokeswoman. "It's still one of the biggest parts of the fair."

Now, what's this about a mermaid? Her name is Melissa and she'll be plying a tank of water.

"She's a 'real' mermaid," Hernandez said, making air quotes with her fingers.

Gosh, a "real" mermaid!

"She wears a 60-pound silicone mermaid tail," Hernandez said.

I prefer my mermaids natural, the way Poseidon made them, but that's me.

"She does a show in a tank with her fellow mermaids," Hernandez continued.

Multiple mermaids? Oh, I'm so there. I might even show up in trunks and flippers.

The same exhibit building will also have sea lions, stingrays and sharks. Note: The fair often has a day or two of odd weather, but no Sharknado is planned.

Seven new carnival attractions are coming, among them rides named Insanity and Mach One. Based on the names, I will not go anywhere near them.

Another ride, probably more my speed, involves farm tractors, and the fact that it's designed for very small children may not deter me. I'm sure if I get scared, a child will tell me it will be over soon and to be brave.

What would the L.A. County Fair be without food? A lot healthier, to be honest. But that won't be an issue, because the fair has all sorts of foods and beverages to sell you. Loan officers will be standing by to help you pay for lunch.

One of the most hotly anticipated items is billed as the world's hottest ice cream, which is made with ghost peppers, reputed to be the world's spiciest.

An item nobody would anticipate is spaghetti ice cream with chocolate meatballs.

"It's specially formulated vanilla ice cream they put through a press," Hernandez explained. "They twirl it on a plate. It has 'marinara sauce,' pureed strawberries, with cookie-dough batter fried, frozen and dipped in chocolate. Grated white chocolate is used for the Parmesan cheese."

I'm picturing an update to the famous romantic scene in *Lady and the Tramp*, where Tramp will nudge an extra meatball toward Lady with his nose, and Lady will take a bite and say, "Mmmm, chocolate."

Other notable items, according to Hernandez: a hot dog inside a waffle bun, a Krispy Kreme doughnut with sloppy joe filling, bacon cotton candy, a double-decker funnel cake and what may be the ultimate nutritionally useless fair food item: a bacon-wrapped, deep-fried pickle.

For those who love shopping at the fair, the Sham Wow is back. New products that you never knew you needed but may decide you can't live without: hair chalk, stretch lids and a steam cleaning mop.

For the more refined among you, the theme at the Flower and Garden Pavilion will be "Mysteries of the Amazon," while the Millard Sheets Center for the Arts will feature "Treasures From the Attic."

Grandstand concert performers include Lynyrd Skynyrd and the Jacksons, neither of whom, we hope, will use holograms of departed members, and Los Lobos.

For the nerdier set, "Pencils 2 Pixels" will teach the art of animation, and "Star Trek: The Exhibition" will, as the name suggests, focus on *Battlestar Galactica*. Not really, but I wanted to make sure you were still paying attention.

Also, the America's Kids building will have the theme "Living Library of Fun" – the phrase "of Fun" is evidently considered necessary to ensure cobwebs don't form over the entrance – and will center on children's books, including the 80th anniversary of *Little House on the Prairie* and 50 years of *Where the Wild Things Are*. Also, the Avengers will appear there on weekends, assuming Iron Man can make it through security. He tends to set off metal detectors.

The fair runs August 30 to September 29. This will be the fourth straight year it has been open for Labor Day weekend, offering an alternative for people who aren't traveling. Due to the holiday falling so early in the month, this will be the second straight year the fair will start in August.

The fair opens at 3 p.m. Friday and admission is a mere $1 the first three hours every day this weekend, through Monday. The fair is open until midnight Friday and Saturday and until 10 p.m. on Labor Day.

After that, it is open five days per week, closed Mondays and Tuesdays, making for 24 days and five weekends of fun.

While some think of it as "the Pomona fair," Fairplex CEO Jim Henwood said that's not really true. There are 17 specific "community days," and other cities, he said, want to get on board.

"Pasadena is saying, how can we be connected?" Henwood said. "This is every community's fair in Southern California. If anybody needed a fair, it's L.A., where everything is so quick and so fast."

There's nothing fast about the fair, other than maybe how fast the money leaves your wallet. And for me, even with 24 days ahead, the fair always seems to end a little too soon.

'STAR TREK' FANS AT THE FAIR WILL BE BEAMING

NORMALLY you can't wear costumes or masks to the L.A. County Fair. (Which makes me wonder if two friends have ever tried to sneak in while dressed as a cow.) Anyway, the fair will make an exception Saturday for *Star Trek* fans.

If you wear some sort of Trek garb between 10 a.m. and 1 p.m., admission is free. Why? It's "Star Trek Day" at the fair. "That can be a T-shirt or a full costume," spokeswoman Renee Hernandez said. But no weapons.

So if you see a man in full Klingon makeup and regalia standing in line at Hot Dog on a Stick, you'll know why. Well, you won't really know why.

"Star Trek Day" should be a great photo opportunity, especially if someone comes dressed as the world's largest Tribble.

Why the Trek tie-in? One feature attraction this year is "Star Trek: The Exhibition," a hall that features costumes, sets and props from all five TV series and 11 feature films. Admission is $5 – even if you got into the fair for free.

At any time during the fair, by the way, fairgoers can buy tickets online using the promotional code "Star Trek" and get in cheaper.

Capping "Star Trek Day," a free screening after dusk of *Star Trek: Into Darkness*, the recent film, will take place on the fair's Picnic Hill.

Unanswered question: Can you still live long and prosper if you eat a deep-fried Twinkie?

CHARITABLE FAIR STAND DOES SOMETHING WARM WITH SOMETHING COLD

H ERE'S the scoop on Colossal Gelato.

The stand at the L.A. County Fair not only sells Italian ice cream, it gives away half its profits to agencies that help children worldwide.

In 2012, that meant $9,000 from the sales of cones, sundaes and shakes in Pomona went toward Feed My Starving Children, which provides meals at 22 cents each for children in the last stages of starvation. Many that year were in Haiti, still suffering after a 2010 earthquake.

Colossal Gelato is one arm of an unusual business venture by Matt Holguin, a 32-year-old Azusa Pacific University alumnus, that is as much about saving the world as it is about satisfying sweet tooths.

The whole operation is called Working to Give, and – wait, let's slow down. No need to give you the factual version of an ice cream headache.

I was introduced to Holguin on a recent blistering afternoon at the fair by reader Beth Brooks, who met him last year and was impressed. The stand is along Broadway in front of the Grandstand.

When I stepped into the stand, Holguin was out, but his brother was taking care of business, making waffle cones from scratch. His name is Cheston Holguin.

(I didn't ask where his parents came up with Cheston. I prefer to think it was a tribute to Charlton Heston.)

Working to Give, based in Atascadero, has two gelato stands that are set up at various California fairs, and three stands at Downtown Disney that sell churros, cinnamon rolls and gelato.

"Fifty percent of profits go back to the company, to grow the company, and the other half we give away," Cheston explained.

This year the company is assisting an orphanage in South Africa named Acres of Love, which attempts to give orphans as normal a life as possible, so that they're indistinguishable from children with parents.

Because Working to Give operates businesses, it doesn't send out fundraising appeals (and waste donor money on doing so).

"It's a new way. It's a different way. The other way, sending out support letters, isn't necessarily wrong. We're using the business-man's approach," Cheston said.

Matt soon entered, fresh from a meeting with Downtown Disney officials about expanding that he said went well.

His brand of philanthropy is, he said, "easy for people to get behind." They might not even know they're getting behind it. They might just want gelato. Prices start at $4 for a scoop of such flavors as cookies and cream, Sicilian pistachio and, the top seller, peach Champagne.

Matt is a traveler, often for missionary work, who estimates he's been to 70 countries. (I've lost count myself, but I've visited either three or four, depending on if I include the United States.)

In 2006 he visited Italy to learn how to make gelato, which he de-scribes as having 70 percent less fat than ice cream and a more in-tense taste. He persuaded an English-speaking gelato maker to teach him and got contacts for suppliers, returning to America with ev-erything he needed to open a gelateria except dough.

He spent two years in a frustrating quest for a bank loan to open a shop in Paso Robles. Twenty-two banks turned him down. Maybe bankers don't eat gelato. Still, this may have been a blessing, in his eyes, because he fears he would have lost everything in the recession.

Instead of a storefront, Matt opted in 2008 for mobile sales, first with a trailer at fairs and festivals, then a second trailer, and in 2011 with his first stand at Downtown Disney.

His travels, especially in Africa, also convinced him that the world has so much poverty, he ought to do something to help.

"You see all these things and it does something to you," Matt said.

The Christian, who got his master's in business administration from Azusa in 2005, says he's trying to heed the admonition of Mark 12:30.

"It's the greatest commandment. Jesus says, love God and love your neighbor as much as you love yourself," Matt said. "Where does 50/50 come from? It's from that verse."

It's profits he's giving away, not revenue. As he explained it, 75 cents of every dollar from the L.A. County Fair goes to rent, ingredients, salaries and taxes. That leaves 25 cents of that dollar as profit. Twelve and a half cents goes back into the company and 12 1/2 to charity. And as I said above, last year, its second year at the fair, that resulted in $9,000 going to charity.

An extra boost has come from donors, whom the Holguins call "give investors," who have provided financial backing. People get inspired after hearing their mission and tell their friends. The investors also make up the difference between whatever Working to Give has pledged to donate and what it can afford.

Working to Give met its 50 percent goal starting in year four. Last year, Matt said, the company gave away 60 percent of its profit.

"This year alone we'll be able to give away $75,000," Matt said. He's pledged $100,000, though, to Acres of Love, which is where donors may come in.

And they probably will, as will customers. The Holguins are upbeat, idealistic and earnest. They could sell gelato to the Eskimos.

BIG BOY LUMBERS TO LIFE AT POMONA FAIRGROUNDS

IN midcentury, No. 4014, the world's largest steam locomotive, traveled up to 70 mph, hauling freight over the mountains between Wyoming and Utah along the intercontinental railroad.

On Thursday, after a half-century of retirement, the Big Boy was on the move again – inches at a time, and under tow.

Movement was almost imperceptible, but the train was pulled 1,000 feet in 90 minutes – is that 0.07 mph? – along temporary track at Fairplex in Pomona, to the excitement of rail fans and railroad officials.

Built in 1941 and operating until 1959, the Big Boy, as it's known, arrived at the Rail Giants train museum on the fairgrounds in 1962, a gift from Union Pacific. Now the railroad is reclaiming the locomotive, with the blessing of the museum, with a plan to restore it and operate it as a passenger train for nostalgia trips.

At 132 feet in length and 1.2 million pounds in girth, it's not only a Big Boy, it's a bad boy.

"It's like an industrial age dinosaur coming back to life," marveled Jim Wrinn, editor of *Trains Magazine*, who traveled from Waukesha, Wisconsin, to cover the story, which for his readers is international news.

Wrinn set up a camera to stream video to his website, *trainsmag.com*, on Wednesday. Given the slow progress, this might seem akin to watching live video of paint drying. But in its first 24 hours, his live webcam had been viewed several thousand times by rail fans across the United States and in Europe.

It's news, Wrinn explained, because the eight surviving Big Boys are inoperable, and rail experts for years had insisted that restoring one to working order was impractical. And yet, here one was, on its way.

"For rail fans, this is nothing short of a miracle," Wrinn said. "It's the biggest thing to happen in rail preservation since the American Freedom Train in 1976," he added, referring to the 20-car train that traveled across America with artifacts to celebrate the Bicentennial.

I appreciated the perspective. For me, it's a local story. I saw the Big Boy in July for a column on its impending move. I was there Thursday for a follow-up.

Word of the photo opportunity had spread among rail fans. Steven Ricotta, 18, of Upland was there with his dad, Rick. The younger Ricotta enjoys taking photos and videos of trains. As we spoke, a friend from San Diego phoned him to inquire about the progress.

"It's nice to see this thing move," Steven told me. "It's beautiful."

Ed Dickens thinks so too. He's the senior manager of Union Pacific's heritage operations. He's leading a crew of eight in getting the Big Boy ready.

They've made small repairs which nonetheless have required disassembling heavy pieces of the complex machinery and then reassembling them.

"You're looking at state of the art steam technology," Dickens said fondly. "It looks old, but it's in good shape, and the core machine is sound."

Two smaller locomotives had to be moved to clear a path for the Big Boy's move, which will take the locomotive northwest across the Fairplex parking lot and National Hot Rod Association grounds to the Metrolink tracks.

Dickens' crew is laying temporary track atop plywood to protect the asphalt. The train will travel a total of one mile. After its short journey Thursday, the track behind the train would be disassembled and then reassembled in front of it for another short journey.

Because Fairplex needs the property for various events, building a full length of track for the days-long pull was deemed a nonstarter.

"We have to use this leapfrog technique," Dickens said. He didn't seem to mind. The Colorado man said he was enjoying the Pomona sunshine and joked that he wouldn't mind stretching out the job until next June.

Dickens expects to have the locomotive up to the Metrolink tracks near Arrow Highway and White Avenue by early next week. The Big Boy will rest there a few days while the crew goes home to see their families.

From there, the locomotive will be towed west on Metrolink tracks to a junction, then travel Union Pacific tracks to Colton for more repairs before eventually heading to Cheyenne, Wyoming, for a projected four years of restoration.

As we spoke, an older gent in classic pinstriped engineer overalls came up and told Perkins he'd like to show him photos of his Big Boy. I think he meant a model, but still, this could be a new tack for Anthony Wiener.

Members of the Southern California Railway and Locomotive Historical Society, which operates the museum, have a mix of emotions: thrilled to see the train in motion, optimistic about its restoration but personally a little sentimental.

Paul Guercio knows the Big Boy better than almost anyone. He's been volunteering on its restoration since 1989, joined a year or two later by Rick Brown.

Guercio, a chemical engineer for Exxon, knew about the Big Boy from childhood, and the museum was one of his first stops when the company transferred him here from Virginia. He signed up with the society and was soon given keys to the gates so he could spend weekends working on the Big Boy.

Little had been done from 1962 to 1989. "Ashes and cinders were still in the firebox and smokebox," Guercio said. He and Brown donated thousands of hours to cleaning the sandbox, firebox and smokebox, greasing and lubing parts, and cleaning the cab for visitors. Some of those activities retarded rust and rot.

Dickens said the duo's attention to the boiler, more than anything else, kept the Big Boy in good enough condition that restoration was deemed feasible.

Now 62, Guercio began tending to the Big Boy when he was 38. He said he almost wondered if he were dreaming when he saw the train in motion Thursday. He welcomes Union Pacific's plans for the Big Boy.

"A lot more people will see it when it's out operating than will ever see it here," Guercio said. "But it's still a little bit of a bittersweet moment."

RAMEN BURGER LESS OF A SENSATION AT L.A. COUNTY FAIR

RAMEN Burger draws long lines at food events in Los Angeles and New York where foodies rave about the taste, and novelty, of an Angus beef patty between Japanese noodles formed into a bun.

The chain sells them on a daily basis at only two places in Southern California: a stand in L.A.'s hip Koreatown neighborhood and a tent at the Los Angeles County Fair in Pomona.

What's hot among hipsters in L.A. and Brooklyn may not translate so well to a county fair environment. One week into the fair, and one day after Ramen Burger got a boost on Conan O'Brien's show, the stand had no line.

"It's a lot slower than we're used to," acknowledged manager Basil Banks during dinnertime on Friday. "The line at 626 Market is around the block."

Well, you don't see a lot of porkpie hats and waxed mustaches in the 909. There was one person ahead of me at the window, and she took her burger to go. (She did not place it in a vintage lunchbox doubling as a purse.)

I paid for a burger, the $10 original ($10.90 with tax), and enjoyed it at a nearby picnic table. It was 15 minutes before someone else ordered.

Last month I was both excited and proud to learn from *LA Weekly* that Ramen Burger was coming to the fair about the same time the first L.A. restaurant was opening. Not only does it save us a trip west, its presence here increases our coolness factor.

At a media preview event two days before the fair opened, Ramen Burger was handing out sample-sized burgers with toothpicks in them. I had one sample and went back for a second, enticed by the unusual combination of flavors: not just the burger and bun but the soy-based Shoyu sauce, arugula and green onions.

Jeff Shimamoto was overseeing the table. His brother, Keizo, created the burger. A computer programmer, Keizo moved to Japan to study ramen, then started a blog, *GoRamen.com*, while experimenting with ways to get ramen to stay together in a bun shape.

He debuted his ramen burger in August 2013 at a Brooklyn flea market, where it sold out and launched a viral sensation akin to the croissant-donut mashup the cronut. *Time* magazine named the ramen burger one of the "17 Most Influential Burgers of All Time."

Ramen Burger has three locations in Brooklyn and has been sold in Southern California at such foodie events as 626 Market in the San Gabriel Valley and DTLA Night Market and Ktown Night Market in L.A.

"They're always the most popular vendor at any event they're at," said Kristie Hang, a food writer who follows the brand avidly.

Jeff Shimamoto said his brother, who grew up in Huntington Beach, may return one day; he's newly married and has a baby.

"There's a huge demand for it in L.A. I want to get the groundwork laid for him here," said Jeff, a hedge fund attorney. He's also busy fending off copycats like the ramen burger from the L&L Hawaiian chain, which has a location in La Verne.

On August 1 he soft-opened Ramen Burger's sole non-Brooklyn location, a walkup window at 239 S. Vermont Avenue in L.A.

Keizo Shimamoto was on *Conan* last Thursday, the night before the grand opening, and the two participated in a cooking segment.

"Basically, what you've done is combine two of the greatest things in the world: ground hamburger meat, which is fried, and ramen noodles," O'Brien declared.

Sherry Flores, the food and beverage manager for Fairplex, saw the Ramen Burger stand at a market event in L.A., got in line for one and the next day contacted Jeff Shimamoto about coming to the fair, Shimamoto told me.

He said he really didn't know what to expect.

"We're prepping for 500 a day. We do 1,200 to 1,400 a day at events," Shimamoto said.

Banks, the manager, declined to say how many they were selling, but clearly it was below expectations.

"It's a different crowd here. But it's the same quality," Banks said. "We're sticking it out."

The stand is hard to find, and the first person at an information booth gave me the wrong location. When I returned, a second person told me exactly where it was, and even then I walked past it and had to double back.

In short, it's near the east side of the Grandstand and barns and the rear of the Grinding Gears nightclub building. The stand is a black tent with a grill in back.

Also, long lines at the fair are unusual. You can get a hot dog within minutes at the Pink's stand, whose Hollywood location often has a two-hour line.

Finally, a couple got one to split and sat at the next picnic table. I let them finish and then introduced myself. Chris and Jennifer Anaya had driven up from Rancho Santa Margarita to explore the fair and try food.

"If I had a choice between this and a regular burger, I'd take this," Chris said. "The flavor of it was really good. Really different. I could actually eat two of these things. The noodles held together really well."

Jennifer, who'd said the burger was too salty for her taste, said Ramen Burger needed more "add-ons" besides bacon, cheese and a fried egg, naming avocado and gorgonzola. Chris said sweet potato fries would be a good side dish.

"I think people in Orange County would like it," Jennifer said of the concept.

In the meantime, people in Pomona have their chance through September 28.

L.A. County Fair: Retro
exhibit swivels visitors
back to '50s

A MOCK lunch counter as part of a nostalgic display at the L.A. County Fair gets people talking. Also, they keep trying to order.

Michelle Pederson stands behind the Woolworth's counter inside the Millard Sheets Art Center as part of its "Midcentury Modern: retro, classic, cool" exhibit. She wears an apron and a paper hat and cheerfully answers questions.

"I tell about Woolworth's. We get kids in here who've never heard of Woolworth's or diners," Pederson told me. A laminated copy of a 1940s menu is there for the perusing. The prices draw interest and sighs from visitors.

"You could get a Coke for a nickel or a sundae for a quarter," Pederson said. Children particularly like that because they have nickels and quarters.

"They say, 'Give me one!' I wish I could," Pederson said.

She may wish she had a nickel or a quarter for every request. Adults ask too. One man wouldn't let it go.

"Do you sell water or soda?" he asked. When she said no, he said, "Are you sure?" He walked away but returned to ask a third time.

The barrier ropes around the display, which keep people from bellying up to the counter in one of the four swivel seats, ought to be a tipoff that it's for show only. But there's no IQ test to get into the fair.

Any visit to the fair is a blast from the past. The "Midcentury Modern" exhibit puts nostalgia front and center.

Walk in and you'll see a living room and entertainment room decorated with 1950s furnishings: mod chairs and lamps, a hi-fi and a starburst mirror. (You can't sit in these chairs either.)

A newsstand is stocked with 1950s magazines, comic books and newspapers. Tupperware, postwar advertising, Revlon dolls, an Electrolux vacuum cleaner, a shoeshine kit and more bring back memories or inspire a smile.

Taking up more floor space is a 1955 Thunderbird convertible, a 1963 Studebaker coupe and a 1960 Cadillac DeVille with enormous tailfins.

An array of vintage LP covers illustrates a small display of popular singers, where you can try to put names to faces. Pop, country, rock and jazz singers are represented.

Claudia Lennear is the docent there. If her name sounds familiar, she's the backup singer featured in the documentary *20 Feet From Stardom* who was profiled in this space earlier this year.

"For me it's wonderful when you get 9- or 12-year-olds who can say 'Elvis,'" Lennear said of the quiz. "This morning I had a 12-year-old girl who recognized Louis Armstrong and Ella Fitzgerald. It almost brought tears to my eyes. Some don't know anything but the 21st century."

Lennear, who lives in Pomona, has been a docent for 10 years. She arranged her schedule at Mount San Antonio College, where she is a language tutor in French, Spanish and Latin, to enable her to volunteer. She's at the center eight hours a day, all five days of the week the fair is open.

This year they've prevailed upon her to sing. When a tour comes through, as it does pretty much every half hour, storyteller Jim Cogan stops them at Lennear's area, introduces her and asks her to sing a couple of vintage numbers.

When I was there, she performed "Blue Suede Shoes" and "Over the Rainbow," both a cappella. It's not quite the same as singing behind Ike and Tina Turner or Joe Cocker, as she did back in the day, but at the fair she's front and center, and she's happy to do it.

Fairgoers seem to be enjoying "Midcentury Modern." (Not to

mention the air conditioning.)

"We're getting good reaction to the exhibit this year," Tony Sheets, the center's director and son of its namesake, said. "It's not so complicated."

Back at the Woolworth's counter, Neal and Rosemary Levin of Montebello, both 76, stopped to chat with Pederson about the old days.

"We're showing our age," Neal quipped.

But he's realistic. Soda prices were low, sure, but so were wages. "You could only buy one once a week because it was a lot of money," Neal said. On the other hand, "they made real malts back then," he said, not the chintzy kind today.

The Levins didn't try ordering anything at the counter. They pass the IQ test.

Pederson, who's 50, said she used to eat at a Woolworth's lunch counter in the San Fernando Valley in the 1970s and into the 1980s. She usually got a club sandwich. But five-and-dime stores faded away, taking their lunch counters with them. You might be able to get a Pizza Hut pizza at Target or a Subway sandwich at Walmart, and sit in the food service area, but it's not the same.

The fair's mockup, which has a small soda fountain, a checkerboard floor, a full-size jukebox as well as a countertop model, was originally going to be static until Pederson volunteered: "Give me a hat and I'll stand back here."

"Michelle's our soda jerk," Sheets said with a smile.

Some visitors ask about Woolworth's darker history. African-Americans couldn't be seated alongside whites, leading to civil rights-era protests. Pederson talks about that too if people ask.

The fair ends Sunday, and at that point, "Midcentury Modern," like everything else at the fair this year, will become part of the past.

TRAIN MUSEUM STILL ON TRACK DESPITE LOSS OF BIG BOY

OLD trains are the featured attraction at the Rail Giants museum at the Pomona fairgrounds, where the departure of the famed Big Boy locomotive two years ago focused attention on the little-known facility.

"Nothing else in our history catapulted us into the national spotlight," reflected John Shatsnider, a museum board member, when we spoke last week.

People came out daily to gaze at the 1941 engine, one of the largest ever built, as it was towed across the parking lot and then was parked along busy Arrow Highway. Union Pacific got it onto the tracks, pushed it to Colton for repairs and then transported it to the rail company's headquarters in Wyoming for restoration.

Along the entire route, rail fans and the curious turned out. Rail Giants members traveled with it, selling merchandise – DVDs, shirts, caps, pins, prints, calendars – and cleaning up. The museum pocketed some $75,000.

"People knew it was a historic event. They wanted to have some memento from it," Shatsnider said. "It was a tremendous windfall for us. We really have to thank Union Pacific."

The metaphorical confetti was swept up long ago, of course.

Curious how the museum is doing in the post-Big Boy era, I ventured over last week during a visit to the L.A. County Fair, which ends Sunday.

It's doing fine, actually. When the Big Boy left, a new piece of equipment replaced it: a 1979 diesel locomotive, the Union Pacific 3105.

In some ways it's the opposite of the Big Boy. It's bright yellow rather than coal black, diesel rather than steam, powered by a battery rather than by coal.

But it's still a locomotive, and it's still big: 150 feet long including a boxcar and caboose.

Unlike the Big Boy, dormant since its 1962 arrival in Pomona, the 3105 works. No tow was necessary.

"The big difference was that 3105 was able to go across the parking lot itself," Shatsnider said.

On weekends during the fair, the engine is started and allowed to run for hours.

"We draw huge crowds whenever it's fired up. They can sit in the cab and feel the vibration. They feel like they're the engineer," Shatsnider said.

The museum is open the second weekend of each month, year-round, from 10 a.m. to 5 p.m., and admission is free. Not only is 3105 started up, museum officials will move it, slowly, down the 150 feet of track behind it, then inch it back.

"Just to stretch its legs, essentially," Shatsnider said. "We have gone through a whole tank of diesel already. We've gone through 1,000 gallons in a year."

3105 is the first operating piece of equipment the museum has had since its 1954 founding, a twist that has rejuvenated everyone's interest.

The museum has a dozen pieces in all, arranged in two long rows, a wide walkway of asphalt in between.

The two rarest are the 5021 and the 3450, each dating to the 1920s and stretching nearly 100 feet in length.

"Both engines are the last ones of their kind," Shatsnider said. "Any museum would be glad to have either of these."

Sam Calderwood was in the cab of the Union Pacific 9000, dressed in a conductor's pinstripes and overalls. He's a new volunteer at the museum but has been involved in other rail societies for years.

"That's the only one of its kind left on the planet," Calderwood said of the 9000 after climbing down to talk to me. "They made 88 of them. They either blew up or were scrapped."

He prefers the 9000, a steam locomotive, to the modern diesel across the way. Some love diesels, the trains of today, but not him. He calls the 3105 "a box with wheels," much of its detail internalized. You can't look at the pieces and figure out how they move together to propel the train.

The steam locomotives might have required 150 people to operate, compared to five on a modern diesel. Temperature in the cabs could reach 120 degrees, whereas a diesel cab is air-conditioned.

"For some people, diesel doesn't have the glamour that steam does. Sure, they're smelly, they're dirty, they're grungy. But you can see what makes the wheels go 'round," said Calderwood, 66, of Burbank. "The old train enthusiasts, they think steam rules, diesel drools."

Train trash talk! This was like being at a car show when the topic of Japanese-made cars comes up.

There are other pieces too, among them an 1887 locomotive, now being restored, and a 1923 Pullman car.

Volunteer Loren Martens, 82, of Montclair gave me and a few others a look inside the Pullman. It seems a bit cramped to modern eyes, and primitive too. "The toilets flushed right out on the tracks," Martens pointed out.

Those aboard were curious as an upper and lower sleeping berth were shown off. Back outside, there was a steady stream of visitors, most of them families with young children.

Earlier, Calderwood had mentioned Thomas the Tank Engine to me, and it wasn't long afterward that a father passed by me with a stroller and said to his young son who was running ahead, "That does look like Thomas."

Shatsnider, who at 25 is part of the next generation of train enthusiasts, said museum officials had made a point of not only promoting the new diesel engine but taking a fresh look at its older equipment.

"We're trying to move past the Big Boy in some ways," he said.

That was clear from signs inside the gift shop, housed in the 1887 train depot from Arcadia. They read: "All Big Boy items 25 percent off."

'LOVE A FAIR'? THEN THIS MIGHT BE FOR YOU

THE Los Angeles County Fair is back, bringing fun and frivolity to the fairgrounds from September 2 to 25.

Meanwhile, three miles away, a sort of shadow fair is taking place.

The dA Center for the Arts is presenting "Love A Fair," an art exhibit that serves as a warm tribute to the fair of the 1950s and '60s, and a gentle rebuke to the fair of today.

Subtitled "a nostalgic walk through the county fair we love," it's devoted to visual reminders of horse racing, the Fun Zone and a hometown feel.

I visited on opening night last month. The dA is familiar itself, a presence in downtown Pomona since the 1980s. You old-timers will remember its 252 S. Main Street location as a furniture store, Wright Brothers and Rice.

The nostalgia, my friends, starts right on the sidewalk. The long front-window display includes a large sign panel from the fair's old Pie A La Mode stand, a cutaway view of a cherry pie. A bale of hay is plopped outside the front door.

Inside, a scale model of the Ranchero sculpture, carved by John Svenson in the 1950s before he went to work on the 22-foot full-size version at the fair, greets you.

On the walls, paintings depict such humble subjects as farm animals, the midway, the Ferris wheel, the clock tower, citrus trees and the monorail. ("Monorail Sunset" is the latter piece's evocative name.) The Lemon Squeezers stand, in the shape of a lemon, is the subject of another.

It's a kick to see fair scenes rendered in watercolors, oils and gouache, like fine art. But it's fine to see.

Inside the front door, two piglets wriggled in the bottom of a metal trough, brought by Amy's Farm, a small farm in Ontario that offers tours.

Memorabilia was displayed: fair posters, prize ribbons, pins, postcards, a pennant with hitchhiking pig mascot Thummer, 4-H correspondence, photos and a horse racing prize cup.

Around a corner, there's a midcentury living room of mod chairs, lamps, coffee tables and accent pieces. It's a tribute to the old "Design for Modern Living" exhibits from the Millard Sheets era.

"Love A Fair" is the brainchild of Cathy Garcia, a Claremont mosaic artist, and was inspired by changes to the art program at the fair that saw Tony Sheets, son of Millard, depart and his stable of art demonstrators left without an outlet.

The dA's executive director, Margaret Aichele, told Garcia that her venue had August and September open. Why not bring the demonstrators there?

The concept snowballed. Garcia wondered if she might be able to build an homage to the fair around the elements she remembered and loved. The interior design showroom was contributed by co-curator David Shearer of Claremont Heritage.

David Svenson, John's son, helped. Two docents from the fair, John Atwater and Michelle Pederson-Tomes, are volunteering. Artist friends pitched in with paintings of orange groves and fair scenes.

"I haven't had a 'no' yet," Garcia told me opening night, tired after having stayed up until midnight making arrangements of paper flowers.

She's been attending the fair since 1952. Her father would sweep the grandstand to earn extra money for family vacations.

She misses the days when Home Arts had its own building, when civic displays were contributed by every city in L.A. County, when there was a rodeo.

If there was a marker for when the fair stopped being the fair to her, it was when the 4-H animals were gone. No longer were youngsters found in the pens with their animals, clipping their hooves or even taking a nap with them. Professionals brought in animals for viewing, timed to maximize the number of live births during the fair.

We didn't discuss the recurring recent exhibit, back this year, of human cadavers, but I'm confident this was not on her must-see list.

For the dA, Garcia arranged for some small-scale contests, including pie and fresh-cut garden flower arrangements.

"It's a heartfelt thing," Garcia said of the efforts.

She and Shearer don't think the fair is lost forever. A search for a new director is underway, and directions can change. "Love A Fair" is a way to remember and honor the old fair, Shearer said, "the way that it was and still could be."

Saturday, a tribute to the fair's old Mexican Village is planned, with a dance performance and homemade salsa contest. Carnival games and children's art projects are slated for September 17. The finale takes place September 24 with art demonstrations, a craft beer garden and a presentation about Richard Petterson, who once ran the fair's art exhibits and for whom a museum at Pilgrim Place is named.

"Love A Fair" isn't the real fair by any stretch, but there are elements in common. Stifling heat, for one: The dA isn't air-conditioned. Unlike the fair, admission is free, and you can find free parking. (Also unlike the fair, the dA's director doesn't pull down a cool million.)

Perhaps the main thing missing is food, dA president Chris Toovey said.

There's no cotton candy, corn dogs or deep-fried anything on a stick. He mused about hiring a mobile barbecue grill for the last weekend.

"Part of the fair is olfactory. That's why we have the hay out front," Toovey said. "Or you can take a good whiff of the piglets."

Mi Poco LA adds hipper, Latino twist to L.A. County Fair

IN the midst of the usual rides, food, farm animals and more that you expect from the L.A. County Fair, there's something unexpected.

A coffee vendor, a street food stand, working artists and live music are all on the enclosed patio of the Millard Sheets Art Center, with tables, chairs and benches plentiful. It's like a block of the downtown Pomona Arts Colony has been transplanted to the fairgrounds.

It's called Mi Poco LA, a name with some wordplay behind it. Formally, Poco stands for Pomona Collective. In Spanish, *poco* means a small piece, and *mi* makes it personal.

"The idea is, this is a piece of L.A.; this is my piece of L.A. It's Pomona's piece. People may come to the fair from Santa Monica and all over. We wanted to specifically feature this part of *LA County*, the eastern San Gabriel Valley," said Miguel Santana, the fair's new CEO.

And the goal is to attract millennials, especially Latinos, who may think that having seen the fair as kids, there's nothing there for them now. (Santana ran into that with some of his own grown children.)

Mi Poco is operating from 3 to 11 p.m. Friday to Sunday through the September 24 end of the fair.

I went there Sunday night to check out the scene. Dia de los Puercos and Mi Cafecito were doing good business while a band from Costa Mesa, Spendtime Palace, performed on the small stage. Their backdrop was a fair standby, the 1952 brick mural "Brahma Bull" by Albert Stewart and John Svenson.

A few steps away, Brandon Roybal was painting an image of Death from a *loteria* card on a tall canvas. It would join cards done by other artists that are displayed around the patio.

At Rick Garcia's Dia de los Puercos stand, the specialty is a dish he calls Mexicorn. It's like *elote* in a cup: corn, cotija cheese, butter, bacon, lime, seasoning and mayo. He also sells tacos, quesadillas, taquitos, bacon-wrapped hot dogs and dessert empanadas filled with peanut butter and jelly. He recommends you take the latter to the adjacent Mi Cafecito stand for a scoop of horchata ice cream.

As a new attraction, Mi Poco got a slow start because people didn't know it existed or where it was. The fair added a painted walkway leading into the venue to make it more visible. Word is getting out.

"We're having a lot of fun," Garcia said. "During the day it's more family oriented. In the evening it's families but a younger crowd. The bands come and they bring their own followers."

He added approvingly: "They're really hitting the target of Chicanos and Latinos with the concept and vibe. It starts with the calaveras – the sugar skulls – and the low rider out front. It sets the tone."

Yes, out front of the Millard Sheets Center, a row of giant, brightly painted skulls like Olmec heads are lined up for Dia de los Muertos, and a lowered 1964 Chevy Impala is parked inside velvet ropes. The center is turned over to the pioneering Chicana artists Judithe Hernandez and Patssi Valdez for a show, "One Path Two Journeys," that is part of the Getty-funded Pacific Standard Time: LA/LA initiative. It's worth your time.

Along the walkway to the east of the center is Handmade LA, a series of vendors selling clothing, jewelry and lamps they've made.

Santana recruited Dia de los Puercos after dining at its restaurant in West Covina, which has been open just over a year, and being impressed. Ditto with Mi Cafecito, a small coffeehouse in downtown Pomona that sells Mexican-styled drinks, pastries and ice cream.

I'm a regular there, but more importantly, so is Santana. Juan Vega, who owns the coffeehouse with his wife, Paola Gonzalez-Vega, said he told Santana that he'd love to be part of the fair. They got invited to join Mi Poco.

"Being part of the community, being able to showcase Pomona, that's something I'm proud of," Vega said.

He and Paola, plus one or two employees, are at the fair selling hot and cold drinks like *cafe de olla* and frozen *tres leches*, a liquid version of the Mexican staple three-milk cake. While business hasn't been as brisk as hoped, the exposure to potential customers who weren't aware of the coffeehouse has made up for it.

"It's a cool place," Vega said of Mi Poco. "The fair wasn't that cool to the millennial crowd."

Surveys of guests are showing that most Mi Poco visitors are between 21 and 24 and most are Latino. (It's a good thing the survey overlooked me or the results might be confusing.) Forty percent came to the fair specifically for Mi Poco.

Thirty-five percent learned about it via Instagram. I'm hopeful the leading answer in the next survey will be "the newspaper."

After Mi Poco's daytime music acts, which tend to be acoustic, three indie rock or fusion bands per night perform as the audience changes. The stage is the purview of Rene Contreras, the founder of the indie music festival Viva! Pomona, who also lent his touch to Coachella earlier this year.

At 8 p.m. about 50 people were there, most seated, some standing, as Spendtime Palace played. The three members of Hana Vu, the next band, watched from a standing table, as if this were a club and not the L.A. County Fair.

"It's like a cafe stage," Vu, the singer, remarked. She was right.

Rolando Leanos, 24, was taking in the band with Crystal Garcia, 22, like him a Pomona resident. Leanos follows Mi Cafecito on Instagram, learned about Mi Poco that way and was curious. "It's mellow, it's not crazy," Leanos said appreciatively.

"It's really cool," Garcia said. "I really like this. Just the environment, the way it's set up, it's really inviting. It's fun to hang out."

It was.

At L.A. County Fair's Garden Railroad, this (tiny) crime scene has been cleared

THE Fairplex Garden Railroad, the sprawling train layout that is one of the L.A. County Fair's oldest and best-loved features, isn't known for offending people. But one of the small displays this year drew the ire of some fairgoers, not to mention the fair's CEO: a miniature crime scene.

In the diorama of downtown Pomona, two small figures were lying face down, hands behind their backs, as if they'd just been arrested. A third man, standing, had his hands behind his back as a lawman in brown prepared to cuff him. Two police vehicles were parked and a second officer was emerging. The scene was set between the Fox Theater and the Masonic Lodge, both inches high.

Oh, brother. Pomona maintains a sense of humor about its flaws, which is refreshing. But police activity in the Garden Railroad is as out of place as a street person vomiting on *Mister Rogers' Neighborhood*.

Daniel Betancourt saw the display Sunday and shot video on his phone. It's shaky because he was laughing. The more he thought about it, though, he decided "it was pretty messed up" to put such an image of Pomona on display within the city's biggest tourist attraction, the fair, which draws upwards of 1 million people per year.

Betancourt is the co-owner of O'Donovan's Pub, a downtown restaurant and bar across from the Fox and two blocks from the Masonic Lodge – the full-size versions. He posted his video on Monday to the Facebook group Eye on Pomona, where he wrote: "doesn't take a genius to realize this was a terrible idea. There's much more to the city than crime."

Later Monday, Fairplex communications director Renee Hernandez posted that CEO Miguel Santana had removed the scene personally. "He found it offensive and not reflective of the Pomona he lives in," she wrote. "We apologize to the residents of Pomona for allowing this to be placed without being noticed sooner."

Santana told me he was at home, a few blocks from the fair, when he received Hernandez's alert about the display Monday. Leaving his dinner half-eaten, he drove to the fairgrounds, hoping the video had been faked or the scene was a short-lived prank that had been taken down.

No such luck. The fair is closed Mondays, so the place was virtually empty, but Santana found the scene just as described.

"I was extremely disappointed and upset. I personally took it down," Santana said. "I was angered to see that." The pieces are in his office.

He continued: "It doesn't reflect our perception of or relationship with this community. We're proud to be in the city of Pomona. A Pomona councilman founded the fair in 1922. It simply doesn't reflect who we are. The Garden Railroad and the entire fair should be about celebrating the best of who we are, the city and the county."

He said he later spoke to the head of the Garden Railroad, whom he said "was extremely apologetic" after Santana pointed out the scene's poor taste. It's apparently been up since the August 31 start of the fair.

Santana said he has fond memories from boyhood of visiting the fair by school bus and the thought that any children may have witnessed the scene this year disturbs him.

Betancourt, asked what he thought of Santana removing the scene, said: "I'm glad he did. I know that he had no idea."

Among those on Eye on Pomona who thanked the fair for taking down the crime scene was Carolyn Hemming, president of the Downtown Pomona Owners Association, the business improvement district. She said she wondered if the scene had been installed without official authorization.

"We have always treasured the railroad exhibit year-round. We've been proud to show it off to relatives and friends from all corners of the world," resident Athena Fristoe wrote. "This was just over the top on someone's part who volunteers for maintaining and/or expanding the exhibit. Not funny. Thank you, Miguel, for saying 'Not on my watch.'"

Not everyone was happy about its removal. Lisa Snider said she had mixed feelings, wondering what the artist who created the scene thought. (I'm wondering what he or she was thinking.) Others said, basically, that's Pomona. "Hey that's how we roll in the P haha I mean come on," Paul Nelson wrote.

"It may be unusual to focus on the ugly side of the city, but it is absolutely ridiculous to call it 'offensive,'" Curt Strength wrote.

To my mind, the scene might be funny in a different context, like an art gallery. If I may speak for fans of the miniature railroad, I don't think we need its idealized, if tiny, version of Americana to begin reflecting the edgy realities of life.

And I have to question what motivated someone to devote hours to painstakingly creating and constructing this grim scene.

Although maybe they didn't spend hours. As Santana pointed out, the law enforcement officers are in brown, like the L.A. County Sheriff's Department, rather than Pomona blue. "The man who's being arrested," Santana added with a chuckle, "is in a suit and tie. Maybe he's being arrested for white collar crime."

KICKS ACHIEVED AT LA COUNTY FAIR'S ROUTE 66 EXHIBIT

ROUTE 66 is a few miles north of the L.A. County Fair, but the Mother Road is coursing through the fairgrounds. "Get Your Kicks on Route 66" is the fair's theme, the first I can recall in my two decades here. It's cool.

Mock versions of old gas stations mark each "neighborhood" of the fair, and all food vendors have a $6.60 special, which is tending to be each stand's best-seller. (Expecting a 66-cent special will show your age.) Even the Millard Sheets art building is taking part with "Alt 66," an exhibit about the route's darker side.

I was at the fairgrounds Wednesday for my first visit. Vacation had kept me away the first part of the fair, and then other commitments kept intruding. It turned out I was cutting it close: Despite my firm belief that the fair ran until the end of September, it actually ends Sunday.

(This would have been embarrassing had I shown up again, say, next Wednesday, notebook in hand. On the other hand, parking would have been a breeze.)

I met two friends for lunch, an annual tradition, our meals accompanied by free cups of water. When one asked if she could have a cup of ice, she was told, "That's $1.25." She declined.

After lunch I toured the Flower and Garden building, which is dedicated to the Southwest's desert landscapes and succulents this year. The theme continues next door in the addition, where animals or plants represent the eight states along Route 66.

A Texas screaming hairy armadillo was, sadly, quiet, but a few of us watched him scuttling around his cage. A North American raccoon, representing New Mexico, scampered around her enclosure as children took photos. "Her name is Luna and she's 4 months old," a handler announced.

Oklahoma's contribution is a Fennec fox. "Why is he losing his hair??" a display card reads. "He looks a little patchy because he is in the process of shedding that thick winter coat."

That's what he tells people, anyway. By the next fair, he'll be growing his remaining fur longer and combing it over.

Going out the back way, I headed up Picnic Hill to see the "Mother Road" exhibit. This entry point meant I was entering it partway through, to what proved to be my detriment.

My first sight was a stand-in for Oklahoma's Blue Whale. The original is a large piece of folk art built in the early 1970s by Hugh Davis as an anniversary present for his wife. History does not record whether she would have preferred flowers.

A woman near me exclaimed, "That's so cool. I want to go to Oklahoma and see the Blue Whale."

Nearby was a replica of an old Route 66 gas station and a scaled-down version of Missouri's Red Rocker, originally a 42-foot-tall red rocking chair built in 2008. Please don't confuse this Red Rocker with Sammy Hagar.

A small version of Texas' Cadillac Ranch was next. In homage to the 1970s art installation of half-buried Caddies, the fair has three, all rusty and graffitied, tamely, with spray paint.

"What happened to these cars?" a mother solicitously asked her two young boys. One replied, "They got dirty."

I passed an abandoned mid-century diner, where the posted prices were more akin to the fantasy of 66-cent fair specials, which is probably why it's abandoned. (No price was listed for cups of ice.) A tribute to Elmer Long's Bottletree Ranch in Oro Grande was next, glass bottles of various hues stuck on wooden "trees."

Around the bend, the exhibit perked to life. A small KOA campground setup had a shiny metal trailer. A sign noted that Route 66 has 21 such campgrounds, including ones in Needles and – who knew? – Pomona.

The fondly recalled Mt. Baldy Drive-In, which operated in La Verne from 1960 to 1984, is recreated after a fashion. There's a replica of the sign, but not in neon, and a screen, log benches and drive-in speakers. Two movies are playing for free after dusk: *Car Wash* and *The Longest Yard*, the latter with Burt Reynolds.

A group of four women recognized me. The quilters said their gripe with the fair is that the winners of the quilting competition always violate the written rules. "That's a shame," I told them, not knowing what else to say. Perhaps someone at the fair can crack down next year on renegade quilters.

Up on the hilltop, past a sign for Dodger Stadium and a Chinatown dragon, was a replica of the Hollywood sign, all the letters spread out like the real thing, if smaller, but also more accessible. People were taking selfies with the sign behind them or with their family arrayed in front of and behind it.

As Miguel Santana, the fair's CEO, told me later: "People love taking pictures by the Hollywood sign. I've never done the hike to see it myself. I'm sure I'm not the only one. It's part of what makes L.A., L.A."

I took that hike for my birthday in 2017 with two friends. It was memorable. Still, I might have saved myself some trouble by waiting to see it in Pomona.

The view, if not as spectacular as in Los Angeles, was helpful: I saw which portions of the exhibit I had missed, including a Wrigley Field homage. Scampering down the hill, much like the North American raccoon, I took a branch of the path that led me past a tribute to the Wigwam Motel chain.

"Have you slept in a wigwam lately?" an old slogan reads. A display offers the detail that originally, "Each wigwam had a radio that would play for one half hour for a silver dime."

A Last Chance Trading Post sells Route 66 merchandise. A painted backdrop lets you pretend to take a selfie at the Grand Canyon. Beyond that is a version of the Mission San Jose from San Antonio, Texas. After that the Blue Whale was in sight again. So I doubled back. I still needed to find Wrigley Field.

I wasn't the only one seeing the exhibit out of order and searching for the Land of Lincoln. Near me in the Texas display, a woman said to her husband: "We still have to go to Illinois."

As a native of Illinois, I found the section for that state gratifyingly large, even if it was entirely about the hated Chicago Cubs. (We downstaters rooted for St. Louis.)

Storyteller Jim Cogan was talking about how Babe Ruth and the Yankees swept the Cubs in four games in the 1932 World Series. That was kind of gratifying too.

"We're going to go all the way from Wrigleyville to Hollywood on Route 66," Cogan promised whoever was listening as he headed off.

But not, of course, on the most direct route: Wrigleyville was about 100 feet from the Hollywood sign. But at the L.A. County Fair, as on the real Route 66, half the pleasure is in the journey.

Sunny Route 66's dark side is explored in art show 'Alt 66' at LA County Fair

ROUTE 66 may call to mind convertibles, diners, tourist kitsch, the open road and freedom. But in contrast to those burnished images, which are all over the L.A. County Fair this year, the route had a side that was less glamorous, even dark.

That's part of the fair too. In the Millard Sheets Arts Center's "Alt 66" exhibit, 13 artists created installations that are sometimes lovely, sometimes stark and always thought-provoking.

"Plastic Tree" by Cat Chiu Phillips uses found plastic, such as lids that might be tossed out a car window, to make hanging strings. A bright, cartoon-like motel room by Marcus Pollitz features a sleepless traveler counting sheep who are cavorting past his bedside. It's called "Insomnia Motel."

The highway wasn't welcoming to all. Thirty Native American tribes lived along the route and "were seen as exotic tourist attractions," as a panel in "In the Pursuit of Dreams" by Doug Pearsall notes.

A silhouette of an African-American female includes text in white that shows how difficult traveling could be: "I had to use the bathroom in the bushes," "Don't go to Sundown Towns," "we have to carry our gas with us" and "The *Green Book* tells me where we're welcome."

A second installation reproduces the cover of a *Green Book*, the 1936-1966 travelers' guide to hotels, restaurants and service stations that were friendly to blacks. Such establishments were few and far between: I looked up one online and there wasn't a single stop between L.A. and Palm Springs.

The Chicano experience is told in "La Ruta Madre," Spanish for the Mother Road, via archival film, a deconstructed vehicle and a wall of family snapshots. It was assembled by Fiona Baler and Margo Gutierrez, both students at Claremont High. I'm sorry I didn't make it to "Alt 66" earlier or I'd have tried interviewing them about this enigmatic, compelling display.

"The thing I'm really proudest of is 'Alt 66,'" fair CEO Miguel Santana told me. "We wanted people to tell the stories of Route 66 that didn't get told."

The works came about after an open competition in which Santana told the artists to be unafraid to make viewers uncomfortable.

The converse, of course, is that some viewers feel welcomed. A half-dozen African-Americans have told Santana how appreciative they were that the Route 66 theme of the fair made room for their experience.

"They got very emotional about it," Santana said. "It's a part of U.S. history most people don't know about." He said with a chuckle: "You don't come to the fair to learn about the *Green Book*. But we like to provide education disguised as fun."

As a reminder, the fair ends Sunday, so if this entices you, don't delay.

There was some undisguised, outright fun too. A series of oversized, semi-abstracted paintings by Tania Alvarez, "That Hits the Spot," pays tribute to roadside food along the route.

I was pleased to see St. Louis' Ted Drewes Frozen Custard, a regular stop for me on visits home, represented. Not to mention a 9-foot-tall rendering of a Donut Man strawberry doughnut from Glendora.

* * *

A family visiting the L.A. County Fair pointed out that their first sight at the Yellow Gate entrance was a dead tree, which didn't quite jibe with the "Welcome to the L.A. County Fair" sign. The fair responded by cutting down the tree and replacing it with flowers planted in the form of the fair seal. Apparently it's a hit. "I stood there for 10 minutes," said fair CEO Miguel Santana, who ordered the work, "and every other family stopped to take a photo."

LA LANDMARKS POP UP AT FAIR

ROLL over, Andy Warhol, and tell Roy Lichtenstein the news: This year the L.A. County Fair has gone pop – that's its slogan, "L.A. County Fair Goes Pop!" – with day-glo colors and Ben-day polka dots. I saw an oversized soup can with Thummer in place of a Campbell kid, an image of Audrey Hepburn in rainbow hues.

Well, the pop artists brought it on themselves. They gleefully sent up commercial images, Elvis portraits and comic book panels. They can't very well object to the fair taking surface elements of their style.

I was at the fair Wednesday for my first visit of the season. Someone with the fair asked how many L.A. County Fairs I'd covered. I was a little surprised myself to realize this is my 23rd.

The fair is in some ways the same every time, in other ways different. The big attraction last year was a tribute to Route 66. The hillside area this time features "L.A. Pop Architecture," a tribute to Los Angeles landmarks like Angels Flight, City Hall, the Santa Monica Pier and the La Brea Tar Pits.

"We're creating what we affectionately call the L.A. Bucket List," Miguel Santana, the fair's CEO, said as we strolled the grounds. "As Angelenos, we don't always experience what tourists do. We put all those icons in one place, so you can check off in one day the L.A. bucket list."

So thoughtful, the L.A. County Fair. You could spend a whole weekend behind the wheel trying to hit Santa Monica, Hollywood, Watts, Long Beach, Mid-Wilshire and downtown, and here it all is within paces of each other in Pomona.

Granted, it's not the same. The Queen Mary is represented by a diorama of a uniformed captain on a ship's deck, Chinatown by an arch and two golden dragon figures, Grand Central Market by oversized cans of vegetables.

Angels Flight isn't bad, an orange trolley and matching arch behind gates. Due to safety issues, the real thing was closed for so long that this version's inaccessibility adds to the realism.

Griffith Observatory is a miniature replica of the building atop a trellis. Maybe if you look up at night, stars in the sky overhead, the effect would improve. Or if there was a tiny, red-jacketed James Dean next to it.

Ain't nothin' like the real thing, baby, as the philosopher Marvin Gaye once opined. That said, not everyone is motivated, industrious or culturally attuned enough to hit all the actual places, and this is the L.A. County Fair. Think of it as Pomona's version of tourist-friendly CityWalk.

So it's all in good fun, and perhaps not for the most demanding audience.

"We want to give people things to take pictures in front of," Santana explained. "We want to give our guests memories, not just of the fair, but the 2019 fair." Sparking conversations among generations – "did you ever buy vegetables at Grand Central Market, grandma?" – is another goal.

An actual Rose Parade float is present in somewhat denuded form. Children can take a cut flower in a water-tube vase and place it on the float to fill it out. Every day the process starts over. "We just keep recycling the roses," employee Marcus Pollitz said.

Santana and I walked past a two-dimensional mockup of L.A. City Hall, where he toiled as city administrative officer before taking the Fairplex job in late 2016. "Where was your office?" I asked. Not visible: It was in the City Hall East annex, on the far side.

Surely Santana's network of contacts made this effort to tie the fair to popular L.A. institutions – the Natural History Museum, the La Brea Tar Pits and the rest – easier to pull off. The children's science center Discovery Cube, on whose board he serves, has its own area at the fair, where Jacob Ockwood was demonstrating a small air cannon to excited Glendora students.

There's a Randy's Donuts too, with a large doughnut perched upright on the roof just like at the famous Inglewood shop. Olde Tyme Donuts runs the stand and is selling the real thing: The owner goes to Inglewood every morning and buys 18 to 25 dozen, an employee told me.

Leaving the hillside, Santana and I walked through the Flower and Garden Pavilion, now a tribute to Grauman's Chinese Theatre, with blooms. Successfully ignoring the tempting smell of grilled meat, we got lunch at Veggie Bomb, the fair's vegan food stand.

Veggie Bomb touts "100% vegan street food." Understandably, there was no line. But it's doing fine, co-owner Vasu Clayton said as he took our orders for a jackfruit taco and a bowl of vegan meatballs, veggies and brown rice.

"People who are looking for vegan food, they're like, 'We're glad you're here,'" Clayton said.

"A lot of people are looking for turkey legs," Santana remarked. "But we have a diverse audience. It's important that people who aren't looking for turkey legs can come here."

The food was fine, but in keeping with the icons theme, perhaps we should have eaten at Pink's Hot Dogs, whose stand may be the most L.A. thing, year after year, about the fair.

The Dodgers are a partner this year, with Blue Gate now branded as Dodger Blue Gate. Inside the entrance are replicas of classic Dodgers anniversary signs, a bobblehead statue and, a bit farther on, official Dodgers merchandise.

Past Dodgers greats, one per hour, will be present near the entrance from 1 to 5 p.m. each day this weekend to sign autographs for free, among them Manny Mota (1 p.m. Friday), Ron Cey (1 p.m. Saturday) and Tommy Davis (3 p.m. Sunday).

A pop representation of the Watts Towers stands outside the Millard Sheets Art Center, which is showcasing the work of 11 Los Angeles contemporary artists. The exhibit is more like an art gallery or museum show than what fairgoers might be used to.

But I liked what I saw, and the first piece, a wall-sized op-art mural, "Emergence" by Darel Carey, is a popular spot for photos.

The piece actually seemed to undulate through my phone's camera lens. "I've heard it makes a few people dizzy," curator Dee Campos told me with a chuckle.

Best to not visit immediately after a Pink's chili dog.

OLDIES ACT HAS NOD TO RITCHIE VALENS' HISTORY AT FAIR

RITCHIE Valens is the pioneering Latino rocker who, in his short eight-month career, happened to perform at the L.A. County Fair in September 1958. In writing about Valens last February, on the 60th anniversary of his death in a plane crash along with Buddy Holly and J.P. Richardson, I suggested the fair commemorate him somehow.

I was visiting the fair Wednesday when Valens popped into my mind, so I inquired of fair CEO Miguel Santana whether anything had been done. He said he believed that had been discussed but may have got lost in the shuffle.

That's how it goes, and of course the fair has played host to many big names in music over the decades. Sometime I'd like to see the records, so to speak, because famous musicians who've performed at the fairgrounds must abound and yet have not been publicly documented. Might be a good project for the fair as its 2022 centennial nears. I'm great with the unsolicited advice, aren't I?

I'd already visited the hillside L.A. Pop Architecture attraction with Santana but returned afterward on my own to take photos. Over near the stand decorated like Randy's Donuts, I was half-listening to the live music from the Santa Monica Pier attraction when singer Jim Lowman started talking between songs.

"Remember when we came over to the fair in '58? Over in Building 10 there was Johnny Cash, Jan and Dean and that young guy, who was only 17 years old. What was his name?" he asked his wife.

Trish Lowman replied on cue: "Ritchie Valens!" Then Jim launched into "La Bamba," solo on electric guitar.

How about that!

It was a good version of the song too, with Jim picking out the familiar melody while singing and bantering in Spanish while a few oldsters and a youngster or two danced or swiveled hula hoops.

When the couple, who perform rock oldies as Jimmy and Sandy, took a break, I asked how they knew about Valens' performance.

Trish recognized my name. The fair's roving storyteller, Jim Cogan, had read my column, told them about the connection to Building 10 and credited me, bless his heart.

"We wanted to tie it into the show somehow," Trish said of the Valens trivia.

When he heard Valens had played at the fair, "I was like, woo-eee!" exclaimed Jim, who's conversant with rock history and remembers seeing the Beatles on *Ed Sullivan* at age 7.

Jim was just acting when he spoke onstage as if the couple were at the fair in 1958. The Lowmans live in Florida and perform at theme parks, where the white-bearded Jim has done duty as Santa. They've come to Pomona to work the fair the past 12 years in various roles.

"We're here two months out of the year. It's a nice break from Florida," Trish said.

Jim pointed to the mountains off in the distance beyond the Ferris wheel, a view that feels magical to the Florida flatlanders. And they look forward to Southern California's excellent Mexican food.

Located on the hill among the other L.A. Pop Architecture features, the couple is ensconced on a small stage past a replica of the vintage Santa Monica Pier sign, in an area that includes seating and sand for that beach-in-Pomona feel.

"Five shows a day and we're lovin' it!" Jim said, beaming.

I don't know how I happened to be in the right place at the right time to catch this impermanent but living commemoration of Ritchie Valens' history at the fair. But I'm lovin' it.

RITCHIE VALENS (CONT'D)

I **WROTE** in September about a casual tribute to musician Ritchie Valens at the L.A. County Fair, where musician couple Jimmy and Sandy cited Valens' 1958 performance at the fair during their stage patter before performing his song "La Bamba."

Reader Russ Cinque from Glendale, an oldies fan who had thanked me after my column about Valens last February, emailed to say he had been at the fair the same day as me and also was inquiring about Valens.

"I did ask a couple of people at the guest information booths about him being remembered at the fair. One lady said she never heard of him, the other lady said she didn't think so," Cinque said. "You were really at the right place at the right time! I am so glad he wasn't forgotten."

I'm not surprised the information booths didn't know one of the free-music acts was remarking about Valens. But I admit I'm still struggling with the concept that someone in Southern California had never heard of Ritchie Valens.

Sky Ride lifts you to great heights ... of anxiety

THE Sky Ride is the snow-less ski lift at the L.A. County Fair that carries passengers high overhead, offering a panoramic view of the fairgrounds.

I'd never been on it. Heights make me nervous.

And yet, seeing people above me traveling in slow motion, I've always been curious about the ride. So are a friend and her mother, who successfully talk themselves out of taking it by reasoning, "It's hotter up there. I don't want to get closer to the sun."

Makes sense. Still, every year I think, oh, I should ride that – next year.

And one day last week, "next year" finally arrived.

I had finished a tour of the fair – it ends Sunday, by the way – with Miguel Santana, the CEO, and Renee Hernandez, the communications director, when Santana asked casually, "Are you afraid of heights?" "Kind of, yeah," I replied.

"Oh, so you wouldn't want to go on the Sky Ride," he said.

"The Sky Ride!" I exclaimed in awe. "I've always wanted to ride that."

Thus, a few minutes later, Santana and I were walking into the Sky Ride entrance near Blue Gate. There was no line. The Sky Ride doesn't stop. You just position yourself in place and let the bench come up under you. An attendant then pulls the safety bar down and you're airborne.

Perhaps wisely, there isn't time to think or orient yourself. Within seconds, we were 30 feet off the ground. Already I was anxious, and the angle of the cable showed that we were only halfway up to the

Sky Ride's full height. This was looking like a mistake.

Absurdly, I scooted back on the bench another inch, to ensure I wouldn't somehow slide out, and gripped the safety bar. "I ride this three times a day," the relaxed Santana was saying.

I still had my notebook in one hand but no interest in jotting notes, which would take two hands. Also, I wanted my phone for photos, but it was wedged into the front pocket of my jeans. Eventually I worked it free while maintaining a hold on my notebook and the safety bar.

Phone in hand, I relaxed enough to take some photos of the fairgrounds – food stands, the Garden Railroad, a surprising number of trees – as we approached the end and began our descent.

You hop off the Sky Ride and move to your right, because the ride doesn't stop. The ride lasted three or four minutes. I have to say, the last minute or so was fun.

"How far up do you think we were?" I asked Santana once we were back on the ground.

"Probably three stories, right? Maybe four," Santana said.

If he'd said that before we'd gone up, he'd have gone up alone. Hernandez, a feet-on-the-ground type, had refused to join us.

A bit later, I spoke to Chris Lopez, the vice president of RCS, the carnival operator. My first question: How far up does the Sky Ride go?

"It takes you approximately 60, 70 feet above the crowd," Lopez said.

That's more like, ulp, four or five stories.

There are two Sky Rides at the fair. One travels roughly north and south between the Clock Tower and Yellow Gate. The second, which I rode, goes roughly east and west, taking people between the Clock Tower and Blue Gate.

The first Sky Ride was installed in 1993 and a second leg was added in 2009, when their locations were shifted.

"They were estimating folks were not seeing 30% of the fair," Lopez said. "We needed a way to get them from Blue Gate to the carnival midway."

Of the 70 rides RCS operates, the top three are, in varying order, the Big Wheel, the roller coaster and the Sky Ride. "It's a very popular ride," Lopez said.

Some ask if it's a round trip. It's not. And you have to transfer, and pay again – a ride is $5, Metro TAP cards not accepted – if you want to do the full L-shape between Blue Gate and the Fun Zone.

Don't bring any liquids, not even a goldfish in water, or any food. They're not allowed. "You don't want to drop anything," Lopez said. "A lot of people get excited and pull out a phone. Can you imagine if that fell from up there?"

And if you spit or throw something, you will not only be ejected from the fair, you may face charges.

"Where can you go? We've got security," Lopez said, patting the radio at his hip. "You're strapped in. We'll be waiting for you."

I went to the Clock Tower to wait for someone exiting at one terminus of the Sky Ride. It was a lazy Wednesday afternoon. Chair after chair off was descending empty. Off in the distance, all the chairs were empty. Either nobody was riding or they'd relaxed their grip on the safety bar – tsk tsk.

During the down time I finally noticed a warning sign for would-be riders: "Do not participate if you have fear of heights."

Finally, here came one lone rider, silhouetted against the sky, approaching at the Sky Ride's leisure. When he disembarked, I introduced myself. He was Pedro Cardozo of Burbank, a confirmed fan of the Sky Ride who's in his 30s.

He likes the Sky Ride for a couple of reasons. He can get an overall look at the grounds and see if there are rides he missed. "When you walk," he said, "it's hard to tell where you've been. Up there, you can see where you want go next."

Secondly, it's tiring to walk the fair, so the ride lets him take a load off and rest his legs. In fact, done for the day, he was going to get on the second Sky Ride to take him back to Blue Gate and his exit.

"It's fun," Cardozo said. "I guess unless you're scared of heights."

Well, yes.

Having got acclimated to the Sky Ride by the end of my journey, I considered taking it to the Fun Zone to see the other leg. That would take me past the Grandstand, Avalon, the rides.

But it would also take me farther from my exit. Also, did I really need to ride this again?

Maybe next year.

Montclair caboose pulls into Pomona museum

A N old train caboose was on permanent display in Montclair for more than three decades, but it's found a new home at Pomona's Rail Giants Train Museum.

The 1955 Union Pacific caboose was hauled to Pomona's Fairplex late last month after the city of Montclair donated it to the nonprofit museum for its outdoor collection of vintage engines and rail cars.

The caboose greeted commuters as they took the eastbound onramp of the 10 Freeway from Monte Vista Avenue and passed Freedom Plaza. The pocket of land holds a sculpture, a cell phone tower, trees, a few parking spots and a bare patch where the caboose had been planted since 2004.

The reason for the move had to do with another form of transportation: the car. Because a lane will be added to the freeway and also to Monte Vista, Freedom Plaza must shrink. (I'm worried this is a metaphor for our actual freedoms.)

In fact, not only did the caboose need to go, but the cell tower obelisk – the white-tiled structure with the Montclair logo that I once dubbed the Montclair Mystery Tower – "will also have to be relocated," Mikey Fuentes of the city manager's office told me. But the tower only has to move a few yards back on the same piece of dirt.

When Loren Martens, a resident who is tuned into city business, heard that the caboose was in the way, he proposed a donation to the Rail Giants Museum, where he is a volunteer and past president. The City Council agreed to the donation in December.

The caboose's departure slipped past me, but Martens let me know about it shortly after the fact. I made a point of taking Monte Vista to the 10 on my way to work and by golly, the caboose was indeed gone from its familiar, if incongruous, spot by the freeway.

With the use of a crane, the 27-ton caboose body was placed on a low trailer and its wheels on a second trailer, Martens told me. Because of low clearance on the overpass, he said, the convoy had to rumble along Holt Avenue and then north on Fairplex Drive over the freeway to get the caboose to its destination north of the 10.

It's now resting comfortably at the museum, where Martens kindly met me Wednesday afternoon for a look. The caboose will join the open-air collection of two diesel engines, seven steam engines, a box car, a refrigerator car and a Pullman dining and sleeping car. "We've got three cabooses now," Martens said.

(I'm pleased to learn from an expert that the plural of caboose isn't cabeese.)

The caboose isn't especially noteworthy, but the museum is glad to have it, Martens said. It will be reassembled and set in a permanent spot by fair time this fall.

Finished in 1955 and last inspected in 1979, the caboose was taken out of service, along with Union Pacific's other cabooses, when new so-called dynamic braking systems meant that a crew was no longer needed to set brakes manually on each car before a downhill grade, Martens explained.

A former Montclair mayor, Harold Hayes, was a train buff who got the railroad company to donate a caboose as a novelty for Alma Hofman Park in 1987. Its dedication drew more than 300 people and it became a focal point for the annual Christmas event in the Civic Center.

Then in 2004, the caboose had to move to make room for a skate park. Like the auto, skateboarding is likewise a modern form of transportation, and as the saying goes, youth must be served.

I covered the caboose's 2-mile move to Freedom Plaza nearly 16 years ago. If you stay in one place long enough, you'll see everything happen twice.

No fair! LA County FAIRGROUNDS SILENT INSTEAD OF LIVELY

I'VE happily attended every L.A. County Fair since my arrival here in 1997. But my annual tradition, and perhaps yours too, has fallen by the wayside. Pomona's fair isn't taking place this year for the first time in 73 years, another victim of coronavirus.

Fair CEO Miguel Santana wouldn't venture a guess as to whether the fair will take place in 2021, although he certainly hopes 2022, the fair's centennial, is a go.

"It's hard to predict anything," Santana told me. "There will always be a need for people to gather and celebrate the best of Southern California. It's been that for 100 years. I hope we can start up that tradition next year and for the next 100 years."

I was at the fairgrounds on Monday evening for a tour with Santana and spokeswoman Renee Hernandez. Does this count as keeping my attendance streak alive?

I felt it was important to honor the loss of an event that drew 1.1 million guests last year, employs 500 seasonal employees and pumps $58 million into the city's economy. The fair needed this fan's fanfare.

The fair would have opened Friday and run through September 27. On a Monday like this before a Friday opening, the grounds would have been "almost a 24/7 operation," Hernandez told me.

Instead, we were virtually the only people on the grounds.

The Midway was devoid of games of chance and carnival rides. (The bumpiest ride is 2020 itself.) The Garden Railroad, the model railroading layout, had no trains. The exhibit halls were devoid of cakes, preserves and crocheting submissions. The colorful structures in what was once known as Fiesta Village were taking a siesta.

"It's a weird feeling to be here and not be seeing anything," Hernandez said.

"It's kind of peaceful, in an eerie way," Santana observed. He walks the grounds at dusk a couple of nights a month. "There are times," he said, "it seems like a zombie movie."

We passed through the Flower and Garden Pavilion, empty of Flower and Garden. The Grandstand's 10,000 seats for concertgoers were unoccupied and would stay that way. No need to hold a seat for a friend.

The Farm had no animals – almost. One barn had its year-round chickens and turkeys, who clucked away. Electric fans were blowing. To my ears, the combination sounded like a sitcom's laugh track to our conversation. It was incongruous but welcome.

I was relieved to not see the Sky Ride, the ski lift-style transport. Last year Santana persuaded me to ride with him and your acrophobic columnist consented, quickly finding himself 70 feet off the ground, legs dangling. A year later and my knuckles are still white.

The fair was canceled in May under orders from Los Angeles County to limit crowds. Even permission for a drive-thru food fair, as Orange County is doing, was denied. OC's positivity rate is lower than L.A. County's, explained Santana, who noted that "we're still leading the state in cases in L.A. County."

Without the fair or its other events, nonprofit Fairplex has pivoted toward using its space to serve the community.

The 240-room Sheraton hotel has been hosting firefighters and other first responders who must quarantine. A drive-thru food pantry takes place on the dragstrip, serving up to 2,000 families a week. The daycare center is watching the children of nurses, firefighters and supermarket employees for free. Drive-thru COVID-19 tests occur at Gate 17.

"We were able to transition our purpose to what the community needed, when it needed it," Santana said.

The fair furloughed 85 percent of its 150-person permanent staff. Executives, including Santana, took pay cuts of 25 to 50 percent. Health insurance is still being provided to employees at least through December 31.

Santana, CEO since 2017, is leaving when his contract expires in January. He recommended that the chief financial officer assume the role of interim CEO until the pandemic is over to save money.

"This will be our reality for all of this year and maybe all of next year. We have to hunker down and protect the asset," said Santana, who spends his days talking to bankers about refinancing debt from construction of the hotel and conference center and finding "passive" sources of revenue, like the rental cars that are parked at Blue Gate.

"It's not fun. This time of year, I'd have the excitement of having a million people come through the campus. This is not what I expected," Santana said. "But it's necessary."

What would the 2020 fair have been like?

Shorter. It would have started later each day – 4 p.m. rather than noon on Wednesdays and Thursdays, 11 a.m. rather than 10 a.m. Fridays to Sundays – in an attempt to avoid the worst of the September heat. 2019's attendance drooped along with fairgoers as the first three weeks of September saw average daily highs of 93 degrees.

New shade structures in the Midway and Farm would have been added to give walkers a break.

The theme was to be "We Light the Night," an attempt to capitalize on more comfortable nighttime temperatures by adding lighted art installations and more entertainment. And country singer Toby Keith was booked to perform.

As we walked around on Monday, the weather was warm but very pleasant.

"Of course the weather is perfect," Santana said ruefully. "I told someone, it'd better get hot later. That would be the perfect 2020 capstone – perfect weather when the fair would be going on."

He can relax: Every day this weekend is predicted to be 100 degrees or above.

The fair last closed on September 11, 2001 and reopened the next day. The last time there was no fair at all was during World War

II. From 1942 to 1947, the grounds were used for such purposes as a holding center for Japanese American internees before they were shipped to internment camps and as a prisoner of war camp for German and Italian Americans.

Six years without a fair. That's a sobering thought. But here's a bright prospect.

When the fair returned in 1948, "that was the first year the fair had a million attendance," Hernandez said. "People were probably just clamoring for something fun to do after all that."

116 DEGREES, BAD AIR, MASKS: LA COUNTY FAIR 2020 MIGHT HAVE BEEN WEIRD

SUNDAY would have been the last day of the L.A. County Fair, had there been an L.A. County Fair. But of course the fair was canceled after a severe outbreak of 2020.

Normally I'd have visited the fair at least a couple of times. I'd have strolled most of the grounds, being sure to see the art in the Millard Sheets Center, the flora in the Flower and Garden Pavilion, the home crafts, the sprawling Garden Railroad layout, the animals in the barn.

While fair food has never held much appeal, I always order a chili dog from the Pink's stand, which beats a trip to Hollywood, and on a brutally hot day – i.e., almost any day at the fair – get ice cream or a grape sno cone, a boyhood favorite.

I went to the fair to look for column items: the diaper derby race, say, where infants are coaxed by their mothers to crawl to the finish line, or the husband-and-wife duo from Florida who travel the fair circuit to perform rock oldies. But I wouldn't bother if I didn't not-so-secretly love the place.

The fair would have opened September 4 to kick off Labor Day weekend, and operated Wednesday through Sunday, 19 days in all, before closing out its run today. Some 1 million guests would have walked through the turnstiles. I wonder what they've done instead. Stuck to their diets, perhaps. Or learned to make funnel cake at home.

This is the first time the county fair hasn't taken place since World War II.

When we toured the fairgrounds August 31, Fairplex CEO Miguel Santana said the cancellation, done on the advice of Los Angeles County health officials, was necessary. He reiterated that to me on Friday: "I think that was the right call, difficult as it was."

On our tour he lamented that the fairgrounds were empty and forlorn. And he joked about the weather, saying that he'd be upset if September ended up with the mild temperatures that always bring out the crowds rather than the withering temperatures that keep them away.

(His three years stewarding the fair have been the hottest in its history, by the way.)

How would the 2020 fair have fared? I checked Accuweather's records.

The four-day opening weekend saw highs of 101, 116, 115 – and, on Labor Day, 92. Who would have visited the fairgrounds when it was 116? Chicken Charlie could have poured cooking oil on the ground and deep-fried his Twinkies on the asphalt.

"Imagine walking around in 100-degree weather wearing a mask," Santana mused on Friday. "Even if we'd been allowed to open, there would've been a requirement to wear a mask, and crowd sizes would have been limited."

What would have been the second week of the fair had more comfortable temperatures, 89 to 95 degrees. But we couldn't breathe: That was the week of the worst of the wildfires. They sprinkled us with ash, clouded the skies and fouled the air.

I checked the air quality index for fairtime days. The air was deemed "unhealthy" September 10 to 13, and "unhealthy for sensitive groups" September 16, based on air quality and amount of particulate matter.

Those first two weeks of the fair, "hot mess" would have been a literal description.

"We would have had to have taken seriously L.A. County Department of Public Health's guidelines and considered closing a day or two of the fair," fair spokeswoman Renee Hernandez said Friday.

"Yes, we could encourage enjoying indoor exhibits and shopping, but when the air is filled with ash and smoke and there is a thick orange-gray cloud hovering over the campus, it would've been uncomfortable just walking from your car to inside the fairgrounds."

The second half of the fair would have fulfilled Santana's rueful prediction: generally nice weather.

Pomona was 93 to 101 degrees September 16 to 20, with comfortable evenings, and with 89 to 94 degrees achieved or predicted for September 23 to 27. That end date would have neatly dodged a bunch of 100-degree days due this week. And air quality was back to normal.

"We would have had a challenging year. Opening weekend was hotter than my first fair, which was the hottest we've had," Santana told me by phone as he took a walk around the empty grounds. Due to air quality, "the second weekend would obviously have been impacted."

Everyone would have tried to go on closing weekend, he said.

Over the run of the fair, Santana said, "I think we would've hit a million, but I would've had a lot of sleepless nights."

Now, about my own attendance.

My column previewing the fair-that-wasn't noted that I'd attended each fair since my arrival here in 1997. Through 2019, that's 23 straight years – far less than those of you who've been going annually since childhood, but respectable.

All our streaks were broken this year. Or were they? There was no fair to attend.

Also, Fairplex's Twitter account tweeted a link to my September 5 column and added: "And we still consider your attendance streak alive, David," with a smiley face.

Is this an official statement from the L.A. County Fair?

"You haven't missed one," Santana affirmed. "This is what the 2020 fair looks like. You experienced it. And you did get on a ride. You rode on a golf cart."

So the tweet was correct?

"That is the official statement of the fair," Santana said. But he added the disclaimer that his last day is December 24 and the next CEO might have other ideas.

If that ruling holds – and let's not forget that the balance on the Supreme Court could tip – that means I've attended 24 straight years. Despite there being only 23 fairs.

Said Twitter follower Annette: "Not too early to think about how to commemorate next year's silver anniversary visit."

Hmm. *Two* Pink's chili dogs?

'Bite-Sized' L.A. County Fair has many small pleasures

MODESTY is not a virtue we associate with the L.A. County Fair, which ballyhoos itself as one of the largest county fairs in North America. But Pomona's first fair in two years is a fraction of the old size and isn't even considered a full-fledged L.A. County Fair.

Instead, it's the Bite-Sized Fair, a kind of sampler platter of the fair's best. It's designed as an appetizer to tide us over until May 2022, when the fair is due to return with its usual buffet of offerings.

"It's a mini version of the L.A. County Fair," spokeswoman Renee Hernandez said. "We'll still have some of your favorite foods, some of your favorite rides."

"Some" beating "none," I beat a path to the fair's door last Sunday during opening weekend. With the Bite-Sized Fair running three weekends only, time has a way of getting past us. And with the attendance streak I have going – more on that later – I didn't want to risk missing out.

It's open 3 to 9 p.m. each Friday, Saturday and Sunday through September 26. Admission is $2, sold online, and parking is $10.

This "fun size" version of the fair is taking place in the northern reaches of the grounds, on a patch of asphalt near the NHRA drag races. You'll find about 20 food or beverage stands, about a dozen rides, midway games and vendors. Everything is outdoors.

What's missing. animals, exhibits and live music. And, for that matter, demonstrations of miracle products like mops and food processors. Nobody, it seems, wants to stand in the hot sun to watch someone slice bell peppers.

I walked down the row of food stands. Your basic fair food groups are represented: kettle corn, bacon, funnel cakes, turkey legs, nachos, ice cream, pork ribs and whatever Dippin' Dots are.

King Taco is back, as is Chicken Charlie's, Texas Donuts, Tasti Chips and my personal favorite, Pink's Hot Dogs, the famous L.A. restaurant.

I got my usual, a chili dog with cheese and onions. My celebrity name for the order was Gerard Butler.

"Gerard Butler!" an employee called out a few minutes later. That would be me, thank you. And the dog was delicious.

All the stands have a Bite-Sized item for $3. I decided to try one of those for dessert. A Dole Whip stand has a $3 tiny cup. First I had to Google "Dole Whip," a name I've heard without knowing what it was. I always pictured whipped cream.

The stand's sign merely boasts that Dole Whip is "gluten free! dairy free! vegan!" As it turns out – pardon for me repeating information that every single one of you already knows – Dole Whip is a low-calorie dessert that resembles sherbet. So I sprung for the $3 version. It was refreshing, not too sweet, and the size, like the price, was right.

Most dining was at picnic tables in the literal shadow of the NHRA grandstand. At 4:30 p.m. it was 97 degrees and the shade was a relief.

Rides were likewise scaled down. The Ferris wheel was small enough that your acrophobic columnist might have boarded – but why chance it?

One ride, fashioned to resemble a round, glowing-green spaceship, is called Alien Abduction. It spins. I imagine that riders exit with no memory of their abduction other than a hazy recollection of a probe that cost five extra tickets.

There are kiddie rides with motorcycles, VW bugs and tractors, all in sparkly colors, going in circles like a carousel. And an actual carousel, of course. These are the only horses at the fair.

Vendors sell such items as jerky, oldies CDs, pistachios and colorful socks. One booth has the banner Jewelry by the Inch. By the inch? "Honey, see this chain I bought you? I love you two whole inches. Wait, why are you crying?"

Forest Lawn has a booth too, with the motto "Take Care of Tomorrow Today." Everyone seemed to be giving it a wide berth. At the fair, no one thinks of tomorrow. We live in the moment.

Attendance was 3,300 on opening day, 10,200 on Saturday and 7,400 on Sunday. The capacity limit of 20,000 was in no danger of being breached.

"It's been a nice, quiet mini-fair," Hernandez said Sunday.

With the fair's staff slashed due to lack of events and revenue, the focus is on putting on a good 100th anniversary fair in May 2022.

But Fairplex's board of directors "still wanted us to do something," leading to the Bite-Sized Fair, Hernandez told me. "We didn't want September to pass by after 99 years. People are so used to the fair in September."

Starting in 1997, the year I arrived here, I attended 23 straight fairs. Last year the fair was dark, and no one's streak was broken. But since I toured the empty grounds last September with Hernandez and then-CEO Miguel Santana, they affirmed that my streak continued.

"This is what the 2020 fair looks like. You experienced it," Santana said at the time. "And you did get on a ride. You rode on a golf cart."

The Bite-Sized Fair isn't considered an official, numbered L.A. County Fair – Hernandez called it "our .5 fair" – but I made a point of going just to cover myself. What if some sanctioning body rules that even unofficial fairs count?

(I don't know what that body would be. The Supreme Court? Texas? The Texas Donuts stand?)

Also, of course, I love the fair, which is all the excuse I need.

True, a lot of my favorites were absent, like exhibits, art and the Garden Railroad. Oh, and the recorded announcements at Juicy's BBQ. Playing on a loop from its loudspeaker, a cheerful, good ol' boy voice would begin: "When yer so hungry yer belly button is gnawin' at your backbone, come to Juicy's!"

The real fair, though, can be overwhelming. The Bite-Sized Fair is not only navigable, it's kind of a relief. There is absolutely no pressure, and at this point in the pandemic, a low-key, uncrowded event is welcome. It's the L.A. County Fair we didn't know we needed.

Could a September Bite-Sized Fair itself become annual?

"Some people have thought of that," Hernandez replied. "We think this will be our only Bite-Sized Fair. But never say never."

Step right up! Fairplex donates archive to Cal Poly

IN advance of its centennial, the L.A. County Fair decided to round up its history – and donate it.

Nearly 100 years of photos, film reels, news clippings, annual cookbooks and more from the Fairplex archives are now in the hands of Cal Poly Pomona. The University Library's Special Collections and Archives is the lucky recipient.

The items deserved a permanent, secure home where they could be accessible to the public, say Fairplex officials, who after all are in the business of putting on an annual exposition, not donning white gloves to slip 1940s brochures into Mylar sleeves. Also, as any of us who've been to the fairgrounds in the September heat can attest, a climate-controlled setting it ain't.

I visited the library archives on Wednesday. The county fair collection fills some 200 white file boxes. And the staff isn't even through packing up and transporting all the ephemera.

"It's one of our largest archival collections. It will probably be our largest," said Katie Richardson, head of Special Collections, who sees the collection growing over time. "The Rose Parade will probably be our runner-up now."

Richardson and archives coordinator Rob Strauss boxed items themselves and lugged them to Cal Poly, often in Strauss' minivan. (All hail the minivan.) Temporary labels on the boxes give a sense of the contents.

"Cattle Drive 1996." "Film Reels." "1971-1972 negatives." "Cookbooks."

An archivist will be hired in February to begin making digital copies of film reels before they deteriorate, organizing the great mass of material and cataloging each item. I'm picturing a tag that reads "representative popsicle stick, ca. 1972."

In general, expect a mix of the fascinating, the curious and the mundane.

When I saw a box labeled "Monorail," I asked Richardson to open it up. I knew the fair had a monorail around the grounds from the 1960s to the 1990s and that the first official rider was Richard Nixon. The former veep got sauteed in his aerial loop around the fairgrounds, by the way, because the monorail windows didn't open and nobody had thought to install air conditioning.

Sadly, the monorail box was full of dull reports about mechanical issues. I don't know what I was hoping for. Maybe a sweat-stained hankie with the initials RN.

But unexpected finds are already turning up. A cardboard box has slender manila envelopes of large-format photo negatives of various sites around California and the West. One is labeled "Capistrano Beach, 1948." The photos have no evident tie to the L.A. County Fair, but that's where the box ended up, mysteriously.

Richardson and Strauss had already pulled a few fun items for me to see. A scrapbook of photos from the 1948 fair. A 1947 planner from the fair's manager. A blue ribbon first prize for sheep from the 1927 fair.

Brochures for the fairs of 1940, 1953, 1963 and 1969 were side by side. Cheerful motto of the 1963 fair: "The nation's most exciting and colorful exposition!" For 1969's groovy cover: "It's where it's happening." In six years the fair went from "exciting" to mellow.

A few items relate to the debut fair of 1922, including a publicity photo of the six founders standing in a field, pointing.

"They were savvy businessmen. They wanted to promote Pomona," Richardson explained. "Pasadena had the Tournament of Roses parade. San Bernardino had the Orange Show. Riverside had a fair. They were trying to think of what would set Pomona apart."

Once they learned there was no Los Angeles County fair, they went with that.

"They incorporated in April 1922 and put the fair on in October. They didn't even break ground until July," Richardson said. "It was amazing how quickly they pulled it off."

The collection has film reels from 1960s and '70s fairs, contents currently unknown. I think those will be a hit. As research progresses, we might learn more about the origins of Thummer, the Porky Pig-like mascot from 1948.

And how about all the musicians who've given concerts at the fair during the rock era? Few of those have been documented in a public way.

For my benefit, Strauss held up a brochure for an unexpected 1952 fair performer: Liberace.

Liberace, in Pomona, at the county fair. The mind boggles. Also, I hope his piano's candelabra was kept away from any hay bales.

As the collection is catalogued, Richardson sees opportunities for exhibits, lectures, web pages, oral histories from fairgoers, and tie-ins with Cal Poly classes in business, agriculture and culinary arts.

She said students could recreate food from fair cookbooks from decades past, or the prize-winning chocolate cake of Alberta Dunbar of San Diego, featured in a news clipping about her back-to-back victories in 1977 and '78.

Richardson said of the collection: "It's going to paint a picture of how the fair evolved."

Meanwhile, the L.A. County Fair is due to return May 5 to 30 as the event shifts away from the broiling late summer to the gentler late spring. The fair, marking its 100th anniversary in 2022, may be part of history, but its evolution continues.

INDEX

ABOUT DAVID ALLEN

David Allen, a native of Illinois, has worked in newspapers for three decades, all in California, his adopted home. His career began in 1987 at the Santa Rosa *News Herald* and continued at the Rohnert Park-Cotati *Clarion*, Petaluma *Argus-Courier* and Victorville *Daily Press*, some of which are still in business. In 1997 he joined the *Inland Valley Daily Bulletin*, where he is a columnist writing about people, places, arts, government and other topics, including, as you may have guessed, the Los Angeles County Fair. His columns now appear as well in the San Bernardino *Sun* and Riverside *Press-Enterprise* as his reach expands to the entire Inland Empire. Find his work online, or impress your friends by buying an actual newspaper. A resident of Claremont, he is the author of three previous books, *Pomona A to Z*, *Getting Started*, and *On Track*, also from Pelekinesis.

112 Harvard Ave #65
Claremont, CA 91711 USA

pelekinesis@gmail.com
www.pelekinesis.com

Pelekinesis titles are available through Small Press Distribution, Baker &
Taylor, Ingram, Bertrams, and directly from the publisher's website.

CPSIA information can be obtained
at www.ICGtesting.com
Printed in the USA
LVHW100059300422
717195LV00003B/16

9 781949 790641